Wow! 365 Stew Recipes

(Wow! 365 Stew Recipes - Volume 1)

Mona Scott

Copyright: Published in the United States by Mona Scott/ © MONA SCOTT

Published on November, 24 2020

All rights reserved. No part of this publication may be reproduced, stored in retrieval system, copied in any form or by any means, electronic, mechanical, photocopying, recording or otherwise transmitted without written permission from the publisher. Please do not participate in or encourage piracy of this material in any way. You must not circulate this book in any format. MONA SCOTT does not control or direct users' actions and is not responsible for the information or content shared, harm and/or actions of the book readers.

In accordance with the U.S. Copyright Act of 1976, the scanning, uploading and electronic sharing of any part of this book without the permission of the publisher constitute unlawful piracy and theft of the author's intellectual property. If you would like to use material from the book (other than just simply for reviewing the book), prior permission must be obtained by contacting the author at author@limerecipes.com

Thank you for your support of the author's rights.

Content

365 AWESOME STEW RECIPES 9

1. 30 SOUPS Recipe 9
2. 44 Clove Comfort Me Soup Recipe 11
3. A Healthy Pot Of Black N Red Recipe 11
4. African Chicken Stew Recipe 12
5. African Peanut Soup Recipe 12
6. Andrews Power Packed Vegan Chili Recipe 13
7. Angel Hair And Three Onion Soup Recipe 13
8. Apple Soup Recipe 14
9. Asian Chicken Noodle Soup Recipe 14
10. Asian Style Lobster Soup Recipe 15
11. Authentic Irish Stew With Lamb And Guinness Recipe 16
12. Authentic New Orleans Gumbo Recipe ... 16
13. Autumn Carrot Bisque Recipe 17
14. Award Winning Chicken Chili Recipe 18
15. BEST REAL ITALIAN MINESTRONE Recipe 18
16. BLACK EYED PEA SOUP Recipe 19
17. BUTTERNUT SQUASH SOUP Recipe . 19
18. Baked Jambalaya Recipe 20
19. Baked White Wine & Onion Soup Recipe 20
20. Barley Stew With Lentils And Swiss Chard Recipe 21
21. Beef And Vegetable Barley Soup Or Krupnik Recipe 21
22. Beef Stew Bourguignonne Recipe 22
23. Beef Stew Moroccan Style Recipe 22
24. Beef Stew Recipe 23
25. Beef Stew And Dumplings Recipe 23
26. Beef And Barley Soup Recipe 24
27. Best Pumpkin Soup Recipe 24
28. Black Bean Chili Cheese Dip Recipe 25
29. Black Bean Soup Recipe 26
30. Black Beans Potage Recipe 26
31. Black Eyed Peas And Veggie Soup Recipe 27
32. Blender Gazpacho Recipe 27
33. Broccoli And Cheese Soup Recipe 28
34. Broccoli Cheddar Soup Recipe 28
35. Broccoli Cheese Soup Recipe 28
36. Brown Stew Recipe 29
37. Brunswick Stew Recipe 29
38. Buffalo Chicken Soup Recipe 30
39. Butternut Squash Soup For The Crockpot Recipe 30
40. CROCKPOT JAMBALAYA Recipe 31
41. Cabbage Soup Recipe 31
42. Canning Country Vegetable Vegan No Meat Soup Recipe 31
43. Carrot Cream Soup With Cream Cheese Dumplings Mohrencremesuppe Mit Klosschen Recipe 32
44. Central Avenue Oyster Bar Stew Recipe ... 33
45. Cheap And Easy Lentil Barley Soup Recipe 33
46. Cheeseburger Soup Meets Potato Soup Recipe 34
47. Chicken And Coconut Soup Recipe 34
48. Chicken Andouille Gumbo Recipe 35
49. Chicken Black Bean Soup Recipe 35
50. Chicken Breasts With Green Chilies Recipe 36
51. Chicken Enchilada Soup Recipe 36
52. Chicken Korma Recipe 37
53. Chicken Noodle Soup Asian Style Recipe 37
54. Chicken Sausage Gumbo Recipe 38
55. Chicken Soup From My Mother In Law Recipe 39
56. Chicken Soup Recipe 39
57. Chicken Soup With Passatelli Chicken Soup With Italian Dumplings Recipe 40
58. Chicken Tortilla Soup Recipe 40
59. Chicken Soup The Jewish Panacea Recipe 40
60. Chicken Tagine Recipe 41
61. Chili Cheddar Potato Wedges Recipe 42
62. Chili Cheese Dip Recipe 42
63. Chili Chicken Stew In A Tortilla Bowl Recipe 42
64. Chili Lime Crab Cakes With Chipotle Avacado Mayo Recipe 43
65. Chili Lime Potato Wedges Recipe 43
66. Chili Parmesan Chicken Recipe 43
67. Chilis Salsa Recipe 44
68. Chili's Baby Back Ribs 44
69. Chilled Avocado Soup Recipe 45
70. Chilled Chicken Yogurt Soup Recipe 45
71. Chilled Peach Soup Recipe 46

72. Chilli Con Carne Recipe 46
73. Chinese Hot And Sour Soup Recipe 46
74. Chinese War Wonton Soup Recipe 47
75. Chipotle Black Bean And Rice Stew Recipe 48
76. Chipotle Blue Chili Took 2nd Place In Chili Contest I Judged Recipe 48
77. Chuck Wagon Soup Recipe 49
78. Cincinnati Chili Skyline Style Recipe 49
79. Coney Island Chili Dogs Recipe 50
80. Copycat A N W Chili Dogs Recipe 50
81. Copycat Chilis Southwest Egg Rolls Recipe 51
82. Copycat Panera Bread Broccoli And Cheese Soup In Bread Bowls Recipe 52
83. Copycat Wendys Chili Recipe 52
84. Corn Chowder The Best Recipe 53
85. Cowboy Soup Recipe 53
86. Crab Cakes With Red Chili Mayonaisse Recipe 54
87. Cream Of Mushroom Soup Recipe 54
88. Cream Of Broccoli Soup Recipe 55
89. Cream Of Broccoli And Cheese Soup Recipe 55
90. Cream Of Mushroom Soup Recipe 56
91. Creamy Chicken Wild Rice Soup In Crockpot Recipe 56
92. Creamy Hungarian Mushroom Soup Recipe 57
93. Creamy Potato Leek Soup Recipe 57
94. Creamy Potato Cheese Soup Recipe 58
95. Creamy Pumpkin Soup Recipe 58
96. Creamy Roasted Cauliflower And Artichoke Soup Recipe 58
97. Creamy Spinach And Potato Soup Recipe 59
98. Creamy Turkey Or Chicken Soup Recipe . 60
99. Creamy Vegetable Chowder Recipe 60
100. Crock Pot French Onion Soup Recipe 61
101. Crock Pot Pork Chili Verde Recipe 61
102. Crock Pot Potato Soup Recipe 62
103. Crock Pot Rustic Beef Stew Recipe 62
104. Crockpot Chicken Creole Recipe 62
105. Crockpot Chili Recipe 63
106. Crockpot Southwestern Pumpkin Soup Aka Korma Soup From Michael Congdons Soups Cookbook Recipe 63
107. Curried Pumpkin Cauliflower Soup Recipe 64
108. Curried Red Lentil Soup Recipe 65
109. DONNAS TACO SOUP Recipe 65
110. Darbars Fantastic Spicy Turkey Chili Recipe 66
111. Darbars Potato Leek Soup Recipe 66
112. Double Bean Bacon Soup Recipe 67
113. Easy Black Bean And Pepper Soup Ci Recipe 67
114. Easy Hungarian Goulash In The Crockpot Recipe 67
115. Easy Microwave Chili Recipe 68
116. Easy Taco Soup Recipe 68
117. Easy Chicken ENCHILADAS Recipe 69
118. Egg Balls For Chicken Soup Recipe 69
119. Egg Drop Soup Recipe 69
120. Eggplant And Lamb Stew Recipe 70
121. Egyptian Swiss Chard Or Beet Green And Rice Soup Recipe 70
122. Elaines Asian Beef Noodle Soup Recipe .. 70
123. Elaines EASY French Canadian Pea Soup Recipe 71
124. Elaines Home Made Scotch Broth Soup Recipe 71
125. Elaines Homemade Beef And Vegetable Soup Recipe 72
126. Extraordinary French Onion Soup Recipe 73
127. Feijouda Recipe 73
128. Firehouse Chili Recipe 74
129. Fish And Cilantro Stew Recipe 74
130. Fish With Coriander Chili And Lemon Sauce Recipe 75
131. Football Killer Dogs Enough Said Recipe 75
132. French Onion Soup 1 Recipe 76
133. French Onion Soup Recipe 76
134. Fresh Artichoke Bisque Recipe 77
135. Fresh Mushroom Soup Recipe 77
136. Fresh Pink Peach Soup Recipe 78
137. Fresh Tomato Soup Recipe 78
138. Friday Night Carrot Leek Parsnip Chicken Orzo Soup Recipe 78
139. Frugal Cabbage Soup Recipe 79
140. Full Minestrone Soup Recipe 79
141. Good Old Chicken With Rice Soup Recipe 80
142. Good Ole New England Clam Chowder

Recipe 80
143. Gosht Do Piaza A Hearty Popular Lamb Stew Recipe 81
144. Goulash I Grew Up With Recipe 81
145. Goulash Recipe 82
146. Grandmas Italian Wedding Soup Recipe .. 82
147. Grandmas Mushroom Bisque Recipe 83
148. Greek Lemon Soup Recipe 83
149. Greek Wedding Soup Recipe 83
150. Green Chili Chicken Recipe 84
151. Green Chili And Chicken Enchiladas Recipe 84
152. Ground Beef Stew Recipe 84
153. Gypsy Soup Recipe 85
154. Ham And Bean Soup With Vegetables Recipe 85
155. Harira Soup Recipe 86
156. Hassenpfeffer German Rabbit Stew Recipe 86
157. Hawaiian Crock Pot Recipe 87
158. Heart Healthy Pumpkin And Black Bean Soup Recipe 87
159. Hearty Broccoli Soup Recipe 87
160. Hearty Flemish Beef Stew Recipe 88
161. Hearty Mexican Stew Recipe 89
162. Hearty Reuben Soup Recipe 89
163. Hearty Vegetable Gumbo Recipe 90
164. Homemade Chicken Noodle Soup Recipe 90
165. Homemade Chicken Stock Recipe 91
166. Homestyle Polish Pickel Soup Recipe 91
167. Honey Chili Shrimp Over Noodles Recipe 92
168. Hot And Sour Cabbage Soup Recipe 92
169. Hot And Sour Soup Recipe 92
170. Hot Chili Cheese Appetizer Recipe 93
171. Hungarian Beef Stew Recipe 94
172. Hungarian Goulash Recipe 94
173. Hungarian Paprika Stew Recipe 94
174. Indian Chili Chicken Recipe 95
175. Irish Stew Recipe 95
176. Italian Beef Soup Recipe 96
177. Italian Sausage And Bean Soup Recipe 96
178. Italian Wedding Soup Recipe 97
179. Jamies Chili Recipe Courtesy Jamie Deen Paula Deens Son Recipe 98
180. Jims Super Bowl Gumbo Recipe 98

181. Julia Childs French Onion Soup Grantineed With Cheese Recipe 99
182. Kapousta Recipe 100
183. Kartoffelsuppe Potato Soup Recipe 100
184. LOBSTER BISQUE Recipe 101
185. Lamb Shank Stew Recipe 101
186. Lamb With Minted Lime Salsa And Chili Roasted Vegetables Recipe 102
187. Lammas Harvest Holiday Soup Aka, Harvest Pepper Soup Recipe 102
188. Lebanese Green Bean Meat Stew Recipe 103
189. Lebanese Lamb And Bean Stew Recipe . 103
190. Leek And Cauliflower Creamy Soup Recipe 104
191. Lemon Chicken In A Crockpot Recipe .. 104
192. Lemon Chicken Velvet Soup For Two Recipe 105
193. Lemon Lentil Soup Recipe 105
194. Lemon Ginger Chicken Soup With Cilantro Recipe 105
195. Lentil Soup Recipe 106
196. Lentil Soup With Swiss Chard And Noodles Recipe 106
197. Lentil And Pea Soup With Bourbon Recipe 107
198. Little Bowl Fins Recipe 107
199. Loaded Baked Potato Soup Recipe 108
200. Lobster Stock Recipe 108
201. Louisiana Chicken And Sausage Gumbo Recipe 109
202. Louisiana Chicken Gumbo Recipe 110
203. Louisiana Jambalaya For A Crowd Recipe 110
204. Make It Yourself Condensed Cream Of Soups Recipe 111
205. Markys Broccoli Cheese Soup Recipe 111
206. Marrow Balls For Beef Soup Recipe 112
207. Mediterranean Pumpkin Soup Recipe 112
208. Mexican Pumpkin Soup Recipe 113
209. Mexican Seafood Cocktail Recipe 113
210. Mi Nanas Albondigas Con Aros Mexicano Mexican Meatball Soup With Mexican Red Rice Recipe 114
211. Microwave Bean And Pasta Chowder Recipe 114
212. Microwave Spaghetti Soup Recipe 115
213. Monkey Stew Recipe 115

214. Moqueca Brazilian Fish Stew Recipe 115
215. Moroccan Beef Soup Recipe 116
216. Moroccan Beef Stew With Dried Fruit Recipe 117
217. Moroccan Chicken & Couscous Soup Recipe 117
218. Moroccan Chickpea Stew Recipe 118
219. Moroccan Harira Soup Recipe 118
220. Moroccan Inspired Vegetable Soup Recipe 119
221. Moroccan Lentil Soup Recipe 119
222. Moroccan Meatball Stew Recipe 120
223. Moroccan Spiced Chickpea And Lentil Soup Recipe 120
224. Moroccan Style Lamb And Chickpea Soup For Two Recipe 121
225. My Baked Potato Soup Recipe 122
226. My Cioppino Italian Seafood Stew Recipe 122
227. My Grandmothers Hungarian Goulash Recipe 123
228. Navy Bean Soup Recipe 124
229. Neighbors Potato Soup Recipe 124
230. North African Chickpea And Kale Soup Recipe 124
231. North African Fish Stew Recipe 125
232. Not Another Pasta E Fagioli Recipe 125
233. Olla Gitana Gypsy Pot Recipe 126
234. Omg Italian Sausage And Potato Soup Recipe 127
235. Oyster Stew With Leeks Recipe 127
236. Oyster Stew Recipe 127
237. Pasta Fazool Recipe 128
238. Paula Deen's Baked Potato Soup Recipe 128
239. Pea Soup With Shiitake Mushrooms Recipe 129
240. Peach Buttermilk Soup Recipe 129
241. Persian Lamb Stew With Basmati Rice Recipe 130
242. Philly Cheese Steak Soup Recipe 130
243. Pizza Soupreme With Garlic Parmesan Puffs Recipe 130
244. Plain Ole Beef Stew Recipe 131
245. Poblano Potato Soup Recipe 132
246. Polish Beetroot Soup Barszcz Recipe 132
247. Polish Sauerkraut Stew Recipe 133
248. Polish Sausage And Bean Soup Recipe ... 133
249. Polish Sausage Stew Recipe 134
250. Polish Sausage Stew Bigosz Recipe 134
251. Polish White Borscht Recipe 134
252. Polski Potato And Sauerkraut Soup Recipe 135
253. Pork Chile Verde Recipe 135
254. Portugese Bean Stew Recipe..................... 136
255. Portuguese Bean Soup Recipe.................. 137
256. Portuguese Traditional Fish Soup Recipe 137
257. Posole Rojo Recipe 138
258. Potato Pinto Bean Soup Recipe 138
259. Pressure Cooker Chili Recipe 139
260. Pretty Darn Good Chili Verde Recipe 139
261. Prize Winning Chicken Sausage Jambalaya Recipe 140
262. Pumpkin Chili Mexicana Recipe 141
263. Pumpkin Pie Soup Aka Pumpkin Soup Recipe 141
264. Quick Chili Cheese Dip Recipe 142
265. Quick N Tender Deer Stew Recipe......... 142
266. REALLY GOOD HOT AND SOUR SOUP Recipe 142
267. Ratatouille My Way Recipe 143
268. Ratatouille The Best Recipe 144
269. Ratatouille Not The Movie Recipe 145
270. Razor Clam Chowder Recipe 145
271. Real Chinese Sweet And Sour Soup Recipe 146
272. Red Bell Pepper And Sweet Potato Soup Recipe 147
273. Red Chili Shrimp Recipe 147
274. Red Lentil Soup Recipe 148
275. Remys Ratatouille Recipe 148
276. Rich Cabbage Soup Recipe 149
277. Rich Roasted Veggie Stock Recipe 150
278. Roasted Butternut Squash Soup Recipe . 150
279. Roasted Garlic Soup Recipe 150
280. Roasted Carrot Ginger Soup With Lemon Yogurt Recipe 151
281. Rockin Morrocan Stew Recipe 151
282. Root Beer Barbecue Beans Recipe 152
283. SLOW COOKER IRISH STEW Recipe 152
284. STOVE TOPSKILLET TAMALE PIE Recipe 153
285. Saltymikes Best Gumbo Recipe 153
286. Saltymikes Oyster Stew Supreme Recipe 154

287. Sauerkraut SoupPolish Style Recipe 154
288. Sausage And Bean Soup Recipe 155
289. Sausage Soup Recipe 155
290. Scallop And Proscuitto Wontons With Safron Broth Recipe 156
291. Seafood Chowder Recipe 156
292. Seafood Chowder Recipe 157
293. Seafood Gumbo Recipe 158
294. Seafood Okra Gumbo Recipe 158
295. Shrimp Rangoon With Chili Garlic Dipping Sauce Recipe 159
296. Simple Cinnamon Stewed Apples Recipe 159
297. Simple Fish Gumbo Recipe 159
298. Slap Your Mama Texas Chili Recipe 160
299. Slow Cooker Asian Inspired Chicken Stew Recipe 160
300. Slow Cooker Beef And Black Bean Stew With Cornmeal Dumplings Recipe 161
301. Slow Cooker Chicken Noodle Soup Recipe 161
302. Slow Cooker Chicken Stock Recipe 162
303. Slow Cooker Chile Verde Recipe 162
304. Slow Cooker Chili Recipe 163
305. Slow Cooker Jambalaya Recipe 163
306. Slow Cooker Kielbasa Stew Recipe 164
307. Slow Cooker Seafood Stew Recipe 164
308. Slow It Down Mediterranean Stew Recipe 164
309. Soothing CHICKEN SOUP Recipe 165
310. Southwest Chicken Chowder Recipe 166
311. Southwest Chicken Soup Recipe 166
312. Spanish Lentil Soup Recipe 167
313. Spicy Cabbage Soup Recipe 167
314. Spicy Chicken Jambalaya Recipe 168
315. Spicy Corn Chowder Recipe 168
316. Spicy Gazpacho Recipe 169
317. Spicy Lentil Soup Recipe 169
318. Spicy Maryland Crab Soup Recipe 170
319. Spicy Peanut Soup Recipe 170
320. Spicy Rustic Red Lentil Soup Recipe 170
321. Spicy Thai Pumpkin Noodle Coconut Soup Recipe 171
322. Spinach And Yogurt Soup Recipe 171
323. Split Green Pea Soup With A Zing Recipe 172
324. Stewed Beef Boat Noodle Soup Gkuay Dtiow Lauy Recipe 172
325. Stroganoff Soup Recipe 173
326. Stupid Easy Crock Pot Chili Recipe 173
327. Super Bowl Super Chili Bowls Recipe 174
328. Sweet And Spicy Black Bean Soup Recipe 175
329. Taco Soup Recipe 176
330. Tamale Filling Green Chili Recipe 176
331. Tex Mex Chili Authentic San Antonio Recipe 176
332. Thai Shrimp And Chicken Soup Recipe. 177
333. The "cure For All Ails" Tomato Soup Recipe 177
334. The BEST Crockpot Potato Soup Recipe 178
335. The Gypsy Stew Recipe 178
336. Three Sisters Stew Recipe 179
337. Tinks Chili Cheese Balls Recipe 179
338. Tom Ka Gai Thai Coconut Chicken Soup Recipe 180
339. Tom Ka Soup Recipe 181
340. Tom Kai Gai Recipe 181
341. Tomato Soup Exotica Recipe 182
342. Tomato Soup Recipe 182
343. Tomato And Cream Cheese Soup Recipe 183
344. Tortellini Soup Recipe 183
345. Turkey Carcass Soup Recipe 183
346. Turkey Chili With Four Beans Recipe 184
347. Under Pressure Split Pea Soup Recipe ... 184
348. Vegan Lentil Stew Recipe 185
349. Vegetarian Chili With Honey Cornbread Recipe 185
350. Vegetarian Tagine Recipe 186
351. Warming Ginger Soup Recipe 187
352. Weight Watchers Taco Soup Recipe 187
353. West African Style Chicken Stew Recipe 188
354. White Bean Turkey Chili Recipe 188
355. White Chicken Chili Recipe 189
356. Winter Minestrone Recipe 189
357. World Championship Chili Cook Off Winning Chili Recipe 190
358. Yayla Yogurt Soup Recipe 190
359. Yummy Homemade Hotdog Chili Or Sauce Recipe 190
360. Yummy Moroccan Lentil Soup Recipe ... 191
361. Zuppa Maritata Wedding Soup Recipe ... 191

362. Zuppa Toscana Soup Olive Garden Recipe 192
363. Butter Chicken Recipe 192
364. Chinese Hot And Sour Soup Recipe 193
365. Chinese Wonton Soup Recipe 193

INDEX 194

CONCLUSION 197

365 Awesome Stew Recipes

***

1. 30 SOUPS Recipe

Serving: 6 | Prep: | Cook: 45mins | Ready in:

Ingredients

- 1. Ravioli Heat canned vegetable broth with a little garlic and a good amount of flat leaf parsley leaves. Add cheese ravioli, cook until done and serve with parmesan cheese and pepper.
- 2. vegetable soup Heat vegetable broth with scallions, garlic and rosemary. Add green beans, diced tomato, sliced mushrooms and thick slices of zucchini. Cook until vegetables are tender and serve with grated cheese.
- 3. pumpkin Heat a couple of cans of vegetable broth with a can of pumpkin puree. Add a touch of ground ginger, a little brown sugar and a splash of cream. Garnish with crushed amaretti cookies or toasted almonds.
- 4. Dad's corn Chowder Take a can of broth, a can of creamed corn, a healthy amount of pepper, some frozen corn kernels and diced red peppers and cook until well combined. Top with oyster crackers.
- 5. Curried cauliflower Soup Sauté scallions and garlic in oil until tender. Add some garam masala, ground ginger and a medium hot curry powder; cook 1 minute. Stir in cauliflower florets until well coated. Add broth and cook until the cauliflower is tender. Puree and add a little milk or cream to thin.
- 6. Congee Add 3 tablespoons of rice to a couple of cans of broth and a cup of water. season with salt, garlic, ginger, and toasted sesame oil and cook until the rice is completely broken down and the soup is thick. Finish with a drizzle of toasted sesame oil and sliced scallions.
- 7. Hot Pot Heat canned broth with scallions, ginger and garlic and cook until flavorful. Add chunks of firm tofu, shredded cabbage, a splash of rice vinegar and hot sauce. Cook until piping hot.
- 8. Carrot-ginger Sauté thinly sliced carrots, fresh ginger and sliced apple in butter and oil until carrots are very tender. Add a combo of carrot juice and vegetable broth and cook a few minutes for the flavors to come together. Puree and serve with a dollop of yogurt or sour cream.
- 9. Mushroom Sauté sliced mushrooms in butter with scallions. Add enough flour to coat and then gradually add milk (about 4 cups for 3 tablespoons flour). Cook until lightly thickened. season with nutmeg and a splash of bourbon.
- 10. Black Bean Soup Sauté sliced scallions with garlic in olive oil until tender. Add canned black beans, canned broth, tomato paste, chipotle chile powder and a splash of sherry. Cook until thickened.
- 11. White Bean, rosemary and garlic Soup Sauté garlic in olive oil, add a can of diced tomatoes, white beans, rosemary, tomato paste, small pasta shapes and canned broth. Cook until pasta is tender.
- 12. Sweet Potato and pepper Soup Sauté red and green bell peppers, a poblano pepper and garlic in oil until peppers are tender. Add peeled-and-sliced sweet potatoes and cook until tender. Finish with lime juice and top with toasted pumpkin seeds.
- 13. minted Pea Soup Sauté a couple of scallions in butter until tender. Add a package of frozen peas, a handful of fresh mint, a handful of shredded lettuce and a couple of cans of broth. Cook until the peas are tender and then puree.

- 14. Summer vegetable soup Sauté onions and garlic in olive oil until tender. Add chunks of yellow squash, green beans, diced peppers and tomatoes along with a can of broth and cook until tender. Serve with a dollop of homemade or store-bought pesto.
- 15. Quick barley Soup Cook chopped onions, garlic and sliced carrots in oil until tender. Add quick cooking barley and broth, along with some rinsed dried mushrooms and a touch of ancho chile powder. Cook until barley is tender. Serve with grated cheese.
- 16. Winter tomato soup Cook diced yellow bell peppers in oil until tender. Add canned tomatoes, fresh ginger and carrot juice, and cook until the flavors blend. Serve with a dollop of sour cream.
- 17. Hot Potato and Leek Soup Clean leeks and slice the tender white and green parts. Sauté in a combo of oil and butter along with a sliver of garlic until tender. Add sliced potatoes, milk and a little broth. season with pepper and nutmeg and cook until the potatoes are almost falling apart.
- 18. butternut squash Soup Halve, seed and peel a medium butternut squash. Cut the squash into chunks and sauté along with a couple of peeled, cored and sliced pears, and garlic until lightly browned. Add broth and cook until the squash is tender. Puree, adding a little half-and-half. Garnish with diced pears.
- 19. Chorizo Sauté onions in olive oil until tender. Add sliced chorizo, diced potatoes, canned pinto beans and canned broth along with smoked paprika and cook until the potatoes are tender.
- 20. Tortilla Soup Jazz up canned chicken broth with cilantro, corn kernels, tomato paste and strips of chicken breast. It's cooked until the chicken is done, then just add toasted tortillas along with lime juice.
- 21. Italian Wedding Soup Add your favorite tiny meatballs to broth along with shredded escarole, elbow macaroni and a healthy amount of parmesan cheese.
- 22. Wonton Add sliced scallions, garlic and ginger to canned broth cooking until flavorful. Toss in a couple of handfuls of watercress and pork pot stickers and cook until done. Finish with a drizzle of toasted sesame oil.
- 23. Winter vegetable soup Combine sweet and white potato chunks, shredded cabbage, a can of white beans, broth and ham in a pot. Cook until the potatoes are tender.
- 24. chicken Noodle Combine chicken thighs and drumsticks in a pot with water to cover, an onion with its skin on, a couple of ribs of celery sliced and cook until the chicken is tender. Remove and shred the chicken. Strain the broth, return the chicken along with a couple of cups of thin egg noodles and let it cook until the noodles are tender.
- 25. ham and edamame Soup Cook a meaty ham bone with carrots and onions in broth. Add frozen edamame and cook until the beans are tender. Shred the meat from the bone and return it to the soup. Serve with toasted bread cubes.
- 26. Hot and Spicy Lentil Soup Cook bacon in a little oil until crisp, then remove bacon and set aside. Add onions, carrots, chopped tomato, chili powder and ginger to the pot and cook for a minute. Add lentils, canned broth and a little water and cook until the lentils are tender. Return bacon to the pot and serve.
- 27. tortellini en Brodo Heat canned broth along with basil and parsley leaves, pepper and a little oregano. Add meat tortellini and cook until tender. Serve with grated parmesan cheese.
- 28. Easy Borscht Cook sliced canned beets, sliced carrots, large white beans and chunks of potatoes in broth until the potatoes are tender. Add thin strips of beef sirloin and cook just until the beef is cooked through.
- 29. Creamy Mussel Soup Heat clam broth and some white wine. Add sliced garlic and cleaned mussels. Cover and cook until mussels have opened. Remove mussels from their shells. Combine a little tomato paste and mayo and whisk into the broth to thicken. Add shelled mussels and croutons.
- 30. shrimp Chowder Sauté onion, garlic and fresh fennel in oil until fennel is tender. Add

chunks of unpeeled red potatoes and broth, and cook until potatoes are tender. Add shelled and deveined shrimp and corn kernels and cook just until shrimp are done.
- 31. Provencal fish Soup Heat clam broth with an equal amount of water. Add strips of orange zest, fennel seeds, garlic and tomatoes. Cook until flavorful. Meanwhile combine roasted red peppers (homemade or jarred) with garlic and hot sauce, then puree. Once the broth is flavorful, add chunks of white-fleshed fish and cook just until tender. Float toasted bread topped with red pepper sauce in the soup.

Direction

- Above
- P.S. That Soup Nazi from the Seinfeld Show cracks me up!

2. 44 Clove Comfort Me Soup Recipe

Serving: 4 | Prep: | Cook: 90mins | Ready in:

Ingredients

- 26 garlic cloves (unpeeled)
- 2 tablespoons olive oil
- 2 tablespoons (1/4 stick) butter
- 2 1/4 cups sliced onions
- 1 1/2 teaspoons chopped fresh thyme
- 18 garlic cloves, peeled
- 3 1/2 cups chicken stock or canned low-salt chicken broth
- 1/2 cup whipping cream
- 1/2 cup finely grated parmesan cheese (about 2 ounces)
- 4 lemon wedges

Direction

- Preheat oven to 350°F.
- Place 26 garlic cloves in small glass baking dish.
- Add 2 tablespoons olive oil and sprinkle with salt and pepper; toss to coat.
- Cover baking dish tightly with foil and bake until garlic is golden brown and tender, about 45 minutes.
- Cool.
- Squeeze garlic between fingertips to release cloves.
- Transfer cloves to small bowl.
- Melt butter in heavy large saucepan over medium-high heat.
- Add onions and thyme and cook until onions are translucent, about 6 minutes.
- Add roasted garlic and 18 raw garlic cloves and cook 3 minutes.
- Add chicken stock; cover and simmer until garlic is very tender, about 20 minutes.
- Working in batches, purée soup in blender until smooth.
- Return soup to saucepan; add cream and bring to simmer.
- Season with salt and pepper. (Can be prepared 1 day ahead. Cover and refrigerate. Rewarm over medium heat, stirring occasionally.)
- Divide grated cheese among 4 bowls and ladle soup over. Squeeze juice of 1 lemon wedge into each bowl and serve.

3. A Healthy Pot Of Black N Red Recipe

Serving: 10 | Prep: | Cook: 480mins | Ready in:

Ingredients

- 1 ½ cups chopped onion
- 1 ½ cups sliced carrots
- 5 cloves garlic, minced
- 3 cups vegetable stock
- 1 teaspoon brown sugar
- 2 cups frozen corn
- 1 cup cooked kidney beans, drained

- 2 cups cooked black beans, drained
- 1 (14.5 ounce) can Italian-style stewed tomatoes
- 2 cups diced tomatoes
- 2 tbsp garlic powder
- 2 tsp cayenne powder
- 2 tsp ground cumin
- 2 jalapeno peppers, chopped

Direction

- Sauté onion, carrots and garlic in a fry-pan spritzed with non-stick cooking spray.
- Add sautéed vegetables and the rest of the ingredients to a crock-pot, and cook on HIGH for the first hour.
- Stir, and turn the temperature down to LOW. Cook 7 more hours.

4. African Chicken Stew Recipe

Serving: 4 | Prep: | Cook: 30mins | Ready in:

Ingredients

- MARINATE OVERNGHT
- ---------------------------------
- 1 lb. skinless and boneless chicken breast, cut in 2-inch pieces
- 1 Tbsp. minced garlic
- 1 Tbsp. grated ginger
- 1 tsp. dried oregano
- 1 Tbsp. fat-free, reduced-sodium chicken broth, or water
- canola oil spray
- 1 spanish onion, half sliced, half finely chopped
- 1 can (28 oz.) tomatoes, with juices
- 1 habanero chile pepper, chopped
- 1/4 cup ketchup
- 1/3 cup reduced-fat peanut butter
- salt and freshly ground black pepper

Direction

- Place the chicken in a 1-quart resealable plastic bag. Combine the garlic, ginger, oregano, and broth in a small bowl. Add the seasoning mixture to the bag and massage it to coat the chicken with the seasonings. Marinate in the refrigerator for 6 hours to overnight.
- Coat a large Dutch oven with cooking spray and set it over medium-high heat. Sear the chicken pieces until they are white on all sides, about 5 minutes. Transfer them to a plate and set aside.
- Coat the pot again with cooking spray. Sauté the sliced onion until limp, 5 minutes, stirring occasionally. Add the tomatoes with half their liquid, the chili pepper and ketchup. Bring to a boil, reduce the heat and simmer the sauce 10 minutes, breaking up the tomatoes with a wooden spoon. Blend the peanut butter in the remaining tomato juice until smooth. Add it to the pot. Return the chicken to the pot. Simmer until the chicken is white in the center, about 15 minutes. Serve, accompanied by cooked brown rice.

5. African Peanut Soup Recipe

Serving: 4 | Prep: | Cook: 20mins | Ready in:

Ingredients

- 1 tablespoon peanut oil
- 1 clove garlic, minced
- 1 28-ounce can chopped tomatoes, undrained
- 1 6-ounce can tomato paste
- 1/2 cup creamy peanut butter
- 4 cups chicken broth
- 1 tablespoon balsamic vinegar
- 1/4 teaspoon cayenne pepper
- 2 teaspoons kosher salt
- 1 cup + 1 tablespoon white rice
- 6 scallions, chopped
- 1/4 cup salted peanuts, roughly chopped

Direction

- In a medium saucepan, over medium heat, heat the oil and garlic for 1 minute.
- Add the tomatoes, tomato paste, peanut butter, broth, vinegar, cayenne, and salt and whisk to combine.
- Bring to a boil.
- Add the rice, reduce heat to low, cover, and cook for 20 minutes. Ladle into individual bowls and garnish with the scallions and peanuts.

6. Andrews Power Packed Vegan Chili Recipe

Serving: 10 | Prep: | Cook: 80mins | Ready in:

Ingredients

- 1 tbsp olive oil
- 1 onion, chopped
- 1 cubanelle pepper, chopped
- 1 green pepper, chopped
- 2 red peppers, chopped
- 20 baby carrots, chopped
- 5 cloves garlic, diced
- 10 button mushrooms
- 2 jalapeños, chopped
- 1 tbsp cumin
- 3 tbsp chili powder
- 2 tsp cayenne pepper
- 2 tsp cinnamon
- 2 tbsp oregano
- 1 tbsp basil
- 1 tbsp paprika
- 2 tsp mustard powder
- ½ cup stout beer
- 28 oz whole tomatoes
- 28 oz crushed tomatoes
- 1 small can tomato paste
- 2 tbsp unsweetened cocoa powder
- 1 cup quinoa
- 2 19-oz cans mixed beans
- water, as required

Direction

- Heat olive oil in a VERY large stockpot.
- Add onion and sweat down thoroughly.
- Add ingredients through to the jalapenos. Cook 5-7 minutes, stirring often.
- Add spices and stir until fragrant.
- Pour in stout, tomatoes, crushed tomatoes and tomato paste. Stir well and add water (or beer) as required (the mixture should be fairly liquid).
- Add cocoa powder and stir.
- Let simmer on low heat 45 minutes.
- Add quinoa, stir and simmer 20 minutes, adding water if required.
- Add beans along with their liquid, stir and simmer at least 15 minutes before serving.

7. Angel Hair And Three Onion Soup Recipe

Serving: 4 | Prep: | Cook: 90mins | Ready in:

Ingredients

- 4 Tbsp olive oil
- 1/2 lb baby (pearl) onions, fresh (or ½ frozen bag, thawed)
- 1 medium red onion, sliced thin
- 1 medium vidalia onion (or other sweet onion), sliced thin
- 6 cups (48 fl oz) chicken stock
- salt (to taste)
- 1/4 tsp red pepper flakes
- 1/2 lb angel hair pasta, broken in 2-inch pieces
- 1/4 cup chopped flat leaf parsley
- 4 tsp grated romano cheese

Direction

- PLACE oil and all onions in a large sauce pan over low heat and sauté, stirring occasionally, about 20 minutes, until onions are golden.
- Add stock and salt to taste.

- Sprinkle with red pepper flakes and simmer for about 1 hour.
- ADD pasta and parsley and cook until pasta is just al dente.
- LADLE into soup bowls.
- Sprinkle with grated Romano cheese

8. Apple Soup Recipe

Serving: 4 | Prep: | Cook: 20mins | Ready in:

Ingredients

- 1 large onion, chopped
- 4 tablespoons butter
- 3/4 tablespoons of curry powder (you can modify this amount)
- 1 quart chicken stock
- 2 large green apples, peeled, cored & chopped
- 1/2 cup light cream
- juice of 1/2 lemon
- 1/4 cup all purpose flour

Direction

- Melt the 1 tablespoon of butter in saucepan over med-high heat. Add onions and sauté until soft but not quite brown.
- Stir in the apples, curry powder, stock, and lemon juice and bring all to a boil. Turn down the heat & let simmer for approximately 10 mins.
- Melt remaining butter in another saucepan over med-heat until the foam subsides.
- Blend in the flour and cook for 1 - 2 minutes, stirring the whole time. Now slowly stir in soup until it is well blended.
- When mixture reaches a boil, remove it from the heat. Strain it into your first saucepan, pressing apple & onion with the back of a spoon.
- Stir in cream.
- Cook just until heated throughout. Now taste and adjust seasonings to your liking.

9. Asian Chicken Noodle Soup Recipe

Serving: 6 | Prep: | Cook: 30mins | Ready in:

Ingredients

- broth
- 2 boneless chicken breasts
- 2 tbsp peanut or canola oil, divided
- 2-inch piece of fresh ginger, sliced
- 2 large garlic cloves, crushed but intact
- 1 onion, thickly sliced
- 2 quarts chicken stock or broth
- 1/2 tsp crushed chili flakes
- 1 stick lemon grass (French Sorrel), crushed at white end
- 2 tbsp fish sauce
- -------------------------------------
- Soup
- One 14 oz pkg fresh udon noodles
- 1 1/4tsp dark sesame oil
- 1 lime
- 6-inch piece white radish or 4 large red radishes, julienned
- 1 carrot, julienned
- 4 cups baby spinach leaves
- 1 cup sliced snow peas or frozen peas
- 1/4 cup each of coarsely chopped fresh mint and Thai or regular fresh basil
- 1 small hot pepper, seeded and very finely minced
- 1 to 2 green onions, very thinly sliced

Direction

- To make broth, remove any clinging fat from chicken.
- Heat 1 tbsp. oil in a large pot over medium-high heat.
- Add chicken; sauté 7 to 8 minutes per side or until golden.
- Remove; cool chicken on a plate.
- Reduce heat to medium.

- Add another tbsp. oil to the pot; sauté ginger, garlic and onion for 5 minutes or until somewhat browned and very fragrant.
- Pour stock over ginger and onion; add chili flakes and lemon grass.
- Bring to a boil.
- Cover; simmer 20 minutes.
- Cool; strain through a sieve, discarding solids.
- Stir in fish sauce.
- [If serving later, cover and refrigerate for up to 3 days or better...freeze.]
- For soup, loosen noodles into a heatproof bowl.
- Cover with boiling water; soak 2 to 3 minutes.
- Drain; toss with sesame oil.
- Thinly slice chicken breasts; cut lime into wedges.
- Heat broth until boiling; add radishes, carrot, spinach, peas and herbs.
- Choose a deep wide bowl for each portion of soup.
- Warm bowls in oven or with hot water.
- Put a small amount of hot pepper in each bowl; top with some of chicken and noodles.
- Pour over piping hot vegetables and broth; sprinkle with green onions.
- Serve immediately
- Pass remaining hot pepper, lime wedges and additional fish sauce to add to personal taste.

10. Asian Style Lobster Soup Recipe

Serving: 23 | Prep: | Cook: 30mins | Ready in:

Ingredients

- 3 live Maine lobsters (you can choose not live), about 1 lb each
- 2 lemongrass sticks
- 1 can of coconut milk (14 oz)
- 2 + 1/8 cups water
- 5 coriander seeds, crushed
- 4 peppercorns, crushed
- 1 medium red onion, sliced thinly
- 2 garlic cloves, crushed
- 1 scallion
- 2 oz ginger root, chopped
- 9 oz romanesco broccoli, (you can use regular)steamed for 2 to 3 min
- 1 corn ear
- A few red radishes, sliced thinly
- 4 Tbsp vegetal oil
- salt
- fresh coriander

Direction

- Boil the lobster for 6 min in rolling water.
- Cool in iced water and then break the claws and tails. Keep the heads and legs of the lobsters.
- Cut the tails open with a scissor and remove the meat. Use a nutcracker to open the claws and remove the meat. Reserve.
- Chop the garlic and ginger.
- Slice the scallion and keep.
- Slice the lemongrass.
- Heat the oil in a large wok and then add the garlic, onion, ginger and lemongrass. Cook for 1 min or 2.
- Add the head and legs of the lobsters. Cook for 2 min while stirring.
- Add the coconut milk and water. Season with salt and the coriander seeds and peppercorns. Cover and cook for 10 to 15 min.
- In the meantime, prepare the vegetables. Boil the corn for 3 to 4 min and cut the kernels. Keep.
- Steam the romanesco broccoli for 3 min and keep.
- Slice the radishes thinly.
- Filter the broth.
- Add the vegetables, lobster meat and serve with fresh coriander and the scallion.

11. Authentic Irish Stew With Lamb And Guinness Recipe

Serving: 6 | Prep: | Cook: 180mins | Ready in:

Ingredients

- 3 pounds lamb shoulder with a little fat, cubed
- 1/2 cup flour
- 3 large russet potatoes, peeled and cubed
- 3 large carrots, peeled and sliced
- 6 stalks celery, cut into 1/2" slices
- 2 large yellow onions, cut into large dice
- 3 - 4 cloves garlic, minced
- 1 bunch fresh rosemary
- 1 bunch fresh thyme
- 1 bunch fresh parsley
- 2 quarts lamb or beef stock, or as needed
- 12 ounces Guinness stout
- 1 cup pearl barley (optional)
- 2 teaspoons corn starch
- salt and freshly ground black pepper, to taste

Direction

- If you are using the barley (which you should do if you want a more authentic Irish country stew), cook it for 20 minutes in 3 cups of lamb or beef stock. You'll add to the stew later.
- Cut off some of the parsley leaves and chop enough to make 2 tablespoons; reserve. Cut off some parsley stems, and tie them into a bundle with a few sprigs of rosemary and thyme; reserve.
- Season the meat with salt and brown the meat in a little oil. Remove and reserve, sprinkling with a little flour, shaking off excess.
- Add the onions, garlic, carrots and celery to the pan and sauté, tossing to coat with the fat.
- Add the Guinness and deglaze, scraping up any caramelized meat juices.
- Add the potatoes, return the meat to the pot -- and the barley if you're using it. Add enough stock to barely cover, cook over medium heat until just boiling, then reduce heat to very low and simmer 2 - 3 hours, until the meat is tender, stirring occasionally.
- Check seasonings, add salt and pepper to taste, then remove from heat, stir in parsley and the cornstarch (mixed into 4 teaspoons water) and stir.
- Cook over low heat for a few more minutes to thicken. Serve with plenty of Irish brown or white soda bread, and more Guinness if you like.

12. Authentic New Orleans Gumbo Recipe

Serving: 8 | Prep: | Cook: 120mins | Ready in:

Ingredients

- 5 Qts. chicken stock (MUST be homemade!)
- 1-1/4 cups flour
- 1 cup oil
- 1 chicken or guinea hen, without giblets, cut up
- 1 to 1-1/2 pounds andouillesausage, sliced about 1/4" thick on the bias (you may substitute hot or mild smoked sausage if good andouille isn't available) and/or fresh Creole hot sausage, browned
- 4 pounds shrimp, peeled and deveined
- 6 blue crabs, cleaned, broken in half and claws pulled off (or for a more elegant looking gumbo, omit and instead add 1-1/2 pounds lump white crabmeat, picked over for shells and cartilage)
- 3 pounds okra, sliced (leave out if you don't like okra, but be sure to add filé at the end if you leave out the okra)
- 2 onions, chopped
- 1 bunch green onions with tops, chopped
- 2 bell peppers, chopped
- 5 ribs celery, chopped
- several cloves garlic, minced
- 3 bay leaves
- 1 bunch fresh parsley, chopped
- creole seasoning to taste, OR
- black, white and cayenne peppers, to taste

- salt to taste
- Few dashes Tabasco, or to taste.
- 1 - 2 tablespoons filé powder (ONLY IF YOU DON'T USE okra!)
- Steaming hot Louisiana long-grain rice

Direction

- For the roux: Blend flour and oil thoroughly in a thick skillet and cook over medium-high to high heat, stirring CONSTANTLY. BE VERY CAREFUL NOT TO BURN IT!! If you see black specks in the roux, you've screwed it up. Dump it out and start over. Keep cooking and stirring until the roux gets darker and darker. It's best to use a very heavy bot or skillet for roux-making, especially cast iron. With a good cast iron Dutch oven or skillet, you can get a beautiful dark roux in only about 20 minutes.
- You should turn the fire down or off as the roux nears the right color, because the heat from the pan will continue cooking it. You can also add your onions, bell peppers and celery to the roux as it's near the end of cooking to arrest the cooking process and to soften the vegetables (this is the way I like to do it). KEEP STIRRING until the roux is relatively cool. Add the roux to the stock.
- Sprinkle the chicken pieces with Creole seasoning and brown in the oven. Slice the sausage and brown, pouring off all the fat (especially if you're using fresh Creole hot sausage).
- Sauté the onions, green onions, bell pepper and celery if you haven't already added them to the roux, and add to the stock. Add the chicken and sausage(s). Add the bay leaves and Creole seasoning (or ground peppers) to taste and stir. Bring to a boil and immediately reduce to a simmer; let simmer for about 45 minutes. Keep tasting and adjusting seasonings as needed.
- Add the okra and cook another 30 minutes or so. Make sure that the "ropiness" or "stringiness" from the okra is gone, add the parsley, crab halves and claws (if you're using them). Cook for another 15 minutes, then add the shrimp (and if you've omitted the hard-shell crabs, add the lump crabmeat now). Give it another 6-8 minutes or so, until the shrimp are just done, turning pink. Be very careful not to overcook the shrimp; adding the shrimp should be the very last step.
- If there is any fat on the surface of the gumbo, try to skim off as much of it as possible.
- Serve generous amounts in bowls over about 1/2 cup of hot rice -- claws, shells, bones and all (if you've made the original "rustic" version). Remember that the rice goes in the bowl first, and it is not an optional step, despite the trend among some New Orleans restaurants to serve a riceless gumbo.
- You may, if you like, sprinkle a small amount of gumbo filé in your individual serving for a little more flavor; just remember that if you're making a filé gumbo, it should be added to the pot off the fire for its proper thickening action.

13. Autumn Carrot Bisque Recipe

Serving: 8 | Prep: | Cook: 30mins | Ready in:

Ingredients

- 3 pounds carrots, peeled and diced into a little smaller than ½-inch pieces
- 1 large onion, chopped
- 2 tablespoons peanut oil (vegetable or olive oil will do)
- 2 cloves garlic, minced
- 1 tablespoon curry powder
- ½ teaspoon salt
- A few dashes fresh black pepper
- 3 cups vegetable broth, or 1 bouillon cube dissolved in 3 cups water
- 1 (13-ounce) can coconut milk
- 1 tablespoon maple syrup

Direction

- In a stockpot over low-medium heat, cook the carrots and onions in the peanut oil for 7 to 10 minutes; cover and stir occasionally.
- You want the onions to brown but not to burn, although if they burn a little bit it's not the end of the world.
- Add the garlic, curry, salt, and pepper; sauté for 1 more minute.
- Add the 3 cups of broth, cover, and bring to a boil.
- Lower the heat and simmer for 10 to 12 minutes, or until the carrots are tender.
- Add the coconut milk and bring to a low boil.
- Turn the heat off. Use a handheld blender to puree half of the soup; if you don't have one, then puree half the soup in a blender and add it back to the soup pot.
- Add the maple syrup and stir. Serve hot.
- *Just A thought*:If you are using a blender to puree the soup, let the soup cool a bit so that the steam doesn't cause the blender lid to pop off and hot soup to splatter everywhere.
- Once the soup has cooled, give it a few pulses in the blender, lift the lid to let steam escape, and repeat.

14. Award Winning Chicken Chili Recipe

Serving: 8 | Prep: | Cook: 50mins | Ready in:

Ingredients

- 3 Tbs olive oil
- 1 1/2 Lb Boneless chicken breast or Thighs, sliced.
- 1 1/2 Cups yellow onions, chopped
- 1/2 tsp red chili Flakes
- 1 Tbs Fresh Minced garlic
- 2 Tsp minced fresh Jalepeno peppers
- 1 1/2 Cups chicken stock
- 3 Tbs chili powder
- 1 Can (28 Oz) whole tomatoes, undrained and broken up
- 1 Can (29Oz) tomato puree
- 2 Cans (15 Oz) dark red kidney beans, drained
- 1 Can (15Oz) hominy
- 1/3 Cup Fresh cilantro, chopped
- 2 Tbs Fresh squeezed lime juice

Direction

- Heat Olive oil in a large stockpot. Sauté' chicken until cooked (about 8 minutes). Add onions and reduce heat. Cook for additional 3 minutes, until onions are tender.
- Add the rest of the remaining ingredients (Except the cilantro and lime juice) and simmer, very low for 30 minutes.
- Add the lime juice and cilantro just prior to serving, stir a few times.
- Top with Sour Cream, Cheddar and tortilla chips. Also a few chunks of fresh pineapple for garnish. Delish.

15. BEST REAL ITALIAN MINESTRONE Recipe

Serving: 8 | Prep: | Cook: 45mins | Ready in:

Ingredients

- 2 pounds bulk Italian sausage
- 2 Tablespoons olive oil
- 1 medium onion, diced
- 2-3 carrots, peeled and chopped
- 2 small zucchini, halved and sliced
- one 28 ounce can diced tomatoes (DO NOT DRAIN)
- one 14 ounce can Swanson's 100% fat-free chicken broth
- 1-1/2 Tablespoons basil
- 1-1/2 Tablespoons parsley
- 1/2 teaspoon ground black pepper
- minced garlic, to taste
- 10 cups water
- two 15 ounce cans cannellini beans, rinsed and drained
- 1 cup uncooked small pasta

- Shredded parmesan cheese

Direction

- Brown sausage in a large skillet. Drain any grease well and set aside.
- In a large pot, sauté onion in olive oil until soft and "clear", but not brown. Add sausage, carrots, zucchini, tomatoes with juice, chicken broth, basil, parsley, pepper, garlic, and water and stir to combine. Simmer 30 minutes. Increase heat and bring mixture to a boil. Stir in beans and pasta. Reduce heat to medium-high and cook until pasta is done, about 10-12 minutes. Top servings with Parmesan cheese.

16. BLACK EYED PEA SOUP Recipe

Serving: 8 | Prep: | Cook: 45mins | Ready in:

Ingredients

- 1 - pound ground beef
- 1 pound Polish sausage, cut into bite-sized pieces(browning the sausage before adding it to the pot adds more flavor)
- 1- cup finely chopped onions
- two- 15 ounce cans blackeyed peas with jalapenos
- 1-14 ounce can beef broth
- 1- 14 ounce can diced tomatoes or (fresh)
- 1- 10 ounce can mild diced tomatoes with green chiles (like rotel)
- 1- 10 ounce can chopped green chiles
- 2-medium jalapenos chiles seeded and chopped
- 1/8 - teaspoon salt
- black pepper to taste

Direction

- Place a Dutch oven or heavy pot over medium - high heat.
- Add the ground beef and onions and cook until beef is browned, stirring frequently.
- Add the sausage, black-eyed peas, broth, diced tomatoes, and tomatoes with chiles, green chiles, jalapenos and salt. Mix well
- Bring the mixture to a boil, reduce the heat, cover tightly
- Simmer for 45 minutes.
- Serves 8.
- Note: can make ahead and refrigerate overnight to allow the flavors to blend, then reheat

17. BUTTERNUT SQUASH SOUP Recipe

Serving: 8 | Prep: | Cook: 30mins | Ready in:

Ingredients

- butternut squash SOUP
- 1 butternut squash, about 2 pounds
- 2 tablespoons peanut oil
- 1 cup chopped onion
- 1 1/2 teaspoons chopped garlic
- 1/2 cup thinly sliced carrot
- 1/2 teaspoons ground cumin
- 1/2 teaspoon salt
- 1/2 teaspoon black pepper
- 2 cups chicken stock
- 1/4 cup heavy cream

Direction

- BUTTERNUT SQUASH SOUP
- Cut the squash in half and scoop out the seeds.
- Peel the squash and cut into 1 inch pieces.
- In a large pot, heat oil over medium heat.
- Add onion and garlic and cook, stirring often, until they begin to brown, about 5 minutes.
- Add the carrot, cumin, salt, and pepper. Cook for 1 minute, and then add squash, and chicken stock.

- Bring to a boil, reduce heat and simmer for 15-20 minutes, or until the vegetables are tender.
- Remove from the heat and puree the soup using an immersion blender, or transfer to a blender or food processor.
- Puree until smooth. Return to the heat, add the cream and adjust the seasonings.

18. Baked Jambalaya Recipe

Serving: 16 | Prep: | Cook: | Ready in:

Ingredients

- 1/2 cup butter
- 1 6 oz can tomato paste
- 1 large diced onion
- 1 large chopped green bell pepper
- 3 cups chopped cooked ham
- 3 cups cooked sliced andouille sausage
- 4 cloves minced garlic
- 3 cups cooked chicken cut into small pieces
- 3 tbspns creole seasoning Blend
- 4 tsps worcestershire sauce
- 2 28 oz cans whole peeled tomatoes
- 7 cups chicken stock
- 4 cups uncooked long-grain white rice
- 4 stalks chopped celery
- 3 cups frozen cooked shrimp

Direction

- Preheat your oven to 350F (175C).
- Melt the butter in large pot. Sauté the onion, celery, green pepper, and garlic until all are tender. Be careful not to burn your garlic. Now add the tomato paste and cook until everything is browned slightly. Be sure to stir repeatedly. Stir in the Worcestershire sauce and Creole seasoning blend. Pour this into a large "roasting" pan. Mash the tomatoes to break them up into pieces and add to the mixture in pan. Now stir in the juice from the tomatoes, ham, chicken stock, chicken, sausage, rice and shrimp. Mix everything up well. Cover (tightly) with foil.
- Finally bake this in your preheated oven for 1 1/2 hours. And be sure to stir it once halfway through the baking time.

19. Baked White Wine & Onion Soup Recipe

Serving: 4 | Prep: | Cook: 2hours | Ready in:

Ingredients

- 2 tbsp butter
- 4 to 5 medium onions, thinly sliced
- 1/2 cup dry white wine
- 4 cups vegetable stock (you can use chicken)
- 1 bay leaf
- 1/4 tsp thyme
- 1/4 tsp marjoram
- 4 rounds toasted French bread
- 1 cup grated gruyere cheese
- salt & pepper to taste

Direction

- Melt butter in large deep skillet. When hot, add onions and cook, uncovered, 30 minutes over medium low heat. Stir a few times during cooking.
- Pour in wine & mix well. Cook over medium heat until wine reduces to half. (About 3-4 minutes)
- Pour in stock, mix well, add bay leaf and all seasonings. Mix well and cook, uncovered, about 35 minutes over low heat.
- Preheat oven to 425 degrees.
- Ladle soup into individual ovenproof onion soup bowls. Cover with toasted rounds, top with grated Gruyere. Bake about 15 minutes or until cheese is bubbly brown.

20. Barley Stew With Lentils And Swiss Chard Recipe

Serving: 6 | Prep: | Cook: 60mins | Ready in:

Ingredients

- 1 tablespoon olive oil
- 4 slices of bacon, chopped
- 1 large onion, chopped
- 3 large carrots, chopped
- 3 large garlic cloves, minced
- 1 Tbsp ground cumin
- 10 cups (or more) low-salt chicken or vegetable broth
- 2/3 cup pearl barley
- 1 14 1/2-ounce can diced tomatoes in juice
- 2/3 cup dried lentils
- 4 cups (packed) coarsely chopped swiss chard (about 1/2 large bunch)
- 2 tablespoons chopped fresh dill
- salt and pepper to taste

Direction

- Heat oil in heavy large nonreactive pot over medium-high heat. Add bacon, onions and carrots; sauté until onions are golden brown, about 10 minutes.
- Add garlic and stir 1 minute. Mix in cumin; stir 30 seconds. Add 10 cups broth and barley; bring to boil. Reduce heat; partially cover and simmer 25 minutes.
- Stir in tomatoes with juice and lentils; cover and simmer until barley and lentils are tender, about 30 minutes.
- Add chard to soup; cover and simmer until chard is tender, about 5 minutes. Stir in dill. Season soup with salt and pepper. Thin with more broth, if desired.
- NOTE: Swiss chard can be substituted for fresh (or frozen) spinach leaves.

21. Beef And Vegetable Barley Soup Or Krupnik Recipe

Serving: 8 | Prep: | Cook: 7mins | Ready in:

Ingredients

- 1-1/2 lbs. lean chuck, cut into chunks
- 1-2 large onions, chopped
- 1/4 cup + 3 Tbsp. cup pearl barley
- 1/4 cup navy/pinto beans, soaked in cold water overnight
- 4 carrots, peeled and diced but not small
- 2 parsnips, peeled and diced, not small
- 1 16-ounce can stewed tomatoes
- 4 cloves garlic, minced or chopped finely
- 1-1/2 tsp. Vegeta seasoning
- 1 packet or cube of beef boullion or use 1 can of low sodium beef broth
- 1/2 pound mushrooms, chopped
- Note: My Mother-in-law always used the dried mushrooms from a Polish/Euro deli. She soaked them for 3 hours and sieved them from the liquid they were soaking in. If you can't find these, a flavourful mushroom should be used - not button mushrooms.
- 2-3 large potatoes, peeled and diced
- 1/2 teaspoon freshly ground black pepper
- fresh parsley to garnish and a crusty loaf of bread to go along with it.

Direction

- Place the meat, onion, barley, beans, carrots, parsnips, tomatoes and garlic in a crockpot and add water and beef cube or beef broth to cover by 3 inches.
- Cover and cook on low overnight.
- Note: When I use my crockpot, I often place a folded tea towel over the top to prevent any vapor from escaping. I have been surprised to see how this method speeds up the cooking process.
- In the morning add the mushrooms and potatoes and cook on low for an additional 8-10 hours, until meat is fork tender and barley and beans are cooked thoroughly.

- Season to taste.
- Makes 8 - 10 servings.

22. Beef Stew Bourguignonne Recipe

Serving: 6 | Prep: | Cook: 90mins | Ready in:

Ingredients

- olive oil
- 1/2 pound bacon, diced
- 2 1/2 pounds beef chuck, cut into 1-inch cubes
- 1 pound carrots, sliced thickly on the bias
- 1 yellow onion, sliced
- 1 red onion, sliced
- 4 cloves garlic, chopped
- 1/2 cup brandy
- 1 bottle dry red wine
- 1 14 1/2-ounce can beef broth
- 1 T. tomato paste
- 1 T. chopped fresh rosemary (or thyme or sage)
- 3 T. butter
- 3 T. flour

Direction

- Preheat the oven to 250 degrees.
- Heat a teaspoon or 2 of olive oil in the biggest skillet (with a lid) you've got or in a Dutch oven. Brown the bacon until it's done, but not crispy. Remove the bacon, but leave the fat; return to medium-high heat.
- Add the cubes of beef in batches, making sure not to overcrowd the pan. Turn the pieces quickly to brown the meat on all sides; remove to the plate with the bacon.
- When all the meat is seared, add the carrots and onions to the pan and cook for about 12-15 minutes, until the onions are golden brown. Add the garlic, and cook for another few minutes. Season with plenty of kosher salt and cracked pepper. Now comes the fun part. Have the half cup of brandy and a match or lighter. Add the brandy, and light it on fire, standing away from the stove. It will burn off in less than a minute, but it's fun to watch!
- Stir in the beef and bacon pieces, and pour in the wine. Stir and season with salt and pepper. Add the beef broth; make sure that the meat is sufficiently covered. Stir in the tomato paste and rosemary. Bring the mixture to a boil, then pop it into the oven to cook for about an hour.
- Remove the pan from the oven and return to the stove top. Mash the butter and flour into a paste, and stir into the stew to thicken. Bring it to a boil; reduce and simmer for about 10-15 minutes. To serve, layer thick slices of crusty bread, rubbed with cut garlic, into bowls; ladle the stew on

23. Beef Stew Moroccan Style Recipe

Serving: 4 | Prep: | Cook: 25mins | Ready in:

Ingredients

- 3 T olive oil
- 1 3/4 Lbs beef tenderloin - 1 in cubes
- 1 LG onion - Chopped
- 1 Large carrot - Chopped
- 2 cloves garlic - chopped
- 1 t paprika
- 2 t ground cumin
- 1 1/2 t ground cinnamon
- 2 C beef broth
- 1 15 oz can garbonzo beans
- 1/2 golden raisins
- 1/2 C fresh cilantro - chopped

Direction

- Heat 2 T oil in a large heavy Skillet. Sprinkle beef with a little salt and pepper and brown on all sides. Transfer to plate and set aside.
- Add remaining 1 T oil to pot and onion, carrot and garlic. Cook till soft, stirring frequently - about 10 min.

- Add spices, stir one minute till well incorporated
- Add beef broth, garbanzo beans and raisins - bring to boil. Simmer until juices thicken a bit - about 5 min.
- Add beef and cilantro to pot and stir till heated through.
- Great served over couscous

24. Beef Stew Recipe

Serving: 6 | Prep: | Cook: 60mins | Ready in:

Ingredients

- 1 cup frozen peas
- 1 1 1/2 pounds bone-less beef chuck roast, cut into 3/4 inch cubes
- 1/3 cup all-purpose flour
- 1 1/2 cups hot water
- 1 large onion, sliced
- 1 bay leaf
- 1 tablespoon instant beef bouillon granules
- 1 1/2 teaspoons salt (optional)
- 1 teaspoon sugar
- 1 teaspoon dried parsley flakes
- 1/8 teaspoon pepper
- 1 8-ounce can tomato sauce
- 6 medium carrots, thinly sliced
- 4 medium potatoes, peeled and cut into eighths
- 2 stalks celery, sliced

Direction

- Measure peas and set aside.
- In a 3 quart casserole toss meat with flour.
- Add water, onion, bay leaf, bouillon granules, salt, sugar, parsley flakes, and pepper.
- Microwave, covered, on high 5 minutes; stir.
- Reduce power to medium (50%).
- Microwave 20 minutes, stirring once.
- Stir in tomato sauce, carrots, potatoes, and celery.
- Microwave, covered, on medium for 40 to 60 minutes or until the meat and vegetables are tender, stirring once.
- Add peas; microwave on medium for 1 to 2 minutes or until peas are heated through.
- Let stand, covered, 10 minutes.
- Makes 4 to 6 servings.
- NOTE: Beef chuck is better marbled and often less expensive then the round sold as beef stew meat. Small uniform pieces you cut yourself will microwave more evenly and be more tender.

25. Beef Stew And Dumplings Recipe

Serving: 46 | Prep: | Cook: 30mins | Ready in:

Ingredients

- Stew
- Half a kilo of stewing beef or any cut you prefer chopped into 1 inch cubes
- 2 or 3 onions Chopped roughly
- 3 carrots sliced (not to thin)
- 1 medium sized swede (chopped)
- 1 fennel bulb (chopped)
- 1 Small pumpkin (skinned and chopped)
- 4 Sticks of celery (de stringed and sliced)
- 4 Meduim to large old potoatos (chopped) or 10 new potatos cut in half.
- 4 Minature marrows (sliced)
- 250 grams button mushrooms left whole
- Half a cup of red lentils
- Half a cup of pearl barley
- Good pinch of salt and pepper
- 2 tablespoons of dried herbs
- 1 vegetable stock cube
- 1 beef stock cube
- gravy thickening granuals
- Enough water to just cover the stew ingredients for cooking
- Dumplings
- 6oz of self raising flour

- 3oz of vegetarian suet or beef suet
- Good pinch of salt and pepper. You can add herbs if you wish but use sparingly.

Direction

- Stew
- Place all the Vegetables, stock cubes, seasoning and beef into a pressure cooker
- Place on the lid and bring to full pressure (as per manufactures instructions) and allow to cook for 5 minutes.
- Dumplings
- Blend the flour suet and seasoning in a bowl.
- Gently add enough water to make to a firm dough.
- Divide into medium sized balls and leave to rest whilst the stew is cooking.
- Stew
- When 5 minutes cooking time is reached depressurise the cooker as per the manufactures instructions.
- Return the cooker back to a reduced heat and add the dumpling balls, gently pushing them under the gravy in the pot.
- Place the lid loosely back on the pressure cooker and leave to simmer for 20 mins.
- When the dumplings are cooked remove them, place in a bowl and keep warm.
- Add thickening gravy granules to the stew and stir until the mixture is thickened and the granules have dissolved completely.
- Put the dumplings on a plate and serve the stew with them.
- Eat with big chunks of fresh bread.
- Great meal for autumn and winter to ward off the chills.
- You can omit the beef and beef stock cube but add another vegetable stock cube and a squeeze of tomato puree to make this a vegetarian dish.

26. Beef And Barley Soup Recipe

Serving: 12 | Prep: | Cook: 40mins | Ready in:

Ingredients

- 2 c. of diced cooked beef
- 10 c. of beef stock
- 3/4 c. of barley
- 1 bay leaf
- 3 sprigs fresh chopped thyme
- 1/2 c. of red wine
- 2 c. of cubed potatoes
- 1 tbsp. of vegetable oil
- 1 1/2 c. of chopped onion
- 1 c. of chopped celery
- 1 c. of chopped carrots
- 2 cloves pf minced garlic
- 1 tsp. of browning sauce (optional)
- 1 1/2 c. of chopped cabbage
- salt and pepper to taste

Direction

- First you want to take some olive oil in medium pot over medium flame.
- Sauté the onions, celery, carrots, and garlic approx. 5 min.
- Now add in the beef stock, barley, bay leaf, and the thyme until barley is tender.
- Next add in the wine, potatoes, and the beef.
- You can add in the browning and seasoning sauce
- Let this simmer approx. 15 min and add the cabbage.
- This will need to simmer another 15 min until all veggies are tender.
- Ladle and serve.

27. Best Pumpkin Soup Recipe

Serving: 10 | Prep: | Cook: 35mins | Ready in:

Ingredients

- 1 large onion, chopped fine
- 1 stick butter
- 6 slices of bacon, cooked to the just crisp stage and crumbled(in m icrowave on paper towels for 3 to 4 minutes)
- 3 to 4 cups fresh cooked pumpkin(This can be done in the microwave!See directions below) or canned pumpkin puree(not pumpkin pie mix kind).
- 1 1/2 Tablespoons minced garlic
- 5 or 6 fresh carrots (chopped)
- 4 cups chicken broth or stock
- 1 cup chopped celery
- 1 pint half-and-half
- 1 teaspoon thyme
- 4 tablespoons chopped parsley
- 1 teaspoon onion salt
- 1 teaspoon cumin
- 1 tablespoon cracked black pepper
- 1/4 teaspoon cinnamon (optional)
- salt to taste
- 1/3 cup sliced green onions
- 1/2 cup heavy cream
- sour cream and roasted pumpkin seeds as a garnish

Direction

- For fresh pumpkin:
- Wash the exterior of the pumpkin in cool or warm water, no soap.
- Cut the pumpkin in half and scrape the insides.
- I find a heavy ice cream scoop works great for this.
- Remove the stem, and put the pumpkin into a microwaveable.
- You may need to cut the pumpkin further to make it fit but try to keep in as big a piece as possible for ease of removing the pumpkin meat.
- Put a couple of inches of water in the bowl, cover it, and put in the microwave\
- Cook the pumpkin until soft, usually anywhere from 15 to 25 minutes depending on size.
- Soup:

- In large soup pot, Sauté onions, garlic, celery in butter until tender.
- Add stock, pumpkin and carrots and bring to a boil.
- Lower heat and cook until carrots are tender, about 20 minutes.
- Puree soup in small batches in blender or food processor until smooth.
- Return to pot and add thyme, cumin, parsley, and cracked pepper and bring to another boil.
- Lower heat to low, stir in half and half, green onions, and bacon and season with salt to taste.
- Continue to cook on low heat for another 10 to 15 minutes.
- Stir in heavy cream.
- Spoon into individual soup bowls or in soup tureen.
- Top with a little sour cream and roasted pumpkin seeds or additional green onions and bacon bits.

28. Black Bean Chili Cheese Dip Recipe

Serving: 10 | Prep: | Cook: 3mins | Ready in:

Ingredients

- 1 can chili without beans (Hormel is my favorite)
- 1 can black beans, drained
- 8 oz colby-Jack cheese, grated or crumbled
- 2-4 oz sour cream
- ground cayenne pepper to taste
- sprinkle of chives

Direction

- Mix chili, beans, cheese and pepper in a 9x9 deep casserole dish.
- Place in microwave oven and heat on high until cheese is thoroughly melted and mix is creamy smooth (usually 3-3½ minutes), stirring often.

- Top with sour cream and chives. Serve hot with tortilla chips.

29. Black Bean Soup Recipe

Serving: 6 | Prep: | Cook: 30mins | Ready in:

Ingredients

- 1 tablespoon vegetable oil
- 1 onion, chopped
- 1 clove garlic, minced
- 2 carrots, chopped
- 2 teaspoons chili powder
- 1 teaspoon ground cumin
- 4 cups chicken or vegetable (for vegetarian) stock
- 2 (15 ounce) cans black beans, rinsed and drained
- 1 (8.75 ounce) can whole kernel corn
- 1/4 teaspoon ground black pepper
- 1 (14.5 ounce) can stewed tomatoes
- juice of one small lime (optional)

Direction

- In large saucepan, heat oil over medium heat; cook onion, garlic, and carrots, stirring occasionally, for 5 minutes or until onion is softened. Add chili powder and cumin; cook, stirring, for 1 minute. Add stock, 1 can of the beans, corn, and pepper; bring to boil.
- Meanwhile, in food processor or blender, puree together tomatoes and remaining can of beans; add to pot. Reduce heat, cover, and simmer for 10 to 15 minutes or until carrots are tender. You can control the thickness by reducing or adding the amount of stock.

30. Black Beans Potage Recipe

Serving: 8 | Prep: | Cook: 452mins | Ready in:

Ingredients

- 1 pound black beans
- 10 cups water
- 1 big green pepper
- 2/3 cup olive oil
- 1 big onion
- 4 garlic cloves
- 1 big green pepper
- 4 teaspoons salt
- 1/2 teaspoon black pepper
- 1/4 teaspoon ground oregano
- 1/4 teaspoon cummin
- 1 laurel leaf
- 3 tablespoons white sugar
- 2 tablespoons vinegar
- 2 tablespoons white dry wine
- 2 tablespoons olive oil

Direction

- Wash the beans and put them in the water, and soak them overnight. You can also put the beans in warm water for about an hour before cooking. Put them to cook in the same water, in a pressure cooker until they are well done and soft, about 45 minutes or so. Without a pressure cooker, cook for about 2 hours or until the beans are tender. Add more water if needed.
- Heat the olive oil, add the onion, finely chopped, and the ground garlic cloves, fry them briefly and then add the green pepper, also finely chopped. Fry them until they are tender.
- Pour about one cup of the cooked black beans in the pan with the onion, garlic and green pepper, grind them well and pour them into the pot with the rest of the black beans. Add the salt, black pepper, oregano, cumin, bay leaf, and white sugar. Simmer them, for about an hour, on very low heat.
- Then add the vinegar and white wine, keep simmering them until they are creamy, just when you are about to serve them, add 2 tablespoons of olive oil.
- Enjoy!

31. Black Eyed Peas And Veggie Soup Recipe

Serving: 8 | Prep: | Cook: 90mins | Ready in:

Ingredients

- 2 cups black-eyed peas, soaked overnight in cold water
- ½ cabbage, thinly sliced
- 2 cups diced pumpkin
- 1 sliced leek
- 1 sliced onion
- 3 red tomatoes, peeled, seeded and diced
- ½ cup red pepper, diced
- 2 Tbsp sweet paprika
- salt to taste
- ¼ cup olive oil

Direction

- Drain peas, place in a casserole with lid and cover with cold water. When boiling, turn heat to low and let simmer covered till tender but firm (1 – 1 ½ hrs.).
- When ready, drain, arrange them in the same casserole and cover again with clean cold water. Add the vegetables and cook till tender, about 15 minutes.
- Add salt to taste and the 2 Tbsp. of sweet paprika. Mix well. Turn heat off and set aside. They are best eaten next day.
- When ready to serve, drizzle some olive oil on (about 2 Tbsp. per person).

32. Blender Gazpacho Recipe

Serving: 10 | Prep: | Cook: 40mins | Ready in:

Ingredients

- 1 28 oz. can of crushed tomatoes in puree
- 1 can of diced tomatoes with green chiles and onion
- 1 english cucumber, peeled diced in big chunks
- 1 red pepper, seeded and chunked
- 2 ribs of celery, trimmed and chunked
- 1 red or yellow onion, cut in large chunks
- 2 cloves of garlic, peeled
- 1 fresh jalapeno, seeded and deveined if you dare (I do)
- 2 tbsp. of olive oil
- 3 inch chunk of day old bread soaked in water and squeezed dry and torn into pieces
- 1 tbsp. of red wine vinegar
- 1 tbsp. of lemon juice
- 1/2 teapoon of salt
- 1/2 teaspoon of black pepper
- several shakes of Tabasco, Chipotle style
- Suggested Garnishes: pickled shrimp/sour cream/herb croutons or minced chives and lemon zest.

Direction

- In a large blender, put the cucumber/pepper/onion/celery/garlic and the can of tomatoes with chilies.
- Process until nearly smooth.
- Pour into a large container.
- Don't rinse the blender, add the big can of tomatoes and the bread and oil, vinegar, lemon juice and seasonings.
- Puree till completely smooth.
- Add to blended veggies and stir until combined.
- Taste and adjust for seasonings, (salt tolerance mostly)
- Chill at least 40 minutes.
- For service, I use a chilled margarita glass, hang a pickled shrimp off the glass with a tiny dollop of sour cream, sprinkled with chives and lemon zest and a tiny pinch of coarse salt.

33. Broccoli And Cheese Soup Recipe

Serving: 6 | Prep: | Cook: 15mins | Ready in:

Ingredients

- 3 cups chopped broccoli
- 3 Tbsp butter
- ¼ cup finely chopped onion
- 4 tsp chicken bouillon mix
- 3 Tbsp all-purpose flour
- ½ tsp paprika
- ½ tsp dry mustard
- 2 cups 1% milk
- 2 cups water
- 2 cups grated old cheddar cheese
- ½ tsp salt

Direction

- Cook broccoli in boiling water until tender crisp. Drain well and reserve water.
- Melt butter in large saucepan and sauté onion until tender.
- Blend in bouillon mix, flour, paprika & mustard. Gradually stir in milk and water. Cook over medium heat, stirring until mixture comes to a boil and thickens.
- Remove from heat.
- Add cheese and stir until melted.
- Add cooked broccoli & salt. Re-heat to serving temperature. DO NOT BOIL.
- Pass more grated cheese to sprinkle over individual servings.

34. Broccoli Cheddar Soup Recipe

Serving: 12 | Prep: | Cook: 30mins | Ready in:

Ingredients

- 1 stick butter
- 1 onion, finely diced
- 2 cloves garlic, minced
- 2 stalks celery, thinnly chopped
- 2 carrots, grated
- about 1lb fresh broccoli, chopped well
- 1 red pepper, finely diced
- 5 cups chicken stock
- 2 cups water
- 2 cups half and half
- 3/4 cup flour
- 16oz cheddar cheese, shredded(shred this yourself...it's worth it :)
- 4oz whipped or very soft cream cheese
- salt and pepper
- dash of hot sauce
- dash of nutmeg

Direction

- In large soup pan or Dutch oven celery, onion, red pepper and carrots in butter until soft.
- Add chicken stock and broccoli and cook at medium heat until broccoli is done (15-20 min)
- Season with salt and pepper (this will need a fair amount of each)
- Whisk together the flour and water to form a slurry
- Add slurry and cream cheese to soup and increase heat to thicken.
- Add cheese until melted.
- Add half and half, nutmeg, hot sauce and more fresh ground pepper and heat through.

35. Broccoli Cheese Soup Recipe

Serving: 10 | Prep: | Cook: 23mins | Ready in:

Ingredients

- 1 large onion, chopped
- 3 tablespoons oil or margarine
- chicken bouillon cubes, dissolved in 6 cups of water
- 2 (10 ounce) packages of frozen chopped broccoli, thawed or 1 bunch fresh broccoli, cut up

- 1/4 teaspoon garlic powder, dried minced garlic or one garlic clove crushed
- 8 ounces of angel hair pasta
- 1 pound of cubed cheddar cheese
- 3 cups of milk

Direction

- In a large pot, sauté onions in oil for 3 minutes.
- Add the dissolved bouillon, broccoli and garlic and cook for about 10 minutes.
- Add the noodles.
- Simmer 5 minutes.
- Add the cheese and heat till soft.
- Add the milk and heat till cheese melts and soup is hot.
- Do not boil!

36. Brown Stew Recipe

Serving: 8 | Prep: | Cook: 60mins | Ready in:

Ingredients

- 6 slices bacon, cut crosswise into eighths
- 2 to 2 1/2 pounds boneless beef chuck roast, cut into 3/4 inch cubes
- 1/3 cup all-purpose flour
- 1 tablespoon soy sauce
- 1 1/2 teaspoons seasoned salt (optional)
- 1/4 teaspoon dried basil, crushed
- 1/8 teaspoon garlic powder
- 1 1/2 cups hot water
- 1/2 cup dry red wine
- 2 medium onions, cut into eight wedges
- 2 cups sliced fresh mushrooms

Direction

- In a 3-quart microwavable casserole cook bacon, covered, on high for 6 minutes.
- Add beef cubes to casserole pan.
- Toss with flour, soy sauce, salt, basil, and garlic powder.
- Stir in water, wine, and onions.

- Microwave, covered, on high for 5 minutes.
- Reduce power to medium heat (50%).
- Microwave, uncovered, 30 minutes, stirring once.
- Add mushrooms.
- Microwave on medium (50%) for another 35 to 45 minutes or until the beef is tender, stirring once.
- Cover and let stand 10 minutes.
- Serves 8.
- NOTE: Beef chuck is better marbled and often less expensive then the round sold as beef stew meat. Small uniform pieces you cut yourself will microwave more evenly and be more tender.

37. Brunswick Stew Recipe

Serving: 6 | Prep: | Cook: 300mins | Ready in:

Ingredients

- 3 medium onions, cut into thin wedges
- 2 pounds meaty chicken pieces, skinned
- 1 1/2 cups diced cooked ham (8 ounces)
- 1 14 1/2-ounce can diced tomatoes
- 1 14 ounce can chicken broth
- 4 cloves garlic, minced
- 1 tablespoon worcestershire sauce
- 1 teaspoon dry mustard
- 1 teaspoon dried thyme, crushed
- 1/4 teaspoon pepper
- 1/4 teaspoon bottled hot pepper sauce
- 1 10-ounce package frozen sliced okra (2 cups)
- 1 cup frozen baby lima beans
- 1 cup frozen whole kernel corn

Direction

- In a 3 1/2- to 4-quart crockery cooker place onion. Top with chicken and ham. In a small bowl combine undrained tomatoes, broth, garlic, Worcestershire sauce, mustard, thyme, pepper, and hot pepper sauce; pour over chicken and ham.

- Cover and cook on low-heat setting for 8 to 10 hours or on high-heat setting for 4 to 5 hours.
- If desired, remove chicken; cool slightly. (Keep lid on the crockery cooker.) Remove meat from chicken bones; cut meat into bite-size pieces. Return chicken to crockery cooker; discard bones.
- Add okra, lima beans, and corn to crockery cooker. If using low-heat setting turn to high-heat setting. Cover and cook 45 minutes more or until vegetables are tender.

38. Buffalo Chicken Soup Recipe

Serving: 6 | Prep: | Cook: 30mins | Ready in:

Ingredients

- 1 2-1/4 to 2-1/2 lb. deli-roasted chicken, skinned, boned, and coarsely shredded
- 2 Tbsp. butter
- 1/2 cup coarsely chopped celery
- 1/2 cup chopped onion
- 2 14-oz. cans reduced-sodium chicken broth
- 1-1/2 cups milk
- 1 tsp. Frank's RedHot Sauce (You are so right, Ray baby!)
- 1-1/2 cups mozzarella cheese (6 oz.)
- 1-1/4 cups crumbled blue cheese (5 oz.)
- 1/2 cup shredded parmesan cheese (2 oz.)
- 1/3 cup all-purpose flour
- 3 chopped green onions, for garnish
- Frank's RedHot Sauce to taste *wink*

Direction

- In 4-quart Dutch oven melt butter over medium heat.
- Add celery and onion; cook and stir until onion is tender, 5-6 minutes.
- Stir in broth, milk, and the 1 teaspoon hot pepper sauce.
- In bowl toss together mozzarella, 1 cup of the blue cheese, Parmesan, and flour. Add gradually to soup, stirring after each addition just until melted.
- Stir in three-fourths of the shredded chicken; heat through.
- Top with remaining chicken, blue cheese, green onions and hot sauce.

39. Butternut Squash Soup For The Crockpot Recipe

Serving: 6 | Prep: | Cook: 390mins | Ready in:

Ingredients

- 2 1/2 pounds butternut squash, peeled, seeded, cubed 1" size (about 1 medium squash)
- 2 cups leeks, chopped (whites and light green only)
- 2 large granny smith apples, peeled, cored, diced
- 2 (14.5 oz) cans chicken or vegitable broth
- 1 cup water
- 1 tsp marjoram, ground
- salt to taste
- heavy cream or plain yogurt (optional)
- white pepper to taste
- parsley or scallion for garnish

Direction

- 1. In a 5 quart electric slow cooker, combine the squash, leeks, apples, broth, and water.
- 2. Cover and cook on Low for 6 to 7 hours or until the squash and leeks are very tender. You can speed up to 3-4 hours on High. Add Marjoram after 5-6 hours on low or 2-3 on High.
- 3. Using a mixing wand, puree the soup in the slow cooker until a smooth uniform texture. Turn on High for another 1/2 hour.
- 4. Serve hot with a dollop of cream or yogurt swirled into soup on top and garnish with a sprig of parsley or sprinkle with chives.

40. CROCKPOT JAMBALAYA Recipe

Serving: 6 | Prep: | Cook: 300mins | Ready in:

Ingredients

- vegetable cooking spray
- 1 cup celery, chopped
- 1 cup green bell pepper, chopped
- 2 cups onion, chopped
- 2 tbsp. minced garlic
- 1/2 cup minced Italian parsley
- 15 oz. canned tomatoes
- 5 lbs. skinless chicken thighs
- 1 lb. smoked sausage – sliced lengthwise, then across in semi circles
- 1 lb. chicken Andouille sausage – sliced lengthwise, then across in semicircles
- 1/2 cup water
- salt and pepper, to taste
- 14 oz. long-grain rice (about 2-1/4 cups)
- 1 tbsp. minced fresh thyme
- 1 tsp. kosher salt
- Above is original... I add lots of cajun seasoning, and less salt.. some red pepper flakes as I like it SPICY! BUT.. start with original and add to your taste...

Direction

- Spray crock-pot with vegetable spray.
- Mix vegetables and seasonings with canned tomatoes.
- Spread over bottom of crock-pot.
- Tuck thighs into vegetable mixture.
- Top with chopped sausages.
- Pour water over, cover and cook on high for 4 hours.
- Remove cover and stir in rice, thyme and salt. Cover and cook for an additional 50 minutes.

41. Cabbage Soup Recipe

Serving: 20 | Prep: | Cook: 220mins | Ready in:

Ingredients

- 1/2 medium head cabbage, chopped
- 4 stalks celery, cut into cubes
- 1 sweet onion, finely diced
- 4 large carrots, cut into cubes
- 1 (14.5 oz) can tomatoes, peeled and finely chopped
- 1 1/2 cups tomato-vegetable juice cocktail
- 3 cups vegetable broth
- 1 (14.5 oz) can chicken broth
- 3/4 cup ketchup

Direction

- Place the cabbage into an 8-qt soup pot.
- Add the carrots to 2 tablespoons of water and microwave on high setting for 6 minutes.
- Microwave celery in 2 tablespoons water on high setting for 4 minutes.
- Stir the microwaved vegetables to the pot with the cabbage. Mix in the celery, sweet onion, and ketchup. Now, add the tomatoes, juice cocktail, and the chicken and vegetable broth. Fill each empty can with water, and add to the mixture. Cover, and bring to a boil, then continue boiling for 30 minutes.
- Lower the heat to simmer and cook for 2-3 hours.
- Serve with sliced French baguette. Place salt, black pepper, and Tabasco sauce at the table to season, as desired.

42. Canning Country Vegetable Vegan No Meat Soup Recipe

Serving: 28 | Prep: | Cook: 75mins | Ready in:

Ingredients

- Canning Country vegetable VEGAN Soup

- 6 Cups water
- 2 Teaspoon salt
- 1/2 Teaspoon pepper
- 2 cloves garlic minced
- 1 Bay leaf
- 1/3 Cup pearl barley or rice
- 1 Quart chopped tomatoes
- 4 Sliced celery stalks
- 4 Sliced carrots
- 1 Cup chopped onions
- 1/2 shredded cabbage
- 1 Pound red kidney beans
- 1 pound yellow split peas (or substitute green split peas)
- Add any fresh garden herbs that you like.

Direction

- Use a large heavy pan
- Soak the kidney beans and peas overnight
- Combine, water, salt and pepper
- Bring to boil, add garlic and bay
- Cover and simmer for 75 minutes
- Add all the of the vegetables
- Simmer for about 20 minutes
- Vegetables will cook more while canning
- Put in jars with 1 inch headspace
- Process in a Pressure Canner

43. Carrot Cream Soup With Cream Cheese Dumplings Mohrencremesuppe Mit Klosschen Recipe

Serving: 4 | Prep: | Cook: 30mins | Ready in:

Ingredients

- For soup:
- 3 T. unsalted butter
- 1 small onion, chopped
- 2 cups carrots, peeled and chopped
- 1 medium yukon gold potato, peeled and chopped
- Freshly squeezed lemon juice, to taste
- 3 cups homemade vegetable stock (recipe follows)
- 1 cup Riesling (or a dry white wine)
- 1 tsp. sugar
- 1/2 cup heavy cream
- kosher salt, freshly grated nutmeg and white pepper, to taste
- chives for garnish
- ~~~~~~
- homemade vegetable stock:
- 1 leek. sliced and rinsed clean
- 3 medium sweet onions, peeled and chopped
- 3 large carrots, scrubbed and chopped
- 2 stalks celery, rinsed and chopped
- 8 ounces crimini mushrooms, rinsed and quartered
- 2 roma tomatoes, rinsed and quartered
- 1 head fennel (about 1 lb.), rinsed, and chopped
- Handful fresh parsley
- Handful fresh thyme
- Handful fresh oregano
- 1 tablespoon black peppercorns
- sea salt to taste
- ~~~~~~For Dumplings:
- 8 oz. natural cream cheese
- 1 egg
- 1/2 c. homemade breadcrumbs, dried and finely ground (or panko, works for me!)
- 2 tsp. fresh parsley, minced
- kosher salt, freshly ground nutmeg and black pepper, to taste

Direction

- For homemade vegetable stock:
- Place leek in an 8- to 10-quart pan. Add onions, carrots, celery, mushrooms, tomatoes, fennel, parsley, thyme, oregano, peppercorns, salt and enough water to cover vegetables (about 2 qt.). Bring to a boil over high heat, then reduce heat and simmer, uncovered, for 2 hours, adding water as needed to keep vegetables barely covered.

- Line a colander with a layer of cheesecloth (or use a large, fine wire strainer); set over a large bowl. Pour stock mixture into colander and drain vegetables well; discard vegetables. Reserve stock for use.
- To make the Carrot Cream Soup:
- Melt the butter in a 4 quart saucepan and sauté the onion for several minutes. Add the carrots and potato and cook for another 3 minutes. Do not brown. Add the lemon juice, wine, broth and a half teaspoon of sugar (optional) and bring to a boil. Simmer for 25 minutes, or until vegetables are soft.
- Make dumplings in the meantime.
- To make the Cream Cheese Dumplings:
- Bring a large pan of water to just under a boil.
- Mix all dumpling ingredients in a bowl and let stand for 5 minutes. If the dough is too thin to form into dumplings, add more bread crumbs.
- Using two teaspoons, form dumplings by taking about 1 tablespoon of dough in one teaspoon and using the second teaspoon to smooth the dumpling. If you transfer the dough several times between the two spoons, you will form a triangular egg shaped dumpling that is common in German cuisine. If you would rather, you may also just form smooth, round balls using your hands---but it looks way cooler to make "quenelles" ;-)
- Drop the dumplings into the simmering water and cook for 3 - 5 minutes, or until done. Dumplings are done when they float to the surface and are firm all the way through. Remove with a slotted spoon and let drain.
- Puree the soup in a blender in 2 batches or with a hand blender (immersion blender) in the pan. Add salt and pepper to taste.
- Ladle the soup into bowls. Place 3 dumplings in each bowl. Garnish with some chopped chives and serve hot.

44. Central Avenue Oyster Bar Stew Recipe

Serving: 2 | Prep: | Cook: 10mins | Ready in:

Ingredients

- 1 pint of oysters, freshest possible
- 3 tablespoons of butter divided
- 1/2 teaspoon of Worchestershire sauce
- 1/2 teaspoon of celery salt
- 1/2 cup of liquid from oysters
- 1/2 cup of bottled clam juice
- 2 cups of milk
- dash of paprika

Direction

- Drain oysters, reserving liquor.
- Heat together 1 1/2 tablespoons of butter, Worchestershire sauce, and celery salt, bring to boil.
- Add oysters and mixed oyster and clam juice.
- Heat until the edges begin to curl.
- Pour in milk and heat just below the boiling point.
- When ready to serve, split the reserved 3/4 tablespoon of butter between the bottom of your two bowls and ladle the stew over top. Sprinkle with a dash of paprika.
- "This is not that, and that is certainly not this, and at the same time an oyster stew is not stewed, and although they are made of the same things and even cooked almost the same way, an oyster soup should never be called a stew, nor stew soup."
- M.F.K. Fisher (1908-1992)

45. Cheap And Easy Lentil Barley Soup Recipe

Serving: 5 | Prep: | Cook: 60mins | Ready in:

Ingredients

- 8 c. water
- 3 small to medium carrots, peeled and diced (about 1 cup diced)
- 1 14.5 oz can diced tomatoes, undrained
- 5 chicken, beef or vegetable bouillon cubes
- ½ tsp. garlic powder or 1 clove garlic, minced
- 1 tbsp onion powder or 1 medium onion, diced
- ½ tsp celery salt or 1 stalk celery, diced
- ¾ cup dried lentils
- ¾ cup barley (not quick-cooking)
- ½ tsp dried rosemary
- ½ tsp ground oregano
- ½ tsp fresh ground pepper
- 1 14 oz. can seasoned Southern kale greens, undrained

Direction

- Put everything except kale greens in a soup pot.
- Bring to a boil, stirring occasionally.
- Reduce heat to low. Cover and simmer 50 minutes.
- Add kale greens.
- Simmer 10 minutes longer to heat through.

46. Cheeseburger Soup Meets Potato Soup Recipe

Serving: 6 | Prep: | Cook: 45mins | Ready in:

Ingredients

- 1 1/2 cups water
- 2 cups potatoes, peeled and cubed
- 2 carrots, grated
- 1 onion, chopped
- 1/4 cup green pepper, chopped
- 1 jalapeno pepper, seeded and finely chopped
- 1 clove garlic, finely chopped
- 1 tbls. beef bouillon granules
- 1/2 tsp. salt
- 1 lb. hamburger, cooked and drained
- 2 1/2 cups milk, divided
- 3 tbls. flour
- 1/2-2/3 lb. Velveeta cheese, cubed
- 1/4-1 tsp. cayenne pepper to taste
- 1/2 lb. bacon, cooked and crumbled
- sour cream and chives to garnish

Direction

- In saucepan, add first 9 ingredients and bring to boil
- Reduce heat and simmer 15-20 minutes or until potatoes are tender
- Stir in beef and 2 cups milk, then heat through
- In mixing bowl, add flour and remaining milk and stir until smooth
- Gradually stir into soup
- Bring to boil and cook, stirring constantly for 2 minutes or until thick and bubbly
- Reduce heat and stir in cheese until melted
- Add desired amount of cayenne and stir
- Top with bacon just before serving
- Garnish with sour cream and chives

47. Chicken And Coconut Soup Recipe

Serving: 0 | Prep: | Cook: 30mins | Ready in:

Ingredients

- 2 cups coconut milk
- 1 1/2 cups chicken stock
- 3 stalks lemongrass, white part only, cut in 1" lengths
- 8 thin slices galangal
- 10 kaffir lime leaves
- 3 shallots, thinly sliced
- 3 boneless, skinless chicken thighs, cut into small cubes (1/2")
- 1 cup thinly sliced fresh mushrooms
- 3 tbsp. fresh lime juice
- 4 tbsp. fish sauce

- 1/2 tsp. palm or granulated sugar (palm tastes truer)
- 2 tbsp. fresh cilantro leaves, chopped
- 1/2 tsp. chopped fresh red chilies

Direction

- In a large saucepan, combine coconut milk, stock, lemongrass, galangal, lime leaves, and shallots. Bring just to a boil. Reduce heat and simmer for 20 minutes.
- Remove the lemongrass, galangal and lime leaves and add the chicken and mushrooms. Simmer for 10 more minutes or until chicken is tender and just cooked.
- Remove from heat and stir in lime juice, fish sauce and sugar.
- Serve soup garnished with cilantro. Stir in chopped chilies, or let guests add their own. :)

48. Chicken Andouille Gumbo Recipe

Serving: 4 | Prep: | Cook: 60093mins | Ready in:

Ingredients

- 2 Tbsp. butter
- 2 Tbsp. flour
- 1/2 large onion, chopped
- 1 med. red bell pepper, finely chopped
- 2 celery stalks, finely chopped
- 4 cloves minced garlic
- 1/2 - 1 tsp. ground cayenne pepper (or more, we like it HOT)
- 12.8 oz. package chicken andouille sausage(4 links) halved, quartered and sliced into bite size pieces (I used Trader Joes brand)
- 1 1/2 tsp dried thyme
- 1/2 tsp marjoram
- 6 cups chicken broth (approx.) I used my own stock, just poured in what I wanted, have made it with Swanson chicken broth before - about 3 cans
- I also threw in my leftover chicken, chopped (not necessary though)
- file powder (optional, not necessary)

Direction

- After all the chopping is done and set aside, melt butter in large pot over med heat;
- Add flour and cook stirring constantly till it's a warm caramel color - PATIENCE REQ.
- You can make it darker, just be careful not to burn, or it will taste burnt.
- When it's the color you like, turn down heat or remove from if using electric, and add onions and cayenne powder, cook stirring till sizzling ends - approx. 2-3 minutes.
- Replace on heat (I use med. low) and add celery and garlic, cook stirring about 2-3 minutes.
- Add peppers and do the same.
- Andouille is already fully cooked, but I like to add it now and brown it a bit.
- Slowly add broth and stir, scraping any bits from bottom of pot.
- Add thyme and marjoram. Adjust seasoning to taste.
- Salt to taste, careful depending on how long you plan to simmer or reduce, it can get saltier.
- Bring to simmer and let simmer as long as you like, it will just reduce and thicken.
- If using file powder, add about 5 minutes before serving while still simmering.
- You can simmer it all day or eat it as soon as you like.
- If it doesn't get as thick as you like, add cornstarch and water mixture to it while simmering, or you can sprinkle Wondra over it. (I've done either before)

49. Chicken Black Bean Soup Recipe

Serving: 6 | Prep: | Cook: 90mins | Ready in:

Ingredients

- 3-4 cooked chicken breasts, cubed (I poached mine with some peppercorns, bay leaves and cilantro)
- 3 cans black beans (drain two of the cans)
- 8-10 cups chicken broth (I use low-sodium)
- 4 stalks celery (sliced)
- 1 onion (diced)
- 3 cloves garlic (smashed/minced)
- 2 green bell peppers (cut into 1in squares)
- 1 habanero (or other small hot pepper), seeded and diced
- 1 tsp thyme
- 1 tbsp cumin
- 1 tsp cayenne
- 1 tsp oregano
- 1/8 cup chopped fresh cilantro
- 1 bay leaf
- 1-2 tbsp olive oil
- salt and pepper

Direction

- Sauté onion, celery and green pepper in olive oil over medium-medium high heat in a large heavy bottomed pot until softened
- Add garlic and habanero, cook for 1-2 minutes or until fragrant
- Add rest of the ingredients to the pot, bring just to a boil then reduce to a simmer, uncovered
- Stir every 10-15 minutes and check spices, add more or less according to taste

50. Chicken Breasts With Green Chilies Recipe

Serving: 4 | Prep: | Cook: 30mins | Ready in:

Ingredients

- 4 Tbs vegetable oil
- 2 whole chicken breasts(about 2 lbs) halved
- 1 c minced onion
- 20 mild green chilies(canned or bottled)
- 1-1/2 c heavy cream
- 1 tsp Tabasco sauce
- 1/2 tsp salt
- black pepper to taste
- juice of 1 lemon or lime
- 1 c grated Moneray Jack cheese

Direction

- Heat oil in sauté pan over med-high heat.
- Sauté chicken breasts 2-3 mins, or till lightly browned on skin side only. Put them in a single layer in an ovenproof casserole, skin side up.
- Add onion to sauté pan and cook till translucent. Add half the chilies, heat through, and pour mixture over the chicken breasts. Preheat oven to 350 degrees.
- In blender or food processor, combine remaining chilies, cream, Tabasco sauce, lemon juice, salt and pepper, combine till slightly thickened. Pour over the chicken and sprinkle on the cheese.
- Bake for 30 mins.

51. Chicken Enchilada Soup Recipe

Serving: 4 | Prep: | Cook: 40mins | Ready in:

Ingredients

- 1 tablespoon vegetable oil
- 1/2 lb. of boneless, skinless chicken (breast or thigh), cut into 1/2" cubes
- 1 small yellow onion, chopped (approx. 1 cup)
- 2 cloves garlic, minced
- 2 C chicken broth
- 1/2 cup masa harina or instant masa mix
- 1 1/2 cups water
- 2/3 cup enchilada sauce
- 6 oz. Velveeta
- 1 teaspoon salt
- 1 1/2 teaspoon chili powder (more if you'd like it spicier, less if you'd like it mild)

- 1/2 teaspoon cumin
- 1 can black beans, rinsed and drained
- 1 can corn, drained
- juice of 1-2 large limes (your preference)
- Garnish: Shredded cheddar cheese; crumbled corn tortilla chips; 1 large tomato, diced; 2 green onions, chopped; diced avocado

Direction

- Add oil to a large pot over medium heat.
- Add chicken breasts, onions and garlic to pot and sauté over medium heat for about 5 minutes to brown the chicken.
- Add the chicken broth.
- Combine masa harina with 1 cup of water in a medium bowl and whisk until blended. The mixture will be thick.
- Add the masa mixture to the pot with chicken mixture.
- Add remaining water, enchilada sauce, cheese and spices to pot and bring mixture to a boil.
- Reduce heat, add beans and corn and simmer soup for 30-40 minutes until thick.
- Add lime juice to taste.
- Serve soup in cups or bowls, and garnish with shredded cheddar cheese, crumbled corn tortilla chips, tomatoes, avocado and green onions.

52. Chicken Korma Recipe

Serving: 8 | Prep: | Cook: 30mins | Ready in:

Ingredients

- 2 Tblsp of vegetable oil or butter
- 3 chicken breast halves (skinless, boneless and diced)
- 1 tsp of ginger (minced or paste)
- 4 garlic cloves (minced or paste)
- 1 small onion (diced)
- ½ green bell pepper (seeded and chopped)
- ½ red pepper (seeded and chopped)
- 1 cup of green peas (thawed if frozen) not canned
- ½ cup of unsalted cashews or sliced almonds
- 1 ½ Tblsp of curry powder (or more to taste)
- 1 Tblsp of brown or white sugar (to taste)
- (8oz.) of plain yogurt
- (16oz.) of coconut milk, heavy cream or milk
- water (if sauce is too thick)
- NOTE- The vegetables can be cauliflower, carrots, potatoes, zucchini, mushrooms, eggplant, etc.

Direction

- Marinate the chicken pieces in the yogurt and some garlic, ginger, salt and pepper for about 2-3 hours.
- Heat the oil or butter in a skillet over medium heat, stir in the onion, ginger and garlic and cook until fragrant.
- Stir in the curry powder and cook stirring for 5 minutes until the onion turns brown.
- Stir in the chicken mixture, the vegetables and the cashews.
- Then add the coconut milk and season with the sugar, salt and black pepper to taste.
- Reduce heat to low, cover and simmer for 15 to 20 minutes.
- Garnish with cilantro and serve with white or brown rice or with parathas.

53. Chicken Noodle Soup Asian Style Recipe

Serving: 4 | Prep: | Cook: 30mins | Ready in:

Ingredients

- 1 oz Dried Shiitake mushrooms; soaked in hot water for 30 minutes, drained, trimmed and sliced
- 1 tb vegetable oil
- 1 c Minced onion
- 2 cloves garlic; minced
- 2 ts Minced fresh ginger

- 1 c Sliced carrot
- 1 1/2 c Sliced napa cabbage or bok choy
- 6 c chicken stock or broth
- 1/2 pk Dried Asian egg noodles
- 1 c broccoli florets (optional)
- 1 c Cooked sliced chicken
- 1 tb soy sauce
- 2 tb rice vinegar
- sesame oil to taste
- Minced whole scallion for garnish

Direction

- In a large saucepan set over moderate heat, heat the oil until it is hot. Add the onion, garlic, and ginger, and cook, stirring occasionally, 3 minutes. Add the carrot and cabbage and toss to combine. Add the broth, reserved mushrooms and salt to taste and simmer 10 minutes
- In a saucepan of boiling salted water cook the pasta until al dente, drain and transfer to stock. Add the broccoli, chicken and seasonings and simmer stirring occasionally, for 3 minutes, or until broccoli is just cooked and chicken heated through.
- Add sesame oil.
- Ladle the soup into bowls and garnish with the scallion.
- Yield: 4 servings

54. Chicken Sausage Gumbo Recipe

Serving: 8 | Prep: | Cook: 95mins | Ready in:

Ingredients

- 1/2 Cup light olive oil
- 2/3 cup all-purpose flour
- 1 cup chopped onions (I use sweet)
- 1/2 cup chopped green bell peppers
- 1/2 Cup chopped celery
- 3 (+) cloves garlic, crushed and chopped
- 2 Tbsp cajun seasoning
- 8 ounces (+) smoked sausage, cut into crosswise slices
- 2 boneless chicken breasts, cubed
- 5-1/2 cups chicken stock
- 1Tbsp worcestershire sauce
- 2 bay leaves
- 2 Cups of rice
- Optional: 1/2 to 1 lb cleaned and deveined med-small shrimp.
- 1 cup okra, cut into crosswise slices
- 1/3 cup loosely packed, chopped fresh parsley
- hot sauce, as desired.. I like Frank's extra hot

Direction

- NOTE: The ROUX: if the roux burns at all, discard and start again.
- Combine the oil and flour together in a large, heavy saucepan. Cook over med-low heat, whisking constantly, for ~ 12 to 15 minutes, until it turns the color of rich milk chocolate.
- Add the onions, bell peppers, celery, garlic, and Cajun seasoning to the roux and continue cooking and stirring for ~ 5 minutes until the vegetables turn tender.
- Add the smoked sausage and raw chicken and continue cooking for about 5 minutes, stirring occasionally.
- Stir in the chicken stock, Worcestershire sauce, and bay leaves into the gumbo, bring it to gentle simmer and cook it uncovered, for 1 hour.
- Cook rice according to the package directions and set aside (I use a rice cooker... so I start it about the time the stock is added)
- Add the okra to the gumbo and continue simmering it for 15 to 20 minutes until the okra is tender. Note: If adding the shrimp. Wait until the okra is almost tender, then cook until the shrimp is pink and translucent)
- Remove gumbo from the heat.
- To serve: Place a scoop of warm rice in a large soup bowl, add ladleful of hot gumbo. Sprinkle with fresh parsley and hot sauce to taste.

55. Chicken Soup From My Mother In Law Recipe

Serving: 6 | Prep: | Cook: 120mins | Ready in:

Ingredients

- 1/4 head of cabbage or 1 head of endive, washed, steamed and chopped to small chunk sized pieces
- 2 hard boiled eggs, chopped
- Note: If you don't like the addition of chopped hard boiled eggs in your soup, my Mother-in-law and I have added 4 eggs in the shell(washed) to the soup and have hard boiled them that way. Then whoever wants hard boiled eggs can have one ;)
- 2 lbs. chicken, cut up
- 1 large onion, coarsely chopped
- about 5 or 6 tops of celery with leaves
- 1 chicken boullion cube or packet of OXO
- Note: If you want to use more cubes or packets or chicken broth then by all means, feel free.
- 2 carrots, chopped
- 2 celery ribs, chopped
- 1-1/2 cups egg noodles or your favourite pasta or Spätzle.

Direction

- Place chicken, onion, celery leaves in a pot.
- Cover with cold water and bring to a rolling boil.
- Reduce heat and simmer until chicken is very tender and falls from the bones. (1-1/2 hours.)
- Remove chicken, celery leaves and onion.
- Discard celery leaves.
- Remove chicken from bones and chop chicken into bite sized pieces.
- Note: You can use boneless chicken but I find with the bone in it adds more flavour to the soup. It's also old world cooking.
- Reserve this delicious broth.
- Add celery and carrots to the broth.
- Cook until tender (10 minutes)
- Add escarole, noodles or spätzle, eggs, and chicken.
- Bring to a low boil.
- Simmer until noodles are cooked.
- Serve hot with a loaf of crusty bread.
- Sprinkle with Parmesan cheese on top and you'll see how delicious this soup is.

56. Chicken Soup Recipe

Serving: 432816 | Prep: | Cook: 7565mins | Ready in:

Ingredients

- 16 cups chicken stock
- 3 cups diced chicken (about 1 3-lb chicken)
- 1-1/2 cups diced celery (about 2 stalks)
- 1-1/2 cups sliced carrots (about 3 medium)
- 1 cup diced onion (about 1 medium)
- salt, optional
- pepper, optional
- 3 chicken bouillon cubes, optional
- 4 quart or 8 pint glass preserving jars with lids and bands

Direction

- PREPARE pressure canner. Heat jars and lids in simmering water until ready for use. Do not boil. Set bands aside.
- COMBINE chicken stock, chicken, celery, carrots and onion in a large saucepot. Bring mixture to a boil. Reduce heat and simmer 30 minutes. Season to taste with salt and pepper, if desired. Add bouillon cubes, if desired. Cook until bouillon cubes are dissolved.
- LADLE hot soup into hot jars leaving 1 inch headspace. Remove air bubbles. Wipe rim. Center hot lid on jar. Apply band and adjust until fit is fingertip tight.
- PROCESS filled jars in a pressure canner at 10 pounds pressure 1 hour and 15 minutes for pints and 1 hour and 30 minutes for quarts, adjusting for altitude. Remove jars and cool.

Check lids for seal after 24 hours. Lid should not flex up and down when center is pressed.

57. Chicken Soup With Passatelli Chicken Soup With Italian Dumplings Recipe

Serving: 6 | Prep: | Cook: 15mins | Ready in:

Ingredients

- 2 slices white bread, torn into rough chunks
- 2 large eggs
- 1 cup freshly grated parmesan cheese (I highly recommend parmigiano-Reggiano), plus more to pass at table
- Pinch of nutmeg
- salt and pepper to taste
- 2 quarts prepared chicken stock
- 2 Tbl minced fresh parsley leaves

Direction

- Preheat oven to 300F. Grind bread in food processor. Measure 1/2 cup bread crumbs onto a small baking sheet. Toast until lightly dried, about 5 minutes. Cool completely. Combine bread crumbs, eggs, Parmesan, nutmeg, and salt and pepper to taste in a medium bowl. Refrigerate mixture until firm, about 15 minutes. With moistened hands, roll teaspoonfuls of bread mixture into grape-sized balls. Bring the stock to a boil in a large stockpot over medium heat, then reduce heat to a gentle simmer. Drop the dumplings into the gently simmering stock and cook until they float to the surface, and are cooked, about 3-4 minutes. Stir in parsley, and adjust seasonings if necessary. Ladle soup and dumplings into bowls and serve immediately, passing extra cheese at the table.

58. Chicken Tortilla Soup Recipe

Serving: 4 | Prep: | Cook: | Ready in:

Ingredients

- 2 chicken breasts, skinless and boneless
- 8 oz tortilla chips, corn
- 2 (14.5 oz) cans of chicken broth
- 1 cup corn kernels, frozen
- 1 cup onion, chopped
- 1 cup salsa, chunky style
- 1/2 tsp chili powder
- 1/4 tsp ground cumin
- 1/2 tsp garlic, finely diced
- 1/2 tsp olive oil
- 1 tbsp lemon juice
- 1/2 cup monterey jack cheese, shredded (this is optional)

Direction

- Add the chicken to a large pot on medium heat, sauté in the oil for 5 minutes. Mix in the cumin and garlic, combine well. Then add the broth, onion, corn, salsa, chili powder, and lemon juice. Lower the heat to low setting and simmer for around 20-30 minutes.
- Break up some tortilla chips and place them into individual bowls. Pour the soup over chips and sprinkle with the Monterey Jack cheese (optional) and some sour cream.

59. Chicken Soup The Jewish Panacea Recipe

Serving: 10 | Prep: | Cook: 120mins | Ready in:

Ingredients

- 3kg chicken parts. The original recipe called for feet but I usually use wings. You can also use a whole chicken.
- 2 large onions
- 4 carrots

- 2 tablespoons of ground ginger. (It sounds like a lot but it isnt.)
- A few bayleaves
- a few peppercorns
- 1/2 cup of chopped parsley.
- water

Direction

- Cut onions coarsely. (1/8ths)
- Peel carrots and cut into segments. (About 5c"m each)
- Spread ginger over all the pieces of chicken
- Put everything in a large pot.
- Fill with water and bring to the boil.
- With a spoon remove all the "stuff" that floats to the top.
- Set flame to low and partially cover pot.
- Cook for at least two hours. (The longer it cooks, the more taste you get).
- Remove pieces of chicken from pot.
- **
- SUGGESTIONS:
- If you cook it long enough you won't need to add anything
- Add soup powder to reduce cooking time.
- If you use a whole chicken, it is a meal in itself after you remove it from the soup.
- If you use wings, put them under the grill for a minute or two, (DELICIOUS)
- Have you ever eaten the meat right off the neck? TRY IT!

60. Chicken Tagine Recipe

Serving: 4 | Prep: | Cook: 61mins | Ready in:

Ingredients

- 3-4 boneless skinless chicken breasts (or thighs if you prefer)
- 1-2 cloves garlic
- 2 shallots
- 1 bell pepper
- 1 summer or zuchinni squash
- 1-2 potatoes
- 2 carrots or 10 baby carrots
- 1 rutubega
- 1 can of fire roasted tomatoes
- Good handful of raisins
- 1 tbsp coriander
- 1 tbsp cinnamon
- 1 heaping tbsp cumin
- garlic salt to taste
- 2 Cups chicken broth
- olive oil or olive oil spray
- slivered almonds for garnish

Direction

- I do this in a pressure cooker, but a large deep skillet with a lid will work
- Cut Chicken into bite size pieces
- Get skillet hot and then spray with olive oil spray, or if you're not watching your weight like me drizzle oil in the hot pan
- Season chicken with garlic salt and sear in pan
- While it is searing finely chop garlic and shallots
- add to pan stirring occasionally while chopping bell pepper, squash, potatoes, carrots and rutabaga into bite size pieces (I don't peel them just wash them, but if you don't like the skins feel free)
- Add to the pan as you chop and make sure and season each layer
- Add can of fire roasted tomatoes (you can roast your own if you like but I think the canned ones are actually better)
- Add chicken broth, raisins and all of the seasonings and stir well
- If you are in a pressure cooker put the lid on and keep on high heat until it whistles, turn heat to low for about 15 minutes and then turn off and let cool.
- If you are in the skillet bring to a boil and then put on lid and bring to low heat and allow to simmer for about 2 hours or until meat is very tender and falling apart. If you use this method it may be necessary to add additional broth as you cook

- Serve over couscous and sprinkle with almonds

61. Chili Cheddar Potato Wedges Recipe

Serving: 6 | Prep: | Cook: 14mins | Ready in:

Ingredients

- 6 russet poatoes(8oz. ea)
- 6Tbs butter,room temperature
- 1 and 1/2c shredded cheddar cheese
- 2 scallions,chopped(1/2c)
- 2Tbs fresh,chopped parsley
- 1/2tsp chili powder
- 1/4tsp salt

Direction

- Pierce potatoes with fork. Microwave on high 10-12 mins. When cool enough to handle, cut each in half lengthwise, scoop out pulp, leaving 1/4" thick shell.
- In bowl, mash potato pulp with butter, 1c cheddar cheese, scallions, parsley, chili powder and salt. Cut each potato shell in half lengthwise. Divide potato mixture evenly among shells, using about 2 Tbs for each. Sprinkle tops with remaining 1/2c cheddar. Microwave on high just till cheese is melted, about 1 to 2 mins.

62. Chili Cheese Dip Recipe

Serving: 8 | Prep: | Cook: 5mins | Ready in:

Ingredients

- 8 ounces cream cheese softened
- 15 ounce can chili without beans
- 1 cup shredded monterey jack cheese

Direction

- Spread cream cheese on bottom and sides of microwaveable pie plate.
- Spread chili over cream cheese then sprinkle with cheese.
- Microwave on high for 3 minutes then serve with tortilla chips.

63. Chili Chicken Stew In A Tortilla Bowl Recipe

Serving: 10 | Prep: | Cook: 50mins | Ready in:

Ingredients

- 3 T. vegetable oil
- 3 boneless, skinless chicken breasts (about 1 1/2 pounds), cut into 1-inch cubes
- 1 c. chopped onion, red, sweet, whatever type you prefer
- 1 green bell pepper, diced
- 1 red bell pepper, diced
- 4 cloves garlic, minced
- 3 (14.5-ounce) cans Mexican-style stewed tomatoes
- 2 (15-ounce) cans pinto beans, drained
- 1 (16-ounce jar medium salsa
- 3 t. chili powder
- 2 t. ground cumin
- 10 (8-inch) flour tortillas
- 2 c. shredded sharp cheddar cheese
- 2 c. shredded monterey jack cheese with peppers
- Garnish: cheddar cheese, sour cream, minced green onions, sliced black olives

Direction

- In a large Dutch oven, heat oil over medium-high heat. Add chicken, onion, peppers, and garlic; cook 7 to 8 minutes, stirring frequently, or until vegetables are tender. Stir in tomatoes, beans, salsa, chili powder, and

cumin; bring to a boil, reduce heat, and simmer 30 to 40 minutes.
- Place 1 tortilla into each of 10 shallow bowls. Sprinkle cheeses evenly over each tortilla. Spoon chicken stew evenly over cheese. Garnish with Cheddar cheese, sour cream, minced green onion, and sliced black olives, if you like. Personally, I take all of the above! =D

64. Chili Lime Crab Cakes With Chipotle Avacado Mayo Recipe

Serving: 4 | Prep: | Cook: 15mins | Ready in:

Ingredients

- crab cakeS
- 1 lb. Backfin crab Meat
- 10 saltine crackers, crushed
- 1 large egg
- 2 Tbsp. ranch dressing
- 2 tsp. Oriental chili garlic paste
- 2 tsp. lime juice
- 1 Tbsp. cilantro
- 2 Tbsp. extra-virgin olive oil
- MAYO
- 1 medium avocado, roughly mashed
- 1/2 tsp. chipotle chili powder
- 1/2 tsp. lemon juice
- Salt and pepper to taste
- 1/4 cup mayonnaise

Direction

- MAYO
- Combine mayonnaise, chili powder, avocado, lemon juice, salt and pepper in a small mixing bowl and blend well.
- Chill.
- CAKES
- In a large mixing bowl, gently combine crab meat, crackers, egg, ranch dressing, garlic paste, lime juice, and cilantro.
- Form into 4-6 crab cakes.
- Sauté in olive oil until golden brown on both sides.
- Serve with dollops of avocado mayonnaise.

65. Chili Lime Potato Wedges Recipe

Serving: 8 | Prep: | Cook: 35mins | Ready in:

Ingredients

- 8 yukon gold potatoes, wedged
- 1 lime, zest and juice
- 1/4 cup olive oil
- 1/2t each of garlic, onion, chili and/or cayenne pepper
- salt
- 1/4 cup fresh cilantro, chopped and divided
- 1/2 cup shredded Mexican or monterey jack cheese
- 8oz sour cream
- 8oz salsa

Direction

- Combine lime zest, juice, oil and spices in large zipper top bag.
- Add potato wedges and toss to coat.
- Bake on well-greased baking sheet for 25 minutes, at 425.
- Sprinkle with cheese and bake until cheese melts.
- Top with half of the cilantro just out of oven.
- **combine salsa, sour cream and remaining cilantro for a dip, if desired**

66. Chili Parmesan Chicken Recipe

Serving: 6 | Prep: | Cook: 25mins | Ready in:

Ingredients

- 1/4 cup Grated parmesan cheese

- 2 teaspoons chili powder
- 6 small boneless skinless chicken breast halves
- Mix cheese and chili powder in pie plate. Add chicken; turn to evenly coat all sides.
- Place chicken in a shallow baking dish.
- Bake at 400 degrees F for 20 to 25 minutes or until chicken is cooked through.

Direction

- Variation
- Coat chicken with cheese mixture as directed; cut into 1-inch-wide strips. Place chicken strips on skewers, then place on rack of broiler pan. Broil 9 minutes or until chicken is cooked through, turning over after 5 minutes. Serve as an appetizer with your favorite salsa.
- Makes 16 appetizer servings.
- This one choice for a side dip
- Maple Apple Barbecue Sauce
- 2/3 cup chicken broth
- 1/3 cup applesauce
- 2 tablespoons maple syrup
- 2 tablespoons balsamic or apple cider vinegar
- 1 tablespoon cornstarch
- 2 teaspoons soy sauce
- 1/4 teaspoon ground ginger
- 1 1/2 teaspoons imitation maple flavor
- In a small saucepan, combine all ingredients except maple flavor. Bring to a boil while stirring with a whisk. Continue to cook 10 minutes. Remove from heat and stir in maple flavor. Use immediately or store in refrigerator up to 2 weeks.

67. Chilis Salsa Recipe

Serving: 10 | Prep: | Cook: |Ready in:

Ingredients

- 1 (14 1/2 ounce) can tomatoes and green chilies
- 1 (14 1/2 ounce) can whole canned tomatoes (plus the juice)
- 4 teaspoons jalapeños (canned, diced, not pickled)
- 1/4 cup yellow onions (diced)
- 1/2-3/4 teaspoon garlic salt
- 1/2 teaspoon cumin
- 1/4 teaspoon sugar

Direction

- In food processor place jalapeños and onions.
- Process for just a few seconds.
- Add both cans of tomatoes, salt, sugar, and cumin.
- Process all ingredients until well blended but do not puree. Place in covered container and chill.
- A couple of hours of chilling will help blend and enrich the flavour.
- Serve with your favourite thin corn tortilla chips.

68. Chili's Baby Back Ribs

Serving: 0 | Prep: | Cook: |Ready in:

Ingredients

- 1/2 cup dark brown sugar
- 2 teaspoons kosher salt
- 1 1/4 teaspoons smoked paprika
- 1/2 teaspoon black pepper
- 1/2 teaspoon onion powder
- 1/2 teaspoon garlic powder
- 1/4 teaspoon cayenne pepper
- 1 slab baby back pork ribs
- 1/2 cup cola soft drink
- 2/3 cup ketchup
- 2 tablespoons water
- 1 tablespoon plus 1 teaspoon molasses
- 1 tablespoon white vinegar
- 1 teaspoon yellow mustard
- 1/8 teaspoon liquid smoke

Direction

- Preheat oven to 275°F. Stir together brown sugar, salt, paprika, black pepper, onion powder, garlic powder, and cayenne in a small bowl. Rub 3 tablespoons of spice blend all over ribs, reserving remaining spice blend. Place ribs in a piece of heavy-duty aluminum foil; pour cola over ribs. Fold edges of foil together, and seal. Place ribs on rimmed baking sheet; bake in preheated oven 2 hours and 30 minutes.
- Combine ketchup, water, molasses, vinegar, mustard, liquid smoke, and reserved spice blend in a small saucepan over medium-high. Bring to a boil, stirring constantly. Reduce heat to medium-low; cover and simmer 10 minutes. Remove from heat.
- Remove ribs from oven. Adjust oven to broil. Line a rimmed baking sheet with aluminum foil. Carefully unwrap cooked ribs, and transfer ribs, bone side up, to prepared baking sheet; discard foil package. Brush ribs with sauce, and broil 2 minutes. Flip ribs, and brush with more sauce. Broil until bubbly, about 2 minutes. Serve with remaining sauce.

69. Chilled Avocado Soup Recipe

Serving: 4 | Prep: | Cook: 65mins | Ready in:

Ingredients

- 3 ripe avocados
- 2 cups low-fat buttermilk
- 1/3 cup walnut halves
- 1/3 cup fresh dill sprigs, plus more for garnish (optional)
- 1/3 cup diced red onion, or half a small onion
- 1 teaspoon coarse salt
- 1/8 tsp ground nutmeg
- ¼ tsp ground black pepper
- 1 tablespoon red wine vinegar

Direction

- Halve and pit two avocados. With a spoon, scoop out flesh and transfer to a blender. TIP: Sprinkle lemon or lime juice over peeled avocados to prevent discoloring.
- Add buttermilk, walnuts, dill, red onion, vinegar, salt, nutmeg, pepper and 1 cup water and puree until smooth.
- Cover the blender and refrigerate until the soup is well chilled, at least one hour. Halve and pit remaining avocado. Cut into four sections lengthwise, and then cut crosswise into 1/2-inch chunks. Divide soup among four bowls and garnish each with diced avocado and dill, if desired.

70. Chilled Chicken Yogurt Soup Recipe

Serving: 4 | Prep: | Cook: | Ready in:

Ingredients

- 1 cup finely chopped cooked chicken
- 1 teaspoon lemon juice
- ¾ teaspoon minced fresh dill or
- ¼ teaspoon dried dill weed
- ½ teaspoon salt
- 1/8 teaspoon garlic powder
- Pinch white pepper
- 2 cups plain yogurt
- 1 small cucumber, seeded and diced
- ¼ cup chopped celery
- 3 tablespoons thinly sliced green onions
- fresh dill sprigs for garnish

Direction

- Place chicken, lemon juice, minced dill, salt, garlic powder and pepper in small bowl; toss lightly.
- Cover; refrigerate 30 minutes.
- Place yogurt in medium bowl. Stir with fork or wire whisk until smooth and creamy.
- Stir chicken mixture, cucumber, celery and onions into yogurt.

- Pour soup into serving bowls; garnish with dill sprigs.

71. Chilled Peach Soup Recipe

Serving: 4 | Prep: | Cook: |Ready in:

Ingredients

- 1/2 cup orange juice
- 1 (16oz) bag frozen peach slices, thawed
- 3/4 cup pineapple juice
- 3 tbsp sugar
- 1 tbsp lemon juice
- 1/4 cup white wine
- 1/2 cup sour cream (or yogurt)
- 1/2 cup half and half (or soymilk)
- A few dashes of nutmeg
- 1/4 tsp cinnamon
- freshly cracked pepper

Direction

- Thaw the frozen peaches and take out about 1/4 of a cup for a topping. Put the rest of them along with all the ingredients in the blender.
- Blend this very well until pureed.
- Slice up the leftover peaches and stir them into the soup.
- Chill this in the fridge for a few hours and serve with cracked pepper.

72. Chilli Con Carne Recipe

Serving: 4 | Prep: | Cook: 40mins | Ready in:

Ingredients

- 500g beef mince
- 2 Large brown onions (diced)
- 2 cloves garlic (crushed)
- 2x 400g tin crushed tomatoes
- 1x 400g tin red kidney beans
- 2tbsp Hot Chilli Powder
- 1tbsp ground cumin Seeds
- 1tbsp ground coriander Seeds
- Dash of worcestershire sauce
- Dash of Tabasco sauce
- salt and pepper to Taste
- Small amount of vegetable oil

Direction

- On a hot burner heat oil in a medium sized saucepan
- Add onion and garlic and cook till semi-transparent
- Add Chill, Cumin and Coriander and cook till fragrant (this doesn't take long)
- Break the mince up and brown in saucepan (3-5 minutes)
- Season the lot with Tabasco and Worcestershire
- Pour in the Tomatoes and Beans, then turn the heat down and allow to simmer for 30 minutes
- Serve with rice, cheese, sour cream, spring onion and whatever else takes your fancy.

73. Chinese Hot And Sour Soup Recipe

Serving: 12 | Prep: | Cook: 6mins |Ready in:

Ingredients

- 8 each   Dried black mushrooms
- 16 each Dried cloud ear (also called tree ear) mushrooms
- water boiling --- amount as needed
- 2 1/2 qt chicken stock
- 8 oz Lean raw pork cut julienne (see note)
- Julienne is simply 'cut into little sticks'.
- 6 oz bamboo shoots cut julienne
- 3 fl oz soy sauce
- 2 tsp white pepper
- 8 tbsp cornstarch
- 8 fl oz Cold water

- 3 fl oz rice vinegar or wine vinegar
- 2 tsp oriental sesame oil
- 2 each eggs lightly beaten
- 1 each scallion, sliced thin
- 2 tbsp Chopped cilantro

Direction

- Place two types of dried mushrooms in separate bowls.
- Add enough boiling water to each to cover the mushrooms.
- Let stand until the mushrooms are soft.
- Drain the mushrooms, squeezing them lightly.
- *****Reserve the soaking liquid.
- Cut off and discard the stems from the black mushrooms.
- Cut the caps into thin strips.
- Cut off any coarse, woody stems from the cloud ear mushrooms.
- Cut the mushrooms into half-inch pieces.
- Combine the stock and the mushroom liquid in a sauce pot.
- Bring to a boil.
- Add the mushrooms, pork, bamboo shoots, soy sauce, and white pepper.
- Simmer 3 minutes.
- Mix the cornstarch with the water until smooth.
- Add the cornstarch mixture to the simmering soup, stirring constantly.
- Simmer until the soup is lightly thickened.
- Add the vinegar and sesame oil to the soup.
- Slowly drizzle in the beaten egg, stirring slowly but constantly, so that the egg coagulates in thin shreds.
- To serve, top each portion with a few slices of scallion and a pinch of chopped cilantro.
- Note:
- To cut the pork into julienne more easily, partially freeze the meat first.

74. Chinese War Wonton Soup Recipe

Serving: 6 | Prep: | Cook: 140mins | Ready in:

Ingredients

- --Chinese Barbecued Pork--
- 1 Tbsp. sugar
- 1/2 Tbsp. plus 3/4 tsp. hoisin sauce
- 1/2 Tbsp. plus 3/4 tsp. soy sauce
- 1/2 Tbsp. plus rice wine
- 1/2 tsp salt
- 1 lb. boneless pork loin, in 1 piece, trimmed of fat
- -------------------------
- --Wontons--
- 1 beaten egg
- 1/4 cup finely chopped onion
- 1/4 cup finely chopped water chestnuts
- 1 Tbsp. soy sauce
- 2 tsp grated fresh ginger root
- 1/2 tsp. sugar
- 1/2 tsp. salt
- 1/8 tsp. pepper
- 1/2 lb. ground pork
- 1/4 lb. small fresh shrimp, finely chopped
- 40 wonton wrappers
- 8 cups water
- -------------------------
- --War Wonton Soup--
- 4 chicken bouillon cubes
- 4 beef bouillon cubes
- 1/2 lb. fresh mushrooms, washed, stems trimmed and sliced
- 3 green onions, diagonally, cut in 1" pieces, tops included
- 1/2 head nappa cabbage
- 1/2 head bok choy
- 1 (10 oz.) pkg. frozen snow peas
- 1 (5 oz.) can water chestnuts, drained and sliced
- 1 (4 oz.) can bamboo shoots, drained
- 1 lb. Chinese Barbecued pork, sliced to thin bite size pieces (recipe above)
- 24 Wontons (recipe above)

- 1 boneless, skinless chicken breast
- 36 medium large shrimp, bitesize, shelled and deveined
- 1/2 lb. lobster meat, cut in bite size pieces (optional)

Direction

- --Chinese Barbecued Pork--
- Place sugar, hoisin sauce, soy sauce, rice wine and salt in a small bowl. Stir until sugar is dissolved. Add pork, turn to coat with marinade. Marinate pork in refrigerator, covered, turning occasionally at least 8 hours, or overnight.
- Heat oven to 375*. Place pork on rack in roasting pan, in centre of oven. Roast until thermometer inserted in thickest part of pork reads 165*, about 45 minutes. Cool completely before slicing.

75. Chipotle Black Bean And Rice Stew Recipe

Serving: 6 | Prep: | Cook: 25mins |Ready in:

Ingredients

- 1 bay leaf
- 1 cup vidalia onion, minced
- 2 celery ribs, chopped
- 2 Knorr Chipolte bouillon cubes (or 1-2 well-minced canned chipotle peppers)
- 1 cup frozen white corn kernels
- 2 tbsp olive oil
- 3 cloves garlic, chopped
- 2 (15 ounce) cans black beans
- 2 tsp chili powder
- 1 (32 ounce) carton vegetable stock
- 1 (15 ounce) can diced tomatoes
- 1 tsp ground coriander
- 1 1/2 tsp cumin
- 1 (8 ounce) can tomato sauce
- 1 cup white rice

Direction

- Put a large pot over medium heat.
- Put in olive oil and sauté your bay leaf, celery, onions, and garlic for about 4 minutes.
- Crumble up your chipotle cubes into the pot and add corn as well as 2 cans of undrained black beans.
- Add chili powder, cumin, and coriander. Stir this well.
- Add in tomato sauce, tomatoes and stock.
- Cover the pot and bring to high-heat and a boil.
- Now add rice and bring back to a boil again. Then lower heat, cover, and let simmer until the rice is tender.

76. Chipotle Blue Chili Took 2nd Place In Chili Contest I Judged Recipe

Serving: 12 | Prep: | Cook: 240mins |Ready in:

Ingredients

- 3 tablespoons extra virgin olive oil
- 6 pounds uncooked stew meat
- 2 pounds pork breakfast sausage with sage
- 2 large white onions chopped fine
- 14 ounce can beef stock
- 2-1/2 ounces canned chipotle peppers in adobe sauce chopped fine
- 2 squares bittersweet chocolate
- 14 ounces canned salsa verde
- 24 ounces bottled dark beer
- 1 ounce top shelf tequila
- 2 limes juiced
- 1 teaspoon salt
- 6 tablespoons freshly ground black pepper
- 3 tablespoons liquid smoke
- 6 tablespoons chili powder
- 6 tablespoons ground cumin
- 1 bunch green onions sliced
- 2 cups 4 blend cheese

Direction

- Heat olive oil in large cast iron pot on high heat.
- Add beef and cook until browned stirring occasionally.
- When browned remove from pot and set aside then drain well.
- Brown sausage and chopped onions until sausage is browned then drain well.
- Return beef to pot along with remaining ingredients then stir well.
- Cover and simmer on medium heat for 4 hours stirring occasionally.
- Serve in bowls with cheese and green onions as garnish.

77. Chuck Wagon Soup Recipe

Serving: 10 | Prep: | Cook: 60mins | Ready in:

Ingredients

- 1 lb 80% lean ground chuck
- 1 1/2 cups diced onion
- 3/4 cup diced celery
- 1 cup sliced mushrooms
- 4 cloves of garlic minced (less if you like or more if you want)
- 3/4 cup diced carrots
- 3/4 cup diced green squash
- 3/4 cup diced yellow squash
- 2 cans dark red kidney beans (drained)
- 1 1/2 cups kernel corn
- 1 chipotle chili chopped fine
- 2 tsps chili powder (adjust to your taste)
- 1/2 tsp red chili
- 2 14 1/2 oz cans Del Monte diced tomato with zesty jalapeno
- 10 cups homemade chicken stock or store bought
- salt and pepper to taste
- 2 cups of pasta cooked seperately (2 cups dry not cooked)
- grated cheese
- sour cream

Direction

- In a large pot add 1 tbsp. oil over medium high heat add onions, celery and mushrooms and cook till onions are slightly tender add ground beef and cook till browned. Make sure you keep the beef from sticking or clumping.
- Add remaining ingredients up to but not including the pasta. Cook over medium heat for 1 hr. or until veggies are somewhat tender.
- Add your cooked pasta and serve with a dollop of sour cream and some grated cheddar cheese.

78. Cincinnati Chili Skyline Style Recipe

Serving: 6 | Prep: | Cook: 60mins | Ready in:

Ingredients

- 1 lb. natural ground beef (85/15 is what I prefer)
- 16 oz. spaghetti noodles
- 8 oz. bag shredded sharp cheddar cheese
- 1 29 oz. can tomato sauce
- 1 cup water
- 1 large diced yellow sweet onion
- 1-2 cloves garlic, minced
- 1 tbsp. Worchestershire sauce
- 1 tbsp. unsweetened powdered cocoa
- 1 cube or tbsp beef boullion
- 1 tsp. cumin
- 1 tsp. cinnamon
- 1 tsp. chili powder
- 1/8 tsp. cloves
- 1/8 tsp. allspice
- oyster crackers and red or sweet yellow onion to top

Direction

- Cook ground beef on stovetop over medium to medium high heat until browned through (about 5 min.) Add about 1/2 to 3/4 cup onion and the 1-2 cloves minced garlic and cook about 2 more minutes or until onion is translucent. The key with the onion is to cut the pieces pretty small, almost minced, so they are not noticeable. This is not your normal chunky chili, should be more of a saucy consistency. Break up the meat while you are cooking also!
- Then, pour into a large (2-3 quart) soup pot. Add other ingredients (except cheese, noodles, crackers, and remainder of onion) and stir well. Bring to rapid boil, stirring frequently.
- Once mixture boils, reduce heat to low, cover, and let simmer for 50-60 minutes. Meanwhile, boil spaghetti to desired tenderness and drain.
- Layer in a bowl as follows: noodles, chili, onion, cheese, oyster crackers. I recommend eating with a knife and fork. Delicious!

79. Coney Island Chili Dogs Recipe

Serving: 8 | Prep: | Cook: 30mins | Ready in:

Ingredients

- 1 pound lean ground beef or ground turkey
- 1 (12oz) jar of chili sauce
- 1 dry packet of chili seasoning
- 1/4 cup of water
- 1 teaspoon worcestershire sauce
- 1 tablespoon yellow mustard
- 1/2 teaspoon onion powder
- 8 hot dogs
- 8 hot dog buns
- Shredded Cheddar to serve
- Chopped white onion to serve

Direction

- In a large pot over medium heat brown the ground beef.
- Stir constantly to break up meat into small pieces.
- Add the chili seasonings, water, Worcestershire, mustard and onion powder.
- Bring to a boil.
- Lower heat and simmer for 30 minutes.

80. Copycat A N W Chili Dogs Recipe

Serving: 6 | Prep: | Cook: 20mins | Ready in:

Ingredients

- A&W chili Dogs
- ~~~~~~~~~~~~~~~~~~~~~~~~~~~~~~
- Level..EASY TRY it..fabulous
- ~~~~~~~~~~~~~~~~~~~~~~~~~~~~~~
- 1 Sabrett brand 2 ounce beef frankfurter (7½" long)
- ~~~~~~~~~~~~~~~~~~~~~~~~~~~~~~
- (I suggest any great quality bun size HD, if unavailable)
- 1 regular hot dog roll
- 3 Tablespoons A&W Coney Island Sauce (see recipe below)
- 1 Tablespoon chopped white onion
- 1/2 Tablespoon Kraft shredded mild cheddar cheese (optional)
- A&W Coney Island chili Dog Sauce
- 1 pound ground chuck
- 1 six ounce can Hunts tomato paste
- 1 Cup water
- 1 Tablespoon sugar
- 1 Tablespoon prepared yellow mustard
- 1 Tablespoon dried, minced onion
- 2 teaspoons chili powder
- 1 teaspoon worcestershire sauce
- 1 teaspoon salt
- 1/2 teaspoon celery seed
- 1/2 teaspoon ground cumin (heaping)

- 1/4 teaspoon ground black pepper

Direction

- Making the Chili Dog Sauce:
- ~~~~~~~~~~~~~~~~~~~~~~~~~~~~~~~~~~
- In a 2 qt. saucepan, brown the ground chuck, breaking into very small pieces.
- Salt and pepper lightly while cooking. Do not drain the fat.
- Add the remaining ingredients.
- Simmer, uncovered, 30–45 minutes until it thickens. Stir occasionally.
- Allow to cool, cover, and refrigerate until "Dog-Time".
- You'll be microwaving what you need later.
- ~~~~~~~~~~~~~~~~~~~~~~~~~~~~~~~~~~
- Cooking your A&W Chili Dog
- Bring a 2 qt. saucepan of water to a rolling boil.
- Remove the saucepan from the heat, and add the desired number of frankfurters to the water. Cover and let sit about 10 minutes.
- After the franks are done, microwave the chili dog sauce until steaming.
- (Only microwave what you need, save the rest) Then microwave each hot dog roll 10 seconds....just enough to warm

81. Copycat Chilis Southwest Egg Rolls Recipe

Serving: 3 | Prep: | Cook: 15mins | Ready in:

Ingredients

- 1 chicken breast fillet
- 1 tablespoon vegetable oil
- 2 tablespoons minced red bell pepper
- 2 tablespoons minced green onion
- 1/3 cup frozen corn
- 1/4 cup canned black beans, rinsed and drained
- 2 tablespoons frozen spinach, thawed and drained
- 2 tablespoons diced, canned jalapeno peppers
- 1/2 tablespoon minced fresh parsley
- 1/2 teaspoon cumin
- 1/2 teaspoon chili powder
- 1/4 teaspoon salt
- dash cayenne pepper
- 3/4 cup shredded monterey jack cheese
- five 7-inch flour tortillas
- avocado-Ranch Dipping Sauce:
- 1/4 cup smashed, fresh avocado (about half of an avocado)
- 1/4 cup mayonnaise
- 1/4 cup sour cream
- 1 tablespoon buttermilk
- 1 1/2 teaspoons white vinegar
- 1/8 teaspoon salt
- 1/8 teaspoon dried parsley
- 1/8 teaspoon onion powder
- dash dried dill weed
- dash garlic powder
- dash pepper
- Garnish:
- 2 tablespoons chopped tomato
- 1 tablespoon chopped onion

Direction

- Sprinkle chicken breast with salt and pepper and grill 4-5 minutes per side, or until done; set aside, when cool, dice the chicken.
- Sauté red pepper and onion in 1 TB oil until soft, about 2-3 minutes.
- Add the chicken to the pan.
- Add corn, black beans, spinach, jalapeno peppers, parsley, cumin, chili powder, salt, and cayenne pepper to pan.
- Cook for 4 minutes, distributing spinach evenly.
- Remove from heat and add the cheese; stir until cheese melts.
- Wrap tortillas in a moist cloth and microwave on high temperature for 1 1/2 minutes or until hot.

- Working on a flat surface, divide the filling evenly among the tortillas, spooning the filling into the centre of each.
- Fold in the ends of the tortilla, then roll up the side closest to you--be sure to roll tightly.
- Set aside, with the fold side down.
- Put the egg rolls on a plate, cover and freeze from 4 hours to 24 hours.
- Preheat 4-6 cups of oil to 375 degrees. (Using an electric skillet is a great way to do this, because you can control the temp of the oil better.)
- Fry the egg rolls for 12-15 minutes and drain on paper towels or a rack.
- To make the dipping sauce, just combine all of the sauce ingredients and mix in a bowl, then garnish with the chopped tomato and onion.
- For presentation, slice each egg roll on the diagonal and place them around the bowl of dipping sauce.

82. Copycat Panera Bread Broccoli And Cheese Soup In Bread Bowls Recipe

Serving: 4 | Prep: | Cook: 45mins | Ready in:

Ingredients

- 1 tbls. butter, melted
- 1/2 onion, finely chopped
- 1/4 cup flour
- 1/4 cup butter, melted
- 2 cups half & half
- 2 cups chicken stock
- 1/2 lb. fresh broccoli
- 1 cup carrots, finely chopped
- 1/4 tsp. nutmeg
- salt & pepper, to taste
- 2 cups grated sharp cheddar cheese
- 4 Breadbowls

Direction

- Sauté onion in 1 tbls. butter
- In another pan, cook melted butter and flour, whisking over medium heat for 3-4 minutes
- Slowly add half & half while continuing to whisk
- Add chicken stock, while continuing to whisk
- Once it starts to simmer, let simmer for 20 minutes
- Add broccoli, carrots and onions
- Cook over low heat until veggies are tender
- Add salt and pepper
- Pour in batches into blender and mix or use immersion blender
- Return to pot and over low heat, add cheese, stirring until well blended
- Stir in the nutmeg
- Cut tops off of bread bowls
- Hollow out
- Pour soup into bowls

83. Copycat Wendys Chili Recipe

Serving: 12 | Prep: | Cook: 180mins | Ready in:

Ingredients

- 2 lbs ground beef
- 1 (29 ounce) can tomato sauce
- 1 (29 ounce) can kidney beans (with liquid)
- 1 (29 ounce) can pinto beans (with liquid)
- 1 cup diced onion
- 1/2 cup diced green chili pepper
- 1/4 cup diced celery
- 3 medium tomatoes
- 2-3 teaspoons cumin powder
- 3 tablespoons chili powder
- 1 1/2 teaspoons black pepper
- 2 teaspoons salt
- 2 cups water

Direction

- Brown the ground beef in a skillet over medium heat.
- Drain off the fat.

- In a large pot, combine the beef plus all the remaining ingredients, and bring to a simmer over low heat.
- Cook, stirring every 15 minutes, for 2 to 3 hours.
- Serve with shredded cheddar and a spoon of sour cream.
- And of course, oyster crackers.

84. Corn Chowder The Best Recipe

Serving: 6 | Prep: | Cook: 25mins | Ready in:

Ingredients

- Ingredients
- 3 medium ears fresh yellow or bicolor corn
- 4 ounces slab (unsliced) bacon, rind removed and cut into 1/3-inch dice
- 2 tablespoons unsalted butter
- 1 medium onion (7 to 8 ounces), cut into 1/2-inch dice
- 1/2 large red bell pepper (6 to 8 ounces), cut into 1/2-inch dice
- 1 to 2 sprigs fresh thyme, leaves removed and chopped (1/2 teaspoon)
- 1/2 teaspoon ground cumin
- 1/8 teaspoon turmeric
- 1 pound Yukon Gold, Maine, PEI, or other all-purpose potatoes, peeled and cut into 1/2-inch dice
- 3 cups chicken stock or chicken broth
- Kosher or sea salt and freshly ground black pepper
- 2 teaspoons cornstarch, dissolved in 2 tablespoons water
- 1 cup heavy cream

Direction

- 1. Husk the corn. Carefully remove most of the silk by hand and then rub the ears with a towel to finish the job. Cut the kernels from the cobs and place in a bowl. You should have about 2 cups. Using the back of your knife, scrape down the cobs and add the milky substance that oozes out to the corn kernels.
- 2. Heat a 3- to 4-quart heavy pot over low heat and add the diced bacon. Once it has rendered a few tablespoons of fat, increase the heat to medium and cook until the bacon is crisp and golden brown. Pour off all but 1 tablespoon of the bacon fat, leaving the bacon in the pot.
- 3. Add the butter, onion, bell pepper, thyme, cumin, and turmeric and sauté, stirring occasionally with a wooden spoon, for about 8 minutes, until the onion and pepper are tender but not browned.
- 4. Add the corn kernels, potatoes, and stock, turn up the heat, cover, and boil vigorously for about 10 minutes. Some of the potatoes will have broken up, but most should retain their shape. Use the back of your spoon to smash a bit of the corn and potatoes against the side of the pot. Reduce the heat to medium and season the chowder with salt and pepper.
- 5. Stir the cornstarch mixture and slowly pour it into the pot, stirring constantly. As soon as the chowder has come back to a boil and thickened slightly, remove from the heat and Stir in the cream. Adjust the seasoning if necessary. If you are not serving the chowder within the hour, let it cool a bit, then refrigerate; cover the chowder after it has chilled completely. Otherwise, let it sit at room temperature for up to an hour, allowing the flavors to meld.
- 6. When ready to serve, reheat the chowder over low heat; don't let it boil. Ladle into cups or bowls and sprinkle with the chopped chives.

85. Cowboy Soup Recipe

Serving: 4 | Prep: | Cook: 20mins | Ready in:

Ingredients

- 1 lb. ground beef
- 1 onion, chopped

- 1 16 oz. can pork and beans in tomato sauce
- 1 can diced tomatoes, undrained
- 1 1/2 cups beef broth
- 1 tbls. chili powder
- salt and pepper to taste
- 1/2 cup wagon wheel pasta
- 1/4 cup shredded cheddar cheese to garnish

Direction

- Brown ground beef and onion until beef is browned
- Drain fat
- Add beans, tomatoes and liquid, beef broth, and chili powder
- Bring to boil
- Lower heat and stir in pasta
- Simmer until pasta is done
- Garnish with cheese

86. Crab Cakes With Red Chili Mayonaisse Recipe

Serving: 8 | Prep: | Cook: 20mins | Ready in:

Ingredients

- 1 cup mayonnaise (I used light mayo)
- 4 teaspoons chili-garlic sauce (available in asian markets or from the ethnic area of some supermarkets).
- 3 1/2 teaspoons fresh lemon juice
- 3 tablespoons olive oil
- 1/2 cup chopped red bell pepper
- 1/2 cup chopped celery
- 1/2 cup chopped red onion
- 2 tablespoons chopped seeded jalapeño chili
- 1 pound crabmeat, coarsely chopped (I used lump crab from cans)
- 1 large egg, beaten to blend
- 5 cups panko breadcrumbs (the recipe called for fresh bread crumbs, but after reading the reviews on the website from people who had made it, I followed their lead and used the panko crumbs. Now I can see why.)

Direction

- Mix mayonnaise, chili-garlic sauce, and 1 1/2 teaspoons lemon juice in small bowl. Cover and refrigerate chili mayonnaise.
- Heat 1 tablespoon oil in heavy medium skillet over medium-high heat. Add bell pepper, celery, onion, and jalapeño; sauté 3 minutes. Transfer to large bowl. Mix in crab, egg, 1/2 cup chili mayonnaise, and remaining 2 teaspoons lemon juice, then 1 1/2 cups breadcrumbs.
- Form crab mixture into eight 1/2-inch-thick cakes, using 1/2 cup for each. Dredge cakes in remaining 3 1/2 cups breadcrumbs, turning to coat. Place on baking sheet. Cover and refrigerate at least 1 hour and up to 8 hours.
- Heat remaining 2 tablespoons oil in heavy large skillet over medium heat. Working in batches, add crab cakes and cook until golden brown and cooked through, about 4 minutes per side. Transfer to plates. Serve, passing remaining chili mayonnaise separately.

87. Cream Of Mushroom Soup Recipe

Serving: 8 | Prep: | Cook: 45mins | Ready in:

Ingredients

- 1 lb. of white button mushrooms
- 1 lb. of crimini mushrooms (baby bellas)
- 1 oz. of dried shitake mushrooms (in produce dept.)
- 1 oz. container of dried imported Polish mushrooms(in the canned veggie department at my local super??)
- 3 large shallots, minced
- 4 tablespoons of butter
- 1/4 cup of flour
- 1/3 cup of vermouth (white)

- 1 package of frozen artichoke hearts, defrosted and chopped
- 6 sprigs of fresh thyme
- a pinch (I mean a little pinch) of powdered sage
- 1/2 teapoon of salt
- 8 to 9 grinds of fresh ground black pepper
- 5 to 6 passes of fresh nutmeg on a microplane
- 24 ounces of chicken stock
- 8 ounces of heavy cream or half and half
- (In a pinch I've used a can of evaporated milk)
- Do not use buttermilk or skim milk, it will curdle and separate)

Direction

- Slice the mushrooms. Heat some of the stock and soak the dried mushrooms at least 10 minutes to soften. Remove tough stems and dice.
- ***When I first started at Rolland et Pierre, the chef came by and dropped 30 lbs. of mushrooms on my station and said, "I need these sliced as soon as possible for our marinated mushrooms" It took me almost 4 hours. When I left the restaurant 3 years later, I could "get 'err done" in under an hour and keep up with all my salad and appetizer service. All it took was lots and lots of practice with a very sharp knife. *****
- Melt the butter in a very large sauté pan, add the shallots and mushrooms and cook over med-high heat until the liquid is released, and reduced. Add more butter if it dries up to much. Sprinkle with flour and toast the flour over the heat until the raw taste is removed.
- Add the vermouth, artichokes, thyme and seasonings.
- Stir and cook to thicken the mushroom base slightly.
- Add stock and cream and cook another 30 minutes over low-medium heat to thicken and reduce slightly.
- Fish out the woody stems of the thyme before you serve this wonderful fragrant woodsy soup.

88. Cream Of Broccoli Soup Recipe

Serving: 6 | Prep: | Cook: 15mins | Ready in:

Ingredients

- 8 c. of broccoli florets
- 3 tbsp. of margarine
- 3 tbsp. of all-purpose flour
- 2 c. of milk
- 2 tbsp. of margarine
- 1 chopped onion
- 1 chopped stalk celery
- 3 c. chicken broth

Direction

- Start by adding 2 tbsp., of butter to your pot.
- Then Sauté the onion and celery until soft.
- Next you can add the broccoli and broth.
- Allow this to simmer approx. 10 min.
- You will want to puree the mixture in a food processor before returning the mixture to the pot.
- In a small pan, make a rough with 3 tbs. of butter, stirring in flour, and adding milk to the rough. After this is thick, pour this into the soup and allow soup to thicken.
- Add salt and pepper to your individual taste.

89. Cream Of Broccoli And Cheese Soup Recipe

Serving: 4 | Prep: | Cook: 1mins | Ready in:

Ingredients

- 3-tbsp unsalted butter, plus 2-tbspn cold unsalted butter, cut into pieces
- 1-cup yellow onions, sliced
- 1/2-tspn salt
- 1/4-tspn black pepper*
- Pinch of nutmeg

- 1 teaspoon jarred minced garlic*
- 1/4-cup dried crushed thyme*
- 3-tbspn all-purpose flour
- 3-cups of chicken broth (I used Swanson's.)
- 2(10-oz)packages frozen chopped broccoli*
- 1/2-cup heavy cream
- 1 1/4-cups freshly shredded mild cheddar cheese
- croutons, to garnish

Direction

- Melt 3-tbspn butter in medium sized pot. Add the onions, salt, pepper and nutmeg and cook, stirring, until soft, 3 minutes. Add the garlic and thyme and cook stirring, until fragrant - about 1 minute. Add the flour and cook, stirring until the mixture is well blended and smells fragrant, 2 minutes. Slowly add the chicken stock, whisking constantly, and bring to a boil. Reduce the heat and simmer until thickened, about 5 minutes. Add the broccoli and cook, stirring, until tender, for 10 minutes. Remove the pot from the heat and puree with a hand-held immersion blender, a food processor or a contour top blender. Return to the pot and add the cream and bring to a bare simmer. Add the cheese and cook over low heat, stirring, until melted. Add the remaining 2-tbspn of cold butter, stirring to blend. Ladle into bowl and serve. Sprinkle with croutons, if desired.

90. Cream Of Mushroom Soup Recipe

Serving: 6 | Prep: | Cook: 30mins | Ready in:

Ingredients

- 5 c. of sliced fresh mushrooms
- 1 1/2 c. of chicken broth
- 1/2 c. of chopped onion
- 1/8 tsp. of dried thyme
- 3 tbsp. of butter
- 1 c. of half-and-half
- 1 tbsp. of sherry
- 3 tbsp. of all-purpose flour
- 1/4 tsp. of salt
- 1/4 tsp. of ground black pepper

Direction

- First you want to sauté your mushrooms in broth with onions and thyme approx. 10-15 min.
- Now in a blender puree this (leave some chunks)
- Now in a pan, make a rouge by melting butter in a saucepan, and whisking in flour. And some salt and pepper, the half and half and the mushroom puree.
- Stir this consistently and let this come to a boil.
- Add salt and pepper (sherry) and ladle up!

91. Creamy Chicken Wild Rice Soup In Crockpot Recipe

Serving: 12 | Prep: | Cook: 360mins | Ready in:

Ingredients

- 1 whole chicken cut in half (about 3-4 pounds)
- 4 medium carrots sliced
- 2 stalks celery sliced
- 2-3 cloves garlic chopped
- 1 large onion chopped
- 1 pepper chopped (red or green, or both)
- 2 tsp dried rosemary
- 2 bay leaves
- 1 tsp paprika
- 1 tsp lemon peel
- 1/2 tsp pepper
- 3 (14 oz) chicken broth
- 3/4 to 1 cup uncooked wild rice, rinsed & drained
- 1 can cream of chicken soup
- 1/4 cup parsley

Direction

- Cut chicken in half and remove as many of rib bones as possible
- In crockpot add veggies, chicken, seasonings, rice, broth, soup
- Turn on high for about 5 hours
- Remove chicken, take off skin, and cut up in to pieces
- Lower to low for another hours
- Done!!
- Enjoy. It's a filling soup

92. Creamy Hungarian Mushroom Soup Recipe

Serving: 6 | Prep: | Cook: 35mins | Ready in:

Ingredients

- 1 lb of fresh sliced mushrooms
- 2 tsp. of dried dill weed
- 1 tbsp. of paprika
- 1 tbsp. of soy sauce
- 2 c. of chicken broth
- 1 c. of milk
- 4 tbsp. of unsalted butter
- 2 c. of chopped onions
- 3 tbsp. of all-purpose flour
- 1 tsp. of salt
- ground black pepper to taste
- 2 tsp. of lemon juice
- 1/4 c. of chopped fresh parsley
- 1/2 c. of sour cream

Direction

- First you want to add some butter to a large pot over medium flame.
- Sauté the onions for approx. 5 min.
- Next add the mushrooms cooking approx. 5 min.
- Now add in the dill, paprika, soy sauce, and the broth.
- Reduce your flame to low, cover with a lid and simmer for approx. 15 min.
- Now in a separate bowl, whisk together the milk and flour
- You can pour this in the soup and stir.
- Next you want to cover this with a lid and cook on low for 15 min.
- Finally, add in salt, pepper, lemon juice, parsley, and sour cream.
- Mix this all together and cook on low for approx. 3-5 in.
- Ladle up and serve!

93. Creamy Potato Leek Soup Recipe

Serving: 6 | Prep: | Cook: 20mins | Ready in:

Ingredients

- 6 potatoes, peeled and cubed
- 2 leeks, trimmed and chopped
- 1 clove garlic, crushed
- 1 TBS butter or margarine
- 1/2 Tsp salt
- 2 cans chicken broth. (4 Cups)
- 1 TBS "Better than Bullion" chicken base
- 2 C Half and Half
- 1/2 C sour cream
- white pepper

Direction

- In a large saucepan or stock pot, sweat leeks and garlic in butter or margarine and salt until soft.
- Add chicken broth, base and potatoes and bring to boil, cook until potatoes are soft.
- Remove from heat, stir in half and half and sour cream.
- Blend soup with immersion blender until smooth and creamy.
- Add pepper to taste.
- Serve hot.

94. Creamy Potato Cheese Soup Recipe

Serving: 6 | Prep: | Cook: 20mins | Ready in:

Ingredients

- 2 cups instant mashed potato flakes
- 1 package (about 1 1/4 oz) dried cheddar cheese sauce mix
- 1 tablespoon dried chives
- 1 teaspoon chicken bouillon granules
- 1/2 teaspoon dry mustard
- 1/4 teaspoon white pepper
- 3 cups water
- 2 cups milk
- 1/2 to 1 cup sour cream or plain yogurt
- hot pepper sauce (optional)
- 1 1/2 cups hearbed croutons (optional)

Direction

- Combine all dry ingredients in a bowl, except croutons.
- Bring water and milk to a boil in large saucepan over high heat.
- Gradually whisk in combined dry ingredients.
- Reduce heat; simmer 5 minutes, stirring constantly.
- Whisk in sour cream.
- Add additional water or milk, 1/2 cup at a time, to reach desired consistency.
- Season with hot pepper sauce, if desired.
- Serve with croutons.
- Variations: Stir in 2 cups cooked broccoli florets or 2 cups cubed cooked ham. Heat through.

95. Creamy Pumpkin Soup Recipe

Serving: 6 | Prep: | Cook: 60mins | Ready in:

Ingredients

- One quarter cup butter
- 1 large onion, chopped
- 2 cloves garlic, minced
- 4 cups chicken broth
- 2 carrots, chopped
- 2 celery ribs, chopped
- 1 can (16-oz.) pumpkin puree
- 1 Tbsp. grated fresh ginger
- One half tsp. curry powder
- One half tsp. ground cinnamon
- One quarter cup cream
- salt and pepper to taste
- fresh parsley for garnish

Direction

- Melt butter in a saucepan and sauté onion and garlic. Place chicken broth and sautéed onion and garlic in a Dutch oven along with carrots, and celery. Bring to a boil then reduce heat and simmer for a couple of hours until vegetables are tender. Place mixture in a blender or food processor and process until smooth. Add pumpkin puree, ginger, curry powder, cinnamon, cream and salt and pepper and mix well. Return to saucepan and heat through. Serve with fresh parsley as a garnish. You may also use grated cheddar cheese, croutons or toasted pumpkin seeds as well.
- The Skinny: Use fat free chicken broth and fat free Half and Half in place of the cream.

96. Creamy Roasted Cauliflower And Artichoke Soup Recipe

Serving: 4 | Prep: | Cook: 40mins | Ready in:

Ingredients

- 1 large head of cauliflower
- 1 cup of artichoke hearts
- 2-3 minced cloves garlic
- extra virgin olive oil
- 1 cup of light cream (or whole milk, half and half, or heavy cream)

- 4 cups of vegetable stock (can substitute chicken broth)
- crushed leaves from a few sprigs of fresh thyme
- zest of a lemon
- fresh ground black pepper
- salt

Direction

- First, preheat your oven to 425 degrees F.
- Wash your cauliflower then cut it into flowerets.
- In a large sized bowl, toss the cauliflower with enough olive oil to just coat all the pieces. Then spread them out over a rimmed baking sheet.
- Now put your cauliflower in a preheated 425 degree oven and roast it. Turn the pieces periodically until almost tender (takes between 20-30 mins)
- Now put the cauliflower pieces in a bowl using tongs and then set aside. There should be some olive oil left on your baking sheet. Oh so carefully pour the oil into a soup pot (or Dutch oven).
- Add in the garlic to the oil in your pot and sauté on medium heat until golden.
- Add the artichoke hearts, cauliflower and vegetable stock to the pot and bring to this to a boil. Turn heat way down and simmer for a few minutes until the cauliflower is fully tender (you can check with a fork).
- Remove the pot from the heat and let cool slightly. Now puree the soup until very smooth with a food processor, or blender. Return to pot.
- Gently reheat the soup then add zest of one lemon (not juice), one cup of light cream, crushed thyme, and a good amount of salt and fresh ground pepper (to taste). The soup can be thinned with extra broth or water if necessary. Remove from heat when soup is heated through again.

97. Creamy Spinach And Potato Soup Recipe

Serving: 4 | Prep: | Cook: 35mins | Ready in:

Ingredients

- 2 medium organic Russet or yukon gold potatoes
- 14 oz organic baby spinach
- 1/2 organic red bell pepper
- 1/2 organic onion
- 1 cup organic vegetable stock
- 2 cups water
- 1/2 cup heavy cream
- 1 tablespoon sea salt
- fresh ground black pepper
- fresh ground nutmeg
- 2 thick slices sesame bread
- cheddar cheese about 2 ounces
- 2 tablespoons olive oil
- 2 tablespoons lemon pepper seasoning
- pinch of sea salt

Direction

- Preheat oven to 450 degrees.
- Cube the russet potatoes coat with vegetable oil and sprinkle with sea salt and fresh ground black pepper, bake them for 35 minutes until soft.
- Dice the onion and half of the red bell pepper and add to pot. Fry for a few minutes on medium.
- Add the Spinach the water and the vegetable stock and bring to a boil.
- Cook down the spinach until it is all wilted, add the heavy cream, sea salt pepper, and fresh ground nutmeg.
- Place the potatoes into a food processor and pulse until rough chopped.
- Reserve half of the rough chopped potato for the soup pot.
- In a food processor blend half the potato with the spinach and cream stock until smooth,

- This may have to be done in batches. Return all the ingredients to the pot and heat thoroughly.
- Fill a soup bowl with spinach potato soup and add the croûtons then grate some cheddar cheese on top.
- Julian the remainder of the red bell pepper add for garnish.
- Serve at once.
- .

98. Creamy Turkey Or Chicken Soup Recipe

Serving: 6 | Prep: | Cook: 60mins | Ready in:

Ingredients

- 1 small carrot; peeled & chopped
- 1 small potato; peeled & cubed
- 1 small onion; peeled & cubed
- 1 turkey drumstick; or 2 lrg chicken legs
- 2 small chicken bouillon cubes
- 1/2 cup orzo pasta
- 2 eggs
- 2 lemons

Direction

- Put prepared vegetables, poultry and bouillon cubes in pressure cooker.
- Add enough water to cover.
- Lock pressure cooker lid.
- Bring to high pressure and cook for an additional 30 minutes.
- Release pressure, remove the meat and set aside to cool.
- Strain broth from pressure cooker into a clean pot.
- Puree vegetables and return to broth.
- Add an additional cup or 2 of water if broth looks a little too thick.
- Heat to boiling and add orzo.
- Meanwhile, remove and discard the bones from the chicken/turkey, cut up the meat and add to pot when the orzo is tender.
- Add eggs and lemon to blender and mix well.
- Slowly add about a cup of soup from the pot to the mixture.
- Pour this back into the soup.
- Serve.

99. Creamy Vegetable Chowder Recipe

Serving: 12 | Prep: | Cook: 90mins | Ready in:

Ingredients

- 3/4 lb sliced bacon,chopped
- 2 large onions,chopped
- 2 med. carrots,chopped
- 2 small turnips,chopped
- 2 med. parsnips,chopped
- 3/4 c flour
- 1/2 tsp salt
- 1/2 tsp cayenne pepper
- 2 cartons (32 oz. ea) chicken broth
- 1 med sweet potato,peeled and chopped
- 3 small red potatoes,chopped
- 2 bay leaves
- 1 Tb worcestershire sauce
- 1/4 tsp hop pepper sauce
- 1 c half and half
- 1/2 c fresh minced parsley

Direction

- In Dutch oven, cook bacon over med. heat until crisp. Remove to paper towels; drain, reserving 3 TB drippings. Chop onions, carrots, celery, parsnips and turnips; add to pan. Cook and stir 6-8 mins or till fragrant.
- Sprinkle vegetables with flour, salt and cayenne; stir till blended. Gradually add broth. Bring to a boil; cook and stir for 2 mins or till thickened.

- Stir in sweet potato, potatoes, bay leaves, Worcestershire sauce and pepper sauce.
- Reduce heat; cover and simmer for 15-20 mins. or till potatoes are tender.
- Stir in cream and parsley; heat through. Discard Bay leaves.

100. Crock Pot French Onion Soup Recipe

Serving: 8 | Prep: | Cook: 40mins | Ready in:

Ingredients

- Soup
- 3 large onions, slice
- 3 Tbl butter, melted
- 3 Tbl flour
- 1 Tbl worcestershire sauce
- 1 tsp sugar
- 1/4 tsp pepper
- 4   14 1/2 ounce cans oc beef broth
- (1/4 cup red wine, brandy or ale can be added as well)
- Cheesy Broiled French bread
- 8 slices French bread 1 inch thick
- 3/4 C shredded mozzarella
- 2 Tbl shredded or grated Parmesan

Direction

- Mix onions and butter in a 3 1/2 to 6 qt. slow cooker
- Cover and cook on high1 to 3 hours or until onions begin to brown slightly around the edges (it depends on your crock pot)
- Whisk flour, Worcestershire, sugar and pepper
- Stir flour mixture and broth into onions
- Cover and cook on low heat 7 to 9 hours or until onions are very tender
- Make Cheesy Broiled Bread and place 1 slice on each bowl of soup
- Set oven to broil
- Place bread slices on rack in broiler pan
- Sprinkle with cheeses
- Broil about 5 to 6 ' from heat about 3 minutes or until cheese is melted

101. Crock Pot Pork Chili Verde Recipe

Serving: 10 | Prep: | Cook: 420mins | Ready in:

Ingredients

- 3 lbs pork shoulder
- 28 oz can of green chili enchilada sauce
- 7 oz can of diced green chili's
- 1 tsp cumin
- pinch of salt
- pinch of pepper
- 2 chopped cloves of garlic
- 1 medium onion
- 1/2 bottle of mexican beer(i use Pacifico)
- 1 cup sour cream
- extras:
- tortillas
- sour cream
- cheese

Direction

- Chop the garlic and dice and brown the onion in a skillet with a little oil. Put into crock pot.
- Cut the pork into cubes. Add to skillet and cook until just brown on sides. Put into crock pot.
- Deglaze pan with beer and pour into crock pot.
- Pour green enchilada sauce, green chilies, cumin, salt and pepper into crock pot.
- Give it a good stir.
- Cook on High for 1 hour.
- Switch to Low and cook for another 7 hours.
- (Crock pot liner works great)
- Stir in 1 cup sour cream at the end of cooking before serving.

- Serve with refried beans and rice. Makes excellent burritos!

102. Crock Pot Potato Soup Recipe

Serving: 12 | Prep: | Cook: 460mins | Ready in:

Ingredients

- 8 lb.of peeled and cubed potatoes
- 1 small chopped onion
- 6 c. of water
- 2 c. of milk
- 1/2 c. of all-purpose flour
- 2 tbsp. of butter
- 2 cubes of chicken bouillon
- 2 tbsp. of dried parsley

Direction

- First you want to add the potatoes, onion, butter, bouillon cubes, parsley, and water over slow flame (crockpot if you have one.)
- Then you will keep it on low for around 6-8 hrs.
- Next you are going to want to stir in some milk around half an hour before serving.
- Now you want to cook this for around 30 min. letting the soup get thick!

103. Crock Pot Rustic Beef Stew Recipe

Serving: 6 | Prep: | Cook: 32mins | Ready in:

Ingredients

- 1-1/2 pounds beef stew meat, cut into 2 inch chunks
- 1/2 teaspoon freshly ground pepper
- 1-1/2 teaspoons paprika
- 1 teaspoon garlic powder
- 2 onions, cut into chunks
- 4 medium - large potatoes, cut in quarters
- 2 carrots, cut into chunks
- 2 parsnips, cut into chunks(optional)
- Note: During the last 1/2 hour of cooking, you can add 1 leek that has been thoroughly rinsed and roughly chopped.
- 1 cup beef broth or water
- Note: You can also add 1/3 cup of red wine
- 2 - 3 tablespoons A1 or Heinz 57 sauce
- 1 tablespoon cornstarch
- 3 tablespoons water

Direction

- Sprinkle beef with pepper, paprika and garlic powder.
- Place in a crock pot with onion, potato, carrots and parsnips.
- Add beef broth / water and steak sauce that have been mixed together.
- Cover and cook on LOW for 8 - 9 hours or until tender.
- Turn to HIGH.
- Dissolve cornstarch in water and add to the crock pot.
- Cover and cook on HIGH for 20 minutes or until slightly thickened.

104. Crockpot Chicken Creole Recipe

Serving: 6 | Prep: | Cook: 480mins | Ready in:

Ingredients

- 2 lbs skinless chicken
- 1 red or green bell pepper, chopped
- 1 lg onion, chopped
- 1 LG bunch green onions,tops and bottoms,chopped
- 2 stalks celery, diced

- 1 15-oz can stewed tomatoes, undrained and chopped
- 3 cloves garlic, minced
- 1 T granulated sugar
- 1 t paprika
- 1 t cajun seasoning
- 1 t salt
- 1 t black pepper
- 1 T lemon juice
- Louisiana hot sauce to taste
- 2 c prepared rice

Direction

- Place chicken in bottom of crockpot.
- Add the remaining ingredients except for lemon juice, hot sauce & rice. Cover; cook on Low for 8-10 hrs. or on Hi for 4-5 hrs.
- In last hr. of cooking, add lemon juice & hot sauce.
- Serve over hot rice.

105. Crockpot Chili Recipe

Serving: 8 | Prep: | Cook: 180mins | Ready in:

Ingredients

- 2-1/2 to 3 lbs. ground beef
- 1 (15.5 oz.) can light red kidney beans, drained
- 1 (15.5 oz.) can dark red kidney beans, drained
- 1 (14.5 oz.) can diced tomatoes
- 1 (14.5 oz.) can stewed tomatoes
- 1/2 large yellow onion, diced
- 2 cloves garlic, finely minced
- 3/4 red pepper, coarsely chopped
- 1-3/4 Tbs. thyme, divided
- 1-3/4 tsp. red pepper flakes, divided
- 6 Tbs. chili powder, divided
- 1 Tbs. steak rub (Yes, steak!, recipe follows)
- 1 cup beef broth
- 5-1/2 pinches kosher salt, divided
- 2 to 2-1/2 Tbs. light brown sugar
- 1 Tbs. butter
- 1-1/2 Tbs. EVOO (extra virgin olive oil)
- steak RUB:
- **(From "Weber's Big Book of Grilling")**
- 2 tsp. black peppercorns
- 2 tsp. mustard seeds
- 2 tsp. paprika
- 1 tsp. granulated garlic
- 1 tsp. kosher salt
- 1 tsp. light brown sugar
- 1/4 tsp. cayenne pepper

Direction

- Preheat large skillet to medium low and heat EVOO and butter.
- Add garlic, sauté for about 1 minute, then add onions, 1/4 tsp. of the red pepper flake and 1 pinch kosher salt; sauté for about 5 minutes. Add chopped red pepper; sauté for another 5 minutes.
- Add 1/4 Tbs. chili powder and 1/4 Tbs. thyme; stir.
- Remove from heat and place in crock pot.
- Place skillet back on burner and increase heat to medium to medium-high, brown beef and drain fat.
- Season with salt, 1 tsp. red pepper, 4-3/4 Tbs. chili powder, 1 Tbs. thyme and all of the barbeque rub.
- Stir to combine and remove from heat.
- Add meat to crock pot with veggies, tomatoes and beans.
- Crank crock pot up to high, add remaining spices, brown sugar and beef broth; stir to combine.
- Put the lid on and walk away for about 2 to 3 hours.

106. Crockpot Southwestern Pumpkin Soup Aka Korma Soup From Michael Congdons Soups Cookbook Recipe

Serving: 6 | Prep: | Cook: 180mins | Ready in:

Ingredients

- 1/4 teaspoon whole cloves
- 2 teaspoons coriander seeds
- 1/2 teaspoon green peppercorns
- 1 teaspoon ground cumin
- 2 teaspoons dried ancho chile powder
- 1/8 teaspoon dried chipotle powder
- 1 teaspoon ground cinnamon
- 1 teaspoon garlic powder
- 1/4 teaspoon fresh ground nutmeg
- 4 cups vegetable stock
- 3/4 cup half-and-half
- 1 (8 fluid ounce) can evaporated milk
- 1 (29 ounce) can pumpkin puree
- 1/2 cup pure maple syrup
- 1 teaspoon kosher salt
- grated cheddar cheese, for garnish
- toasted cashews, for garnish

Direction

- In a hot skillet, toast the cloves, coriander seeds, and peppercorns.
- Add the ground spices to the whole ones in the skillet- the cumin, chili powders, cinnamon, garlic powder, and nutmeg, and toast the mixture over high heat, stirring occasionally, for about 3 minutes or until the spices begin to smoke.
- Remove from heat, let cool, and grind together to a powder (an electric coffee grinder works well for this); set aside.
- Pour the stock, half and half, and evaporated milk into the crock pot; stir well, cover, and turn on high.
- Put the pureed pumpkin into a large bowl, then add the maple syrup, salt, and the now-powdered spice mixture; use a whisk to incorporate the mixture well.
- Add the pumpkin mixture to the liquids in the crockpot, whisking it well to make sure there are no lumps.
- Cover and let simmer on high for 2 to 3 hours.
- Garnish servings with grated cheddar cheese and toasted cashew pieces.

- Many thanks to Michael for creating this wonderful soup! :)

107. Curried Pumpkin Cauliflower Soup Recipe

Serving: 6 | Prep: | Cook: 25mins | Ready in:

Ingredients

- 2 tbsp. unsalted butter
- 2 cups cauliflower florets (can use frozen)
- 1 tsp. chicken (poultry) seasoning
- 1 large onion, chopped
- 3 tsp. mild curry powder
- 4 cups chicken or vegetable stock (broth)
- 1 can (16 oz.) solid-pack pumpkin puree
- 1 tsp. salt
- 1/2 cup heavy cream, or half and half
- 1 tbsp. sugar
- 1/3 cup chopped cashew nuts
- plain yogurt for garnish

Direction

- Melt butter in a large, heavy saucepan or Dutch oven over medium heat. Add cauliflower, sauté about 5 minutes or until almost tender. Sprinkle with 1 tsp. chicken (poultry) seasoning. Remove to a bowl, set aside.
- Add onion to the sauce pan. Sauté for about 4 minutes, or until tender. Add more butter if needed. Stir in curry powder. Cook and stir 1 more minute. Deglaze with 2 cups of broth. Transfer the onion mixture to the blender or food processor. Process to a smooth puree.
- Return broth mixture to saucepan (or Dutch oven). Add remaining 2 cups of broth, pumpkin and salt. Stir well to combine and bring to a boil. Reduce the heat and simmer for about 10 minutes.
- Add the cauliflower and cook, stirring occasionally, for another 5 minutes, or until cauliflower is tender.

- Stir in heavy cream, or half and half, and 1 tbsp. sugar. Heat through until sugar dissolves. Turn off the heat.
- To serve, ladle hot soup in a bowl, dollop with plain yogurt, and sprinkle with cashew nuts. *Note: Do not add cashews until serving time.

108. Curried Red Lentil Soup Recipe

Serving: 6 | Prep: | Cook: 20mins | Ready in:

Ingredients

- 1 tbsp. olive oil
- 1 onion, finely chopped
- 1 carrot, finely chopped
- 1 garlic clove, minced
- 1 tbsp. curry powder
- 2 tsp. minced peeled fresh ginger
- 1/8 tsp. cayenne pepper
- 4 cups chicken broth
- 1 cup red lentils, picked over, rinsed and drained
- 1 14 1/2-ounce can diced tomatoes in juice
- 1 tart apple, finely chopped

Direction

- Heat the oil in a large non-stick saucepan, then add the onion. Sauté until translucent. Add the carrot and sauté until softened. Add the garlic, curry powder, ginger and cayenne pepper sauté until fragrant, about 1 minute.
- Stir in the broth, lentils, tomatoes and apple; bring to a boil. Reduce the heat and simmer until the lentils are very tender, about 20 minutes.
- Serves 6.

109. DONNAS TACO SOUP Recipe

Serving: 8 | Prep: | Cook: 1mins | Ready in:

Ingredients

- 2 LBS hamburger CHUCK
- 1 LARGE ONION CHOPPED
- 1 BUNCH OF green onions CHOPPED
- 1CAN OF whole kernel corn DRAINED
- 1 CAN OF Rotel tomatoes
- 1 CAN OF STEWED OR diced tomatoes
- 1 6.5 OZ CAN OF mushrooms OR mushroom pieces & STEMS
- 1 CAN OF kidney beans
- 1 CAN OF ranch style beans
- 1 CAN OF pinto beans
- 1 PKG. OF taco seasoning
- 1 PKG. OF RANCH STYLE DRESSING
- parsley
- seasoning OF YOUR CHOICE SUCH AS HOUSE seasoning, NATURES SEASONINGS, TONYS, ETC...
- black pepper
- water TO YOUR DESIRED CONSISTENCY
- YOU CAN ALSO ADD chili powder TO TASTE
- IF YOU ARE IN SOUTH LOUISIANA AND HAVE ACCESS TO CREOLE beans YOU CAN ADD THOSE ALSO
- ENJOY!

Direction

- BROWN THE HAMBURGER CHUCK WITH THE LARGE ONION, DRAIN
- THEN ADD THE REST OF YOUR INGREDIENTS
- BRING TO A BOIL STIRRING OFTEN SO IT WON'T STICK
- BRING DOWN TO A MEDIUM HEAT AND COOK FOR 45 MINUTES
- YOU CAN DOUBLE THIS RECIPE AND FREEZE IF YOU LIKE
- SERVE OVER TORTILLA CHIPS
- WITH CRACKERS

- OR TOP WITH SHREDDED CHEESE & SOUR CREAM

110. Darbars Fantastic Spicy Turkey Chili Recipe

Serving: 10 | Prep: | Cook: 60mins | Ready in:

Ingredients

- 1 lb. ground turkey
- 1 tbsp. vegetable oil
- 1 onion, diced, or two if you want to
- 6 cloves garlic, minced or pressed
- 14.5 oz. can pinto beans
- 14.5 oz. can cannellini beans
- 14.5 oz. can black beans
- 2 - 14.5 oz. cans diced tomatoes
- 16 oz. tomato sauce
- 1 tbsp. red wine vinegar
- 8 oz. red wine
- 2 tbsp. Chipotle Tabasco sauce
- 2 tbsp. chili powder
- 1 tbsp. cumin
- 1 tbsp. dried oregano
- 1 tbsp. dried basil
- 1 tbsp. black pepper
- 1 tsp. hot paprika
- 2 tbsp. brown sugar
- 1 tbsp. crushed red pepper

Direction

- Heat the oil in a large heavy pot over medium heat; cook onion and garlic until onions are translucent. Add turkey and cook, stirring, until meat is browned. Stir in all other ingredients. Reduce heat to low, cover and simmer gently 60 minutes or more, stirring occasionally, until flavors are well blended.
- Serve with a bowl of diced onions or shredded cheddar cheese and plenty of buttered crackers.
- Note: This is very spicy. If you don't like it real spicy, cut back on the crushed red pepper, Chipotle Tabasco, and hot paprika. If you already made it and it's too spicy, peel a couple of potatoes, cut them in half lengthwise, and cook them in the chili for 30-45 minutes and then discard them. They will soak up some of the heat.

111. Darbars Potato Leek Soup Recipe

Serving: 4 | Prep: | Cook: 30mins | Ready in:

Ingredients

- The white and pale green part of 4 large leeks, split lengthwise, washed well, and chopped (rinse in a colander after chopping)
- 4 cloves of garlic, crushed
- 2 tablespoons unsalted butter
- 2 cups chicken broth
- 2 cups water (or more chicken broth)
- 1 cup white wine
- 2 pounds yukon gold potatoes
- 4 tablespoons minced fresh parsley leaves
- Handful of fresh chives, chopped

Direction

- In a large heavy saucepan cook the leeks and garlic in the butter with salt and pepper to taste, covered, over moderately low heat, stirring occasionally, for 8 to 10 minutes, or until they are softened but not browned. Add the water, the broth, the wine, and the potatoes, peeled and cut into 1/2-inch dice, and simmer the mixture, covered, for 30 minutes, or until the potatoes are tender. In a blender, puree 3-4 cups of the soup, stir the puree into the remaining soup with the parsley, and season the soup with salt and pepper. Pour into bowls and garnish with the chives. Serve with hunks of crusty bread or in a bread bowl.

- Feel free to experiment with other veggies too, like parsnips, turnips or carrots.

112. Double Bean Bacon Soup Recipe

Serving: 4 | Prep: | Cook: 30mins | Ready in:

Ingredients

- 4 strips bacon cooked and chopped
- 1 can white kidney beans
- 1 can black beans
- 1 fresh tomato crushed
- 3 cups vegetables stock
- 1 medium red onion
- 4 cloves garlic
- 4 green onions
- 4 stalks celery
- 1 large carrot
- 3 ears fresh corn kernels cut off ears
- 1/4 cup fresh coriander
- 1 teaspoon salt
- 2 teaspoons freshly ground black pepper
- 3 tablespoons grated pepper jack cheese
- 1 large fresh jalapeno pepper minced

Direction

- Combine all ingredients in a large soup pot and simmer for 30 minutes. When ready to serve put into soup bowls and sprinkle cheese and jalapenos over top and serve immediately.

113. Easy Black Bean And Pepper Soup Ci Recipe

Serving: 6 | Prep: | Cook: 60mins | Ready in:

Ingredients

- 30-45oz black beans, undrained(depending on the size of the cans :)
- 1/2 cup red onion, diced
- 4-6 cloves garlic, minced
- 1-4T jarred jalapeno peppers, diced(this will determine most of the heat, so use to your taste)
- 1 cup beef stock
- 2t brown sugar
- juice from 1 lime
- couple dashes red wine vinegar
- 1-2t chili powder
- 1t/2-1t cayenne
- 1/4 cup fresh cilantro, chopped
- salt
- sour cream for serving

Direction

- Combine all ingredients besides lime juice, salt, cilantro and sour cream in large saucepan and heat to high simmer.
- Simmer 30-60 minutes, adding salt cilantro and lime juice in the last few minutes.
- Garnish with sour cream.
- *This can also be made in a slow cooker but will only need to cook a couple of hours, adding juice, salt and cilantro just prior to serving.

114. Easy Hungarian Goulash In The Crockpot Recipe

Serving: 6 | Prep: | Cook: 3mins | Ready in:

Ingredients

- 2 pounds beef chuck roast, cubed
- 1 large onion, diced
- 1/2 cup ketchup
- 2 tablespoons worcestershire sauce
- 1 tablespoon brown sugar
- 2 teaspoons salt
- 2 teaspoons Hungarian sweet paprika

- 1/2 teaspoon dry mustard
- 1 1/4 cups water, divided
- 1/4 cup all-purpose flour

Direction

- Place beef in slow cooker, and cover with onion. In a medium bowl, stir together ketchup, Worcestershire sauce, brown sugar, salt, paprika, mustard, and 1 cup water. Pour mixture over beef and onions.
- Cover, and cook on Low for 9 to 10 hours, or until meat is tender.
- Mix 1/4 cup water with flour to form a paste, and stir into goulash. Cook on High for 10 to 15 minutes, or until sauce thickens.

115. Easy Microwave Chili Recipe

Serving: 4 | Prep: | Cook: 10mins | Ready in:

Ingredients

- 1 lb ground beef
- 1 8 oz can tomato sauce
- 1 pk chili seasoning mix
- 2 tbsp Original Louisiana red chili Hot Sauce
- 1/2 cup water
- 1 15 oz can Casa Fiesta chili beans

Direction

- Break ground meat into smaller portions and place in a 2 quart microwavable bowl.
- Microwave on high for 3 - 5 minutes, rotating dish.
- Drain excess oil.
- Add remaining ingredients and mix well.
- Cover bowl, microwave on high 6-8 minutes, rotating bowl and stirring every 3 minutes during cooking.
- Remove from oven and sprinkle shredded cheese.
- Serve

116. Easy Taco Soup Recipe

Serving: 8 | Prep: | Cook: 60mins | Ready in:

Ingredients

- 2 pounds of hamburger (or ground turkey), cooked, drained (I use 4% fat beef)
- 1 medium onion, chopped
- 1 package taco seasoning
- 2 cups of water
- 6 green scallions, chopped
- 1 16-ounce can kidney beans, drained
- 1 16-ounce can corn, drained
- 1 16-ounce can of diced tomatoes (or use rotel with chiles!)
- 2, 8-ounce can tomato sauce or tomato soup
- 1 Tb cumin
- 1 bag or tortilla chips
- Optional: sour cream, fresh cilantro, chopped cabbage, sliced radishes, chopped scallions AND a handful of monterey jack cheese for each bowl to top soup

Direction

- In a large heated cooking pot, add the beef, scallions and chopped onions and cook for five minutes over high heat.
- Reduce heat to medium and add taco mix, water and tomatoes.
- Add tomato sauce and the rest of the canned ingredients.
- Add the cumin.
- Bring to a boil then reduce heat and simmer for 40 minutes.
- Place tortilla chips in individual serving bowls and pour soup over chips.
- Top with your favorite toppings!
- Serve!

117. Easy Chicken ENCHILADAS Recipe

Serving: 8 | Prep: | Cook: 30mins | Ready in:

Ingredients

- 1 whole roasted chicken from grocery deli
- 12 corn or flour tortillas. I like corn
- 16 ounces monterey jack cheese shredded
- 3/4 cup chopped onion
- 1/4 cup butter
- 1/4 cup flour
- 2 cup chicken broth Canned works great with added 1 tsp soup base
- 1 cup sour cream
- 1 can green chilies

Direction

- De-bone chicken and cut into pieces.
- If using corn tortillas soften in hot oil for about 20 sec... I spray and heat.
- Place 2 tablespoons cheese, 1 1/2 tablespoons chicken and 1 tablespoon onion in each tortilla. Roll up.
- Place seam side down in a 9x13 inch casserole that has been sprayed with non-stick oil.
- Melt butter in saucepan; blend flour; slowly add chick broth; cook stirring constantly until mixture thickens and bubbles.
- Stir in Sour Cream and Peppers; cook until heated through, but do not boil. Pour over tortillas.
- Bake at 350 degrees for 30 minutes. Sprinkle remaining cheese on top and cook for 5 more minutes or until cheese melts.
- I add minced hot peppers (not a lot) with the cheese.
- Easy and Very Good!

118. Egg Balls For Chicken Soup Recipe

Serving: 24 | Prep: | Cook: 10mins | Ready in:

Ingredients

- 1 doz eggs
- salt pepper to taste
- flour
- dash cumin
- finely chopped basil

Direction

- Hard cook eggs
- Peel and remove yolks
- Place yolks, cumin, salt, pepper and mix well
- Add white of egg
- Cumin and basil
- Add flour until you get consistency to where you can make small balls about the size of a nickel
- Bring broth to rolling boil
- Roll balls gently in more flour, salt and pepper
- Drop one at a time into boiling soup...
- Will pop to the top in about a minute
- Very colorful and tasty

119. Egg Drop Soup Recipe

Serving: 4 | Prep: | Cook: 25mins | Ready in:

Ingredients

- 3 cups of homemade chicken broth
- 2 teaspoons of cornstarch
- 2 tablespoons cold water
- 1 scallion, including some of the green part, cut into 1/4 inch pieces
- 1 egg, well beaten
- freshly ground pepper

Direction

- Bring the broth to a boil.
- Blend the cornstarch and water.
- Add to the broth slowly, stirring.
- When thickened, add the scallion.
- Stirring the soup rapidly, gradually add the beaten egg.
- Remove from the heat immediately and season with pepper.

120. Eggplant And Lamb Stew Recipe

Serving: 6 | Prep: | Cook: 120mins | Ready in:

Ingredients

- 1 1/2 pounds lamb shoulder
- 2 green bell peppers, chopped
- 2 large tomatoes, diced
- 2 large eggplants, peels removed and chopped
- 2 large onions, chopped
- 1/2 cup water
- 2 tbsp butter
- 1 tbsp tomato paste
- 1 tsp allspice
- 10 garlic cloves, diced
- 2 tsp salt
- 1 tsp ground black pepper

Direction

- Melt the butter in a large pot, over a medium heat. Add the lamb and brown on all sides. Stir in the peppers, tomatoes, eggplants, onions, and garlic. Cook, and stir until tender and browned lightly.
- In a small bowl, mix the tomato paste and water. Add to the pot with the lamb and season the lamb with allspice, salt, and pepper. Lower the heat, and simmer for about 1 1/2 hours, stirring from time to time, until you can easily shred the meat with a fork. (Add some small amounts of water as needed to keep the ingredients moist.)

121. Egyptian Swiss Chard Or Beet Green And Rice Soup Recipe

Serving: 4 | Prep: | Cook: 20mins | Ready in:

Ingredients

- 1 onion, peeled and chopped
- 4 cloves garlic, finely chopped
- 1/2 tsp. cumin seeds
- 2 T. olive oil
- 1 bunch swiss chard, chopped
- 1 can chick peas
- 1/4 cup rice
- 4 cups water
- 1 cup plain yogurt
- juice of 1/2 lemon
- 1/2 tsp. salt
- Preparation

Direction

- Sauté the onion, 2 cloves of garlic, and cumin seeds in the olive oil. When soft, add the chard and fry for about 5 minutes.
- Add the chick peas with their juice, the rice, and water. Stir well and simmer until rice is cooked, about 15 minutes.
- Meanwhile, mix remaining garlic with yogurt and lemon juice.
- Take soup off heat and stir in yogurt. Season to taste.

122. Elaines Asian Beef Noodle Soup Recipe

Serving: 4 | Prep: | Cook: 30mins | Ready in:

Ingredients

- 2 cups beef, thinly sliced
- 1 cup thinly sliced carrots

- 1 package rice noodles
- 2 cups beef bouillon
- 1 cup chicken stock
- 1/2 tsp salt
- 2 cups trimmed snow pea pods
- 6 green onions, chopped coarsely
- 1/2 tsp Chinese five-spice powder
- 1 tbsp grated fresh ginger or 1 tsp ground ginger
- 2 garlic cloves, finely minced
- 2 tsp soy sauce
- 2 tsp fresh lemon juice
- 1/4 tsp sesame oil*

Direction

- Bring 2 cups water to boil in a large saucepan.
- Add the beef bouillon and chicken stock.
- Reduce heat to simmer.
- Boiling rapidly will only cloud the broth.
- Add carrots.
- Add the peas, onions, garlic, ginger and beef.
- Simmer 20 minutes.

123. Elaines EASY French Canadian Pea Soup Recipe

Serving: 10 | Prep: | Cook: 25mins | Ready in:

Ingredients

- 1 medium sized ham bone with some meat left intact
- 1 tsp dehydrated onion flakes
- salt to preference (I used none here because the ham had enough)
- 1/4 tsp black pepper
- 4 cups dehydrated peas
- 3/4 cup heavy cream
- 6 cups cold water

Direction

- Place the cold water and the ham bone with meat intact into the pressure cooker
- Clamp the lid
- Bring to a boil slowly, then increase flame to high to produce steam and pressure.
- When the little indicator post rises, the pressure release will shoot off some steam.
- Turn heat off, and allow to cool enough to remove the clamped lid. DO NOT attempt to rush this, as SERIOUS burns could result.
- When the lid is safely removed, add the onion, pepper, and dried peas (and salt if you're using any)
- Clamp the lid again and bring to boil until steam and pressure begins to escape.
- Turn off heat immediately, and again allow to cool until the lid can be loosened safely.
- When the lid is removed, slowly add the heavy cream and combine well.
- The beauty of this is that the peas rehydrate very quickly and literally 'explode' in the pressure cooker, bringing out every bit of flavor, resulting in a hearty, thick soup.
- ENJOY! :D

124. Elaines Home Made Scotch Broth Soup Recipe

Serving: 8 | Prep: | Cook: 180mins | Ready in:

Ingredients

- About 1 – ½ lbs cooked lamb, coarsely cut. RESERVE THE BONES!
- 3 – 4 raw potatoes, medium sized, coarsely chopped
- 1 – ½ cups carrots, coarsely chopped
- approx ½ cup dried onions, or 1 cup fresh
- about 7 cups of chicken broth. It's equivalent equals two boxes of ready-made, store-bought broth in the 900 ml tetri-packs if you have no homemade broth or stock
- ½ tsp salt. (For no salt recipe, use 1 tsp of McCormicks 'No salt Added Citrus Pepper')
- 1 –1/2 cups raw barley
- 2 oz dry red wine

Direction

- Combine all ingredients into the stock pot and slowly bring to a boil.
- Reduce to half heat, stirring often.
- In another pot, put in the bones, and add about 2 cups of water.
- Add 2 tsp vanilla extract.
- Bring to the boil rapidly, then reduce to simmer. Stir often.
- Allow to cook until the meat falls off the bones, and the broth is reduced.
- Remove all the bones, then add the bone broth to the stock pot.
- This soup is also very easily made in the slow cooker, and all measurements are the same.
- The vanilla might sound strange, but believe me, it heightens the flavor tremendously in the finished product!
- As for the wine, for those who do not use alcohol, have no concerns, as the alcohol is evaporated during the cooking process. The wine, like the vanilla, heightens the flavor of this hearty soup.

125. Elaines Homemade Beef And Vegetable Soup Recipe

Serving: 8 | Prep: | Cook: 180mins | Ready in:

Ingredients

- 1 lb lean stewing beef, cut into bite-sized pieces
- 4 beef shank bones, marrow in
- about 2 quarts cold water
- 1 tsp pure vanilla extract
- 1 tsp salt
- 1/2 tsp pepper
- 1 tsp dried basil
- 1 tsp italian seasoning
- 3 medium sized potatoes, washed and unpeeled, cut into bite-sized pieces
- 1 can (28 oz size) tomatoes
- (if additional tomato richness is desired, add 1/2 small can unsalted tomato paste)
- 1 1/2 cups carrots, chopped
- 1 1/2 cups celery, chopped
- 1 cup corn niblets
- 1 large onion, diced
- 1 cup peas
- =========================
- For the mirepoix:
- finely dice one large onion
- add 1/2 (roughly) the amount of finely diced carrots
- add 1/2 (roughly the amount of celery

Direction

- Place the beef shanks into the cold water
- Slowly bring to the boil
- Add the vanilla (the vanilla dramatically heightens the flavor of the beef)
- Skim off any 'scum' that rises from the bones
- In another saucepan, brown the beef, and when browned, add to the soup pot, drippings and all.
- In the meantime, in a separate saucepan, caramelize the onion, and add a mirepoix of one part finely chopped onion, 1/2 part carrots, and 1/2 part celery in a little canola oil
- Cook until tender
- Usually, mirepoix is not served, but in this soup, the mirepoix is added to the soup, adding terrific flavor, texture, and making the soup more economical in these dollar-stretching times!
- While cooking the mirepoix, make vegetable stock from clean leftover pieces of veggies you have cut. It should be in a water bath of about 2 cups.
- When the veggie stock is cooked, and the veggies tender, strain the liquid through a colander, and discard the veggies used in the stock.
- Add the veggie stock to the soup pot.
- Add the mirepoix to the soup pot, and add the additional vegetables as indicated... more carrots, celery, onion, corn, potatoes, tomatoes, peas...

- Allow to simmer for at least two hours, stirring periodically.
- Taste, and adjust the seasoning, adding more salt and pepper if desired.
- This recipe makes a very HEARTY soup, and is a meal in itself.
- Served with garlic toast, your family will be asking you to make this more often!

126. Extraordinary French Onion Soup Recipe

Serving: 4 | Prep: | Cook: 50mins | Ready in:

Ingredients

- 4 slices French bread
- 2 tablespoons butter
- 3 medium onions thinly sliced
- 1 clove garlic mined
- 1/4 teaspoon sugar
- 1/4 cup dry white wine
- 2 tablespoons flour
- 1 bay leaf
- 4 cups beef broth
- 2 cups water
- 1 teaspoon salt
- 1 teaspoon freshly ground black pepper
- 1 cup grated gruyere cheese
- Grated parmesan cheese

Direction

- Toast bread in 350 oven for 15 minutes. In a large heavy saucepan melt butter over medium heat until it begins to foam. Reduce heat to low and add onions and garlic then simmer uncovered for 15 minutes stirring occasionally, adding butter during cooking process if necessary. Increase heat to medium then add sugar and sauté for 30 minutes. Increase heat to high then pour the wine into the onions and reduce the liquid by 2/3. Reduce heat to medium and sprinkle flour onto the onions and stir until all traces of flour disappear. Gradually stir in broth and water then add bay leaf and season with salt and pepper. Bring to boil then reduce heat and simmer uncovered for 30 minutes stirring occasionally. Remove bay leaf then pour hot soup into bowls and float bread on top. Sprinkle generously with gruyere cheese and a little grated parmesan. Broil soup in the middle of the oven for 20 minutes.

127. Feijouda Recipe

Serving: 68 | Prep: | Cook: 120mins | Ready in:

Ingredients

- 1 large onion
- 1 head of cabbage(couve de bruxels)
- I can tomatoes sauce
- (portuguese sausage meat)
- Chorizo red or black
- Linguica(portuguese sausage)
- Farinheira(soft - portuguese smoked sausage)
- Entrecosto (pork chops)
- Touchinho (bacon) - copped in bit size pieces
- rice
- 1 orange
- Red, black or white beans soaked

Direction

- Sauté onions in olive oil.
- Add meat (entrecosto) and tomatoes sauce and cook for 10mins.
- Then add beans and water, and bay leaf and simmer for 50 mins
- Add chorizo, linguica and toucinho and some herbs and spices of your choice simmer for another 40 mins until beans are almost done.
- Then add farinheira.
- Do not add salt to the feijoada until it is done.
- Serve with steamed cabbage, rice and orange slices.

128. Firehouse Chili Recipe

Serving: 15 | Prep: | Cook: 90mins | Ready in:

Ingredients

- 1 pound bacon, diced
- 2 medium onions, chopped
- 6 cloves garlic, peeled and crushed
- 2 jalapeno peppers, seeded and diced
- 2 red chili pepper, seeded and diced
- 1 habanero pepper, seeded and diced
- 3 pounds beef chuck, cut in small cubes (about 1-inch cubes)
- 4-5 Louisiana spiced sausage links
- 1 can (28 ounces) crushed tomatoes
- 1 can (28 ounces) diced tomatoes
- 1 can (6 ounces) tomato paste
- 8-10 tablespoons chili powder
- 2 tablespoons cumin seeds
- 1 tablespoon oregano
- 1 tablespoon thyme
- 2 tablespoons sugar
- 3 cups beef stock
- 3 cans (15 ounces each) pinto beans
- 1 can or SMART PAK(tm) carton of Hormel® chili with beans
- 2 tablespoons Masa (corn flower)
- 1 tablespoon crushed red pepper
- Add to taste:
- cayenne pepper
- salt
- ground black pepper
- For garnish:
- Chopped green onions
- Grated cheddar cheese
- sour cream

Direction

- In a large saucepan or Dutch oven over medium heat, fry bacon until fat is rendered and bacon is crisp. Drain off all but 2 tablespoons of the bacon fat. Add diced onions, crushed garlic, and seeded and diced peppers and cook until soft, 10-15 minutes. Meanwhile, in a large skillet over medium-high heat, brown the chuck and sausage links in the reserved back fat as needed (or use vegetable oil). If the skillet is not large enough to hold all of the meat in one layer, brown in several batches, removing each batch to a plate or bowl as it is finished. Use 1 cup of the beef stock to deglaze the browning pan. When the onions and vegetables are soft, add the browned meat to the pan. Then add the crushed and diced tomatoes, tomato paste, seasonings, 1 cup of beef stock used to deglaze the meat browning pan, the remaining 2 cups stock, the pinto beans and the Hormel® Chili. Bring to a simmer. Add to 2 tablespoons of Masa flour. Reduce heat, cover and simmer over low heat about 1 hour or until meat is tender.
- Season to taste with 1 or 2 dashes of cayenne pepper, salt and ground black pepper. Serve with garnishes on the side.

129. Fish And Cilantro Stew Recipe

Serving: 6 | Prep: | Cook: 30mins | Ready in:

Ingredients

- 1 T olive oil
- 2 cups chopped onion
- 1 cup sliced celery
- 1 cup sliced carrot
- 3-4 cloves garlic, crushed
- 1 jalapeno, minced
- 2 cups cubed potato
- 5 cups chicken stock
- 15 oz can crushed tomatoes
- 1/2 cup chopped cilantro
- 1 pound cod, cut into bite sized pieces
- 1 pound medium shrimp, shelled, deveined
- 1 lime, zested and juiced
- salt and pepper to taste

Direction

- Heat olive oil over med high heat. Sauté onion, celery, carrot, garlic and jalapeno about 5 minutes.
- Add potato, tomatoes, and stock. Simmer till potatoes are tender.
- Add fish, shrimp, lime juice and zest and cilantro. Cook about 5 minutes till shrimp are pink and fish is cooked. Season to taste with salt and pepper.

130. Fish With Coriander Chili And Lemon Sauce Recipe

Serving: 6 | Prep: | Cook: 30mins | Ready in:

Ingredients

- You will need a food processor for this recipe. If you do not have one, all the ingredients will have to be diced very finely by hand before mixing them with the meat.
- swordfish steaks, boned washed and pat dry
- salt and pepper
- vegetable oil
- paper towel
- 2 tblspns washed and chopped fresh coriander (cilantro)
- 6 cloves garlic peeled
- 1/2 - 1 fresh red chili, seeds removed and finely diced or 1 tsp dried red chili flakes
- 1 tsp salt
- 1 tblspn olive oil
- juice of 2 lemons
- water
- 3 potatoes, peeled &cut in wedges
- vegetable oil

Direction

- Season fish steaks with salt and pepper.
- Heat vegetable oil in shallow fry pan.
- Fry fish steaks until golden.
- Drain on paper towel.
- In mortar and pestle (or small food processor), grind garlic, coriander and chili to a paste, with a tsp of salt.
- Heat 1 tbsp. olive oil in a large, deep sided fry pan or saucepan on top of stove over medium heat.
- Fry the garlic paste until garlic 'just' starting to turn golden. Be careful NOT to burn garlic.
- Add the lemon juice, simmer for 1 min, then add the fish steaks.
- Add just enough water to cover the fish.
- Simmer on medium heat.
- Meanwhile fry the potato wedges until golden.
- Drain on paper towel, then add to the fish.
- Cover and simmer till the sauce has reduced slightly, and the potatoes are tender.
- Add water as necessary to prevent drying.
- Serve with rice
- PS: try it with my recipe Rice in fish broth.

131. Football Killer Dogs Enough Said Recipe

Serving: 1 | Prep: | Cook: 15mins | Ready in:

Ingredients

- hot dogs, your choice
- hot dog buns, your choice
- mustard
- swiss cheese, sliced in half
- Kraut
- chili
- Chopped onions
- jalapenos
- FORKS ON STAND-BY
- LOTS OF NAPKINS

Direction

- 1 hot dog, cooked, your choice (steamed, grilled, sizzled)
- 1 hot dog bun, good quality
- Spread mustard on bun

- Place hot dog on bun
- Place Swiss cheese on both sides of bun with hot dog in middle
- Spoon Kraut on hot dog
- Spoon heated chili on top
- Top with onions and jalapenos
- WOW, WOW, WOW
- Serve with your favorite chips and a long slice of kosher pickle

132. French Onion Soup 1 Recipe

Serving: 46 | Prep: | Cook: 50mins | Ready in:

Ingredients

- French onion soup
- 1/2 cup unsalted butter
- 4 onions, sliced
- 2 garlic cloves, chopped
- 2 bay leaves
- 2 fresh thyme sprigs
- kosher salt and freshly ground black pepper
- 1 cup red wine
- 3 heaping tablespoons all-purpose flour
- 2 quarts beef broth
- 1 baguette, sliced
- 1/2 pound grated gruyere

Direction

- Melt the stick of butter in a large pot over medium heat. Add the onions, garlic, bay leaves, thyme, and salt and pepper and cook until the onions are very soft and caramelized, about 25 minutes. Add the wine, bring to a boil, reduce the heat and simmer until the wine has evaporated and the onions are dry, about 5 minutes. Discard the bay leaves and thyme sprigs. Dust the onions with the flour and give them a stir. Turn the heat down to medium low so the flour doesn't burn, and cook for 10 minutes to cook out the raw flour taste. Now add the beef broth, bring the soup back to a simmer, and cook for 10 minutes. Season, to taste, with salt and pepper.
- When you're ready to eat, preheat the broiler. Arrange the baguette slices on a baking sheet in a single layer. Sprinkle the slices with the Gruyere and broil until bubbly and golden brown, 3 to 5 minutes.
- Ladle the soup in bowls and float several of the Gruyere croutons on top.
- Alternative method: Ladle the soup into bowls, top each with 2 slices of bread and top with cheese. Put the bowls into the oven to toast the bread and melt the cheese.

133. French Onion Soup Recipe

Serving: 6 | Prep: | Cook: 60mins | Ready in:

Ingredients

- 4 Tablespoons butter (1/4 cup)
- 5 med sweet onions (about a pound)
- 1 tsp sugar
- 2 tsp flour
- 1/2 tsp dry mustard
- 5/8 cup of white wine
- 3-3/4 cups beef-stock.html">Oxtail Consomme Beef Stock">oxtail beef consomme (or 2 cans of beef consommé) oxtail beef consomme">
- 6 slices of swiss cheese, provolone, gruyere, or fresh parmesan
- 1/2 loaf of French bread
- 6 T butter

Direction

- Peel and slice onions. In a deep heavy stock pot, over med heat, sauté onions in butter and sugar till caramelized (golden brown). BE PATIENT and stir frequently as this will take a while to do it properly.
- Add mustard and flour, stir well. Add consommé and wine. Simmer 30 minutes.

- Slice, butter, and lightly toast French bread under broiler in oven. Put soup into 6 ceramic (oven safe) bowls. Float a slice on soup in each bowl. Cover bread with cheese. Broil 1-2 min. Serve.
- Note – Chateau Ste. Michelle Johannisburg Riesling works especially well in this soup.
- USE THIS STOCK RECIPE and adjust the amount of wine to taste since the stock recipe uses wine to deglaze the roasting pan.

134. Fresh Artichoke Bisque Recipe

Serving: 8 | Prep: | Cook: 60mins | Ready in:

Ingredients

- 8 large artichoke hearts
- 8 Tbsp butter
- 1 medium size leek, white-and-light green part, sliced and rinsed
- 6 garlic cloves, chopped
- 1/2 cup chopped shallots
- 2 medium size yukon gold potatoes, peeled and diced
- 8 cups of homemade vegetable stock
- 1 bay leaf
- 2 sprigs fresh thyme
- 4 sprigs of parsley
- 1/2 teaspoon cracked white peppercorns
- 1/4 teaspoon freshly grated nutmeg
- 1/2 cup of cream
- kosher salt to taste
- lemon and parsley for garnish

Direction

- Prepare the artichoke hearts. Cut the artichokes lengthwise into quarters. With a small knife, remove the thisly choke part and discard. Cut away the leaves from the artichoke heart. Cut or peel with a vegetable peeler the tough outside skin of the stems and discard. (Leave an inch to two inches of stem with each of the hearts) Slice the hearts or chop to a quarter inch thickness. Squeeze lemon juice all over them to help control discoloration (turning brown).
- In a large pot, melt half of the butter and cook the artichoke hearts, leek, garlic, and shallots on medium heat until tender but not brown. Add the potatoes and stock. Tie up the bay leaf, thyme, parsley, and peppercorns in cheesecloth and add to the pot. Increase heat to bring to a simmer, then lower heat and continue to simmer uncovered, 1 hour.
- Remove and discard the herbs. Purée the soup, adding more stock to thin if needed. Pour back into soup pot.
- When ready to serve, heat the soup and whisk in the remaining butter and the cream. Season with salt and nutmeg. Garnish with lemon slice floating on top and a sprig of fresh parsley and serve.

135. Fresh Mushroom Soup Recipe

Serving: 6 | Prep: | Cook: 25mins | Ready in:

Ingredients

- 8 oz. Shitake or button mushrooms
- 6 oz oyster mushrooms
- 1/3 cup chopped shallots
- 2 Tbl butter
- ½ tsp salt
- ¼ tsp pepper
- flour, enough to absorb liquid
- 1 14 ½ oz can vegetable or chicken broth (1 ¾ cup)
- 2 cups half & half or light cream

Direction

- Remove any tough or woody stems from mushrooms. Cut the mushrooms into medium to small pieces.

- In a large saucepan cook mushrooms and shallots in melted butter, uncovered, over medium high for 4 – 5 minutes or until tender, stirring occasionally.
- Stir in flour, salt and pepper. Add broth. Cook and stir over medium heat until slightly thickened and bubbly. Cook and stir 1 minute more.
- Stir in half & half, heat through, ladle into bowls
- Makes 6 generous side dish servings.

136. Fresh Pink Peach Soup Recipe

Serving: 4 | Prep: | Cook: | Ready in:

Ingredients

- 2 cups sliced fresh strawberries
- 2 peaches, pitted, peeled, and sliced
- 1/2 cup fresh orange juice
- 1/2 cup plain yogurt (or sour cream)
- 3 tablespoons sugar, or to taste
- 1 tablespoon fresh lemon juice
- 1/8 teaspoon nutmeg, preferably freshly grated
- Dollops of plain yogurt/sour cream and fresh blueberries for garnish

Direction

- Purée all the ingredients, except the garnishes, in a blender until smooth.
- Taste and adjust the sweetening.
- Refrigerate in a covered container until chilled, at least 3 hours, before serving.

137. Fresh Tomato Soup Recipe

Serving: 4 | Prep: | Cook: 20mins | Ready in:

Ingredients

- 3 medium tomatoes, peeled and quartered, or one 14 1/2 ounce can tomatoes cut up.
- 1 1/2 cups water
- 1/2 cup chopped onion
- 1/2 cup chopped celery
- 1/2 of a 6 oz can of tomato paste
- 2 tablespoons fresh cilantro or parsley chopped
- 2 teaspoons chicken bouillon granules
- 2 teaspoons lime juice or lemon juice
- 1 teaspoon sugar
- Few dashes of louisiana hot sauce
- Snipped fresh clinatro or parsley (optional)

Direction

- If desired you can seed the tomatoes.
- In a large saucepan combine fresh or undrained tomatoes, water, onion, celery, tomato paste, parsley or cilantro chopped.
- Add bouillon granules, lime juice, sugar, and hot sauce.
- Bring to boiling; reduce heat.
- Cover and simmer about 20 minutes or until celery is tender.
- Cool slightly.
- Place half of the tomato mixture in a food processor and blend until smooth.
- Repeat with other half of mixture.
- Return to pan and reheat.
- Serve hot or served chilled.
- Garnish with extra cilantro or parsley

138. Friday Night Carrot Leek Parsnip Chicken Orzo Soup Recipe

Serving: 8 | Prep: | Cook: 60mins | Ready in:

Ingredients

- 1 large bunch of carrots washed and tops off
- 1 large bunch of parsnips washed and tops off

- 3 leeks tops cut off and discarded
- 1 chicken or chicken parts washed and excess fat removed
- skin on or off as preferred
- 4 teaspoons granulated chicken boullion
- white pepper
- fresh dill
- fresh bread or crackers

Direction

- Put chicken, whole parsnips, whole carrots and leeks in pot
- Fill with water to cover chicken and veggies
- Cook on med/high till hot
- Add bouillon crystals, pepper and dill
- Stir gently
- Lower to high simmer
- Remove chicken pieces when done
- Remove all veggies
- Separate into 2 groups
- Slice 1/2 carrots and parsnips add to soup
- Place rest in blender and puree in 1 cup of soup
- Add puree to soup

139. Frugal Cabbage Soup Recipe

Serving: 4 | Prep: | Cook: 8hours | Ready in:

Ingredients

- 1 head shredded cabbage
- 1 package of frozen spinach
- 4 carrots
- 1 head of garlic smashed
- 2 tomatoes
- 1 cup of water
- cracked black pepper

Direction

- Place all ingredients in slow cooker (crockpot) for 8 hours on LOW.

140. Full Minestrone Soup Recipe

Serving: 8 | Prep: | Cook: 50mins | Ready in:

Ingredients

- 1/2 c. of seashell pasta
- 2 tbsp. of grated parmesan cheese for topping
- 1 tbsp. of olive oil
- 2 chopped onions
- 2 c. of chopped celery
- 5 sliced carrots
- 2 c. of chicken broth
- 2 c. of water
- 4 c. of tomato sauce
- 1/2 c. of red wine (optional)
- 1 c. of canned kidney beans, drained
- 1 (15 oz.) can of green beans
- 2 c. of baby spinach, rinsed
- 3 quartered and sliced zucchinis
- 1 tbps. of chopped fresh oregano
- 2 tablespoons chopped fresh basil
- 3 cloves garlic, chopped
- salt and pepper

Direction

- Add some olive oil to a large pan over medium flame.
- Sauté garlic 3 min.
- Next add in the onion and cook for approx. 4-5 min.
- Then add in your celery and carrots, cook for about 1-2 min.
- Add in your broth, water, and tomato sauce, letting this come to a boil (stir).
- You can add your wine at this point.
- Now reduce your flame to low and then ad in your kidney beans, green beans, spinach leaves, zucchini, oregano, basil, salt and the pepper.

- You will want to let this simmer for around 30-40 min.
- Now in a separate pan, fill with water and bring the flame to medium (you want a full boil.
- Add in the macaroni coon till al dente.
- Drain macaroni and add to soup.
- Ladle into bowls with sprinkled parmesan on top.

141. Good Old Chicken With Rice Soup Recipe

Serving: 6 | Prep: | Cook: 35mins | Ready in:

Ingredients

- 8 cups chicken broth
- 1 onion, chopped
- 2 stalks celery, diced
- 2 carrots, diced
- 2-3 garlic cloves, minced
- 1 cup uncooked rice
- 1 1/2 teaspoons dried thyme
- 2 cups cooked chicken, diced
- salt and pepper (to taste)

Direction

- Combine broth, onion, celery, carrots and garlic in a large soup pot.
- Bring to a boil.
- Add rice and thyme.
- Reduce heat to low and simmer, uncovered, 30 minutes, stirring occasionally.
- Add chicken and heat through.
- Thin with more broth if necessary.
- Add salt and pepper to taste.

142. Good Ole New England Clam Chowder Recipe

Serving: 6 | Prep: | Cook: 25mins | Ready in:

Ingredients

- 1/2 cup butter
- 2 cups chopped onions
- 2 cups chopped celery
- 1 cup chopped green bell peppers
- 2 cloves garlic, chopped
- 2 teaspoons dried thyme
- 1/2 cup flour
- 1 cup white wine
- Three 8 oz. cans clam juice
- Three 12 oz. cans chopped clams
- 1 quart milk
- 2 cups cubed peeled potatoes
- 3 cups heavy cream
- 1/4 cup chopped parsley + 1 Tablespoon for optional garnish
- salt & pepper, to taste
- oyster crackers for garnish (optional)

Direction

- In a 5-quart soup pot melt the butter over medium heat.
- Add the onions, celery, green bell peppers, garlic, and dried thyme. Sauté until tender.
- Add the flour and cook for 3-4 minutes.
- Add the wine, clam juice, milk, and heavy cream; stir to combine and bring to a boil.
- Reduce to a simmer and add the clams and potatoes. Cook until potatoes are tender (5-10 minutes).
- Salt and pepper to taste.
- Stir in the 1/4 cup of chopped parsley.
- For optional garnish, sprinkle with oyster crackers and 1 Tablespoon of chopped parsley and serve.

143. Gosht Do Piaza A Hearty Popular Lamb Stew Recipe

Serving: 6 | Prep: | Cook: 25mins | Ready in:

Ingredients

- lamb - 1/2 kg (on the bone/shoulder cut preferably)
- onions - 1 kg (8-10 medium)
- garam masala - Cloves-5; Black Cardamom-5;Whole pepper-10;Bay leaves -2
- Red Chilli powder - 1 /2 tsp (optional)
- yogurt - 1/2 cup
- garlic - 1 small bulb / chopped fine
- ginger - 2" piece / chopped fine
- tomatoes - 2-3 medium / chopped
- paprika - 1 tsp
- Whole Red Chillies - 2-3 / broken into large pieces (optional)
- Green chillies - 2 / deseeded if desired (optional)
- fresh coriander leaves for garnishing

Direction

- Finely slice 2-3 onions.
- Roughly chop the remaining onions & keep aside with the chopped ginger, garlic & tomatoes.
- Heat about 1/2 cup oil in a pressure cooker.
- Fry the finely sliced onions till golden brown.
- Add the lamb & roast for 5-7 minutes, followed by the yogurt. Roast well till the sides leave oil.
- Add the whole garam masalas + paprika + red chili powder (if using) and roast for a minute or two.
- Now add the remaining onions with the chopped ginger, garlic, tomatoes & whole red chilies (if using).
- Add salt, mix well cook under pressure, on low heat, for 25 minutes/or until done.
- Open only once cool, i.e. steam dies down completely.
- Roast well to dry excess water.
- Add 2 slit & deseeded green chilies for flavour if desired.
- Garnish with fresh coriander. (Remove bay leaves before serving).
- Serve hot with naan, tandoori roti, paratha etc.

144. Goulash I Grew Up With Recipe

Serving: 6 | Prep: | Cook: 60mins | Ready in:

Ingredients

- 1 pound cooked ground beef
- 1/2 onion - chopped
- 1/2 green bell pepper - chopped
- 1 T canola oil (or butter)
- 3 cups water
- 3 beef boullion cubes
- 2 14.5 oz cans diced tomatoes
- 2 4 oz. cans tomato sauce
- 1 teas garlic powder
- 1 teas chili powder
- 1 1/2 teas cumin
- 1/4 teas salt (more to taste)
- 1/4 teas pepper
- 2 cups large elbow macaroni

Direction

- Brown ground beef - then drain and rinse
- In a large pot cook onion and green pepper in oil till softened
- Add all ingredients to the pot except macaroni and bring to a boil over medium heat
- Stir in the macaroni and reduce the heat to simmer. Let simmer until the macaroni is done, stirring occasionally to make sure macaroni doesn't stick.
- Great with crusty bread.
- Feel free to adjust the spices as you like, of course!

145. Goulash Recipe

Serving: 4 | Prep: | Cook: 90mins | Ready in:

Ingredients

- 4 tbs olive oil
- 4 rashes bacon, cut into strips
- 1 kg diced beef
- 2 diced onions
- 3 garlic cloves, crushed
- 2 roasted capsicums, peeled and left whole
- 3 tbs hot paprika
- 1 can diced tomatoes
- 6 cups unsalted beef stock
- 2 tbs red wine vinegar
- 6 medium peeled and sliced potatoes

Direction

- In a heavy pot on a medium heat fry the bacon in the oil. Remove and set aside.
- Add the beef and cook until brown.
- Add flour and stir.
- Add onions, garlic and capsicum. Add paprika, can of tomatoes, beef stock and vinegar. Simmer for 1 hour, stirring occasionally.
- Add potatoes and fried bacon. Stir and simmer for 30 minutes, semi-covered, stirring occasionally.

146. Grandmas Italian Wedding Soup Recipe

Serving: 15 | Prep: | Cook: 120mins | Ready in:

Ingredients

- SOUP:
- 5-6lb. stewing chicken
- 6-8qts. of water
- 4-5 sticks of celery
- 5-6 whole carrots
- 1 onion; quartered
- 5-6lbs. endive; boiled, drained & chopped
- MEATBALLS:
- 2lbs. ground chuck
- 2-3 eggs
- 1/2c. parmesan cheese
- salt & pepper
- CROUTONS:
- 6 eggs
- 1/2c. parmesan or romano cheese
- 1c. bread crumbs
- 1T. parsley
- salt & pepper

Direction

- SOUP:
- In stockpot boil the chicken, water, celery, carrots & onion for 90min. to 2 hrs. until chicken is tender.
- Clean chicken from bones removing all fat & skin.
- Strain broth.
- Add shredded chicken, carrots (which you have cut up) & chopped endive.
- Salt to taste.
- Add meatballs.
- Ladle soup into bowls and add croutons before serving.
- MEATBALLS:
- Mix together & roll into little balls the size of marbles.
- Brown on a cookie sheet in a 350F oven.
- Add to soup.
- CROUTONS:
- Beat eggs.
- Add bread crumbs, parsley, cheese and salt & pepper.
- If batter is runny, add a little more bread crumbs until batter is thick but still pourable.
- Pour into well-greased 9x13 pan.
- Bake 350F for 30 min. or until browned.
- Cut into small cubes and add to soup before serving.

147. Grandmas Mushroom Bisque Recipe

Serving: 4 | Prep: | Cook: 20mins | Ready in:

Ingredients

- 3 tbsp diced onion
- 1/4 cup water
- 1/2 lb sliced mushrooms
- 2 tbsp flour
- 3 cups rich vegetable stock
- 1 tbsp sherry
- 1/2 cup lowfat (not fat-free) plain yogurt
- 1/4 tsp salt
- 1/2 tsp black pepper

Direction

- Sauté the onion in 2 tbsp. of the water until translucent.
- Add mushrooms and remaining water, cook 7-8 minutes, stirring constantly.
- Sprinkle in flour and stir in well.
- Slowly add the stock and sherry, stirring constantly. Cook 5 minutes longer.
- Remove from heat and stir in yogurt, salt and pepper just before serving.

148. Greek Lemon Soup Recipe

Serving: 8 | Prep: | Cook: 35mins | Ready in:

Ingredients

- 6 cups Vegitable broth
- 2 cups cooked rice
- zest of one lemon
- 12 oz silken tofu
- 2 Tbs dill, snipped
- 1/4 cup lemon juice
- white pepper to taste

Direction

- In large pan/pot, bring broth, rice, and lemon zest to a boil, then reduce to simmer for 15 minutes.
- Remove 2 cups of broth and rice to a blender, add tofu, and blend (carefully, as it's hot) till smooth.
- Return to pot, whisking it into the broth and rice soup in the pot. Whisk in dill and lemon juice. Heat through, and serve.

149. Greek Wedding Soup Recipe

Serving: 4 | Prep: | Cook: 10mins | Ready in:

Ingredients

- Two (32oz) cans (8 cups) chicken broth
- 3/4lb. ground lamb or beef
- 2/3c finely chopped flat-leaf parsley
- 1/3c breadcrumbs
- 1/4c feta cheese, chopped or crumbled
- 1 large egg
- 2 cloves garlic, grated or finely chopped
- 2 sprigs oregano, finely chopped
- salt and pepper
- grated peel and juice of 1 lemon
- 1/3c chopped mint leaves

Direction

- In a deep skillet or Dutch oven, bring chicken broth to a boil. Lower heat and bring to simmer.
- Meanwhile, in a large bowl, combine lamb, half the parsley, breadcrumbs, feta, egg, garlic and oregano; season with salt and pepper. Form into 1" balls. Add to the broth along with orzo and cook 8 mins. Stir in remaining lemon peel, remaining parsley and the mint.

150. Green Chili Chicken Recipe

Serving: 4 | Prep: | Cook: 50mins | Ready in:

Ingredients

- 4 chicken breast halves
- 1 c. of chicken broth
- 2 tbsp. of chopped cilantro
- 4 oz. of chopped green chilies
- 1 c. of heavy cream
- 4 oz. of chredded monterey jack cheese
- 2 slices bacon
- 2 cloved of minced garlic

Direction

- First you want to preheat oven to 350°F.
- Now take an ovenproof skillet, you can now fry the bacon until crisp.
- Drain on paper towel.
- Now sauté chicken in bacon fat turning only once, till brown.
- Remove chicken, but you need to keep warm.
- Then add the chicken broth and scrape up any browned bits on bottom of skillet, simmer until reduced to half.
- Now you can put chicken back in skillet.
- Now add the garlic, cilantro, undrained chilies and cream.
- This needs to bake uncovered, until chicken is done approx. 30 minutes. Take this out of the oven, then you need to put oven to broil, sprinkle chicken with cheese, set under broiler until cheese melts and browns.
- Add the crumbled bacon to chicken.
- Serve.

151. Green Chili And Chicken Enchiladas Recipe

Serving: 4 | Prep: | Cook: 12mins | Ready in:

Ingredients

- 1-1/4 lbs. chicken breast tenders
- 1-1/2 c bottled green salsa
- 1 4 oz. can green chilies
- 1-1/2 c shreddded Mexican-style four-cheese blend (6oz.)
- 8 6 to 7 " flour tortillas
- refrigerated fresh salsa
- lime wedges(optional)

Direction

- Preheat broiler. Cut chicken into 1" pieces. In large microwave-safe bowl, micro cook on high 7 mins. or till no pink remains, stirring twice. Drain liquid. Break up chicken slightly in bowl with back of wooden spoon. Add salsa and chilies. Cook 3 mins. more or till heated through, stirring once. Stir in 1 c cheese.
- Spoon chicken mixture evenly down the center of tortillas. Roll tortillas around filling and place in 9x13" baking pan. Sprinkle remaining cheese over enchiladas. Broil 3 to 4" from heat 1 to 2 mins. or till cheese is melted.
- To serve, top with salsa and pass lime wedges.

152. Ground Beef Stew Recipe

Serving: 6 | Prep: | Cook: 480mins | Ready in:

Ingredients

- 2 large potatoes, sliced
- 2 medium carrots, sliced
- 1 can (15 oz) peas, drained
- 3 medium onions, sliced
- 2 celery ribs, sliced
- 1 1/2 lbs ground beef, cooked and drained
- 1 can (10 3/4 oz) condensed tomato soup, undiluted
- 1 1/3 cups water

Direction

- In a slow cooker, layer the first 6 ingredients in the order listed. Combine soup and water; mix well. Pour over beef. Cover and cook on LOW for 6-8 hours or until vegetables are tender.

153. Gypsy Soup Recipe

Serving: 10 | Prep: | Cook: 30mins | Ready in:

Ingredients

- 1 c. chopped fresh tomato
- 1 1/2 c. cooked garbanzo beans
- 3/4 c. chopped green bell pepper
- 1 small pinch ground cinnamon
- cayenne pepper
- 1 bay leaf
- 3 c. chicken stock
- 1 tbsp. tamari
- 2 c. diced peeled sweet potatoes
- 2 tsp. paprika
- 1 tsp. ground turmeric
- 1 tsp. dried basil
- 1 tsp. salt
- 4 tbsp. olive oil
- 2 c. chopped onion
- 1/2 c. chopped celery
- 2 cloves garlic, crushed

Direction

- You will heat EVOO in a pot over medium heat.
- Next you will sauté your onion, the garlic, celery, and the sweet potatoes for around 5 min.
- You will then add the paprika, turmeric, basil, salt, cinnamon, cayenne, and finally your bay leaf.
- Stir this and add while stirring your chicken stock and the tamari.
- You will then cover the pot and let it simmer for at least 15 min.
- Next, you will add the tomatoes, garbanzo beans, and your green pepper.

- Let this simmer for around 10 min, letting the veggies get tender.
- Add salt and pepper and enjoy!

154. Ham And Bean Soup With Vegetables Recipe

Serving: 4 | Prep: | Cook: 2hours | Ready in:

Ingredients

- 1 cup dry navy beans
- 1-1/4 to 1-1/2 pounds meaty smoked
- pork hocks or one 1- to 1-1/2-pound meaty ham bone
- 1 cup chopped onion
- 1/2 cup sliced celery
- 1 tablespoon instant chicken bouillon granules
- 1 tablespoon snipped fresh parsley
- 1 tablespoon snipped fresh thyme or
- 1 teaspoon dried, crushed
- 1/4 teaspoon pepper
- 2 cups chopped parsnips or rutabaga
- 1 cup sliced carrots
- 1 10-ounce package frozen chopped spinach, thawed and well drained.

Direction

- Rinse beans. In a Dutch oven combine beans and 5 cups cold water. Bring to boiling. Reduce heat and simmer, uncovered, for 2 minutes. Remove from heat. Cover and let stand 1 hour. (Or, skip boiling water and soak beans overnight in a covered pan.) Drain and rinse beans.
- In the same pan combine beans, 5 cups fresh water, pork hocks or ham bone, onion, celery, bouillon granules, parsley, thyme, and pepper. Bring to boiling. Reduce heat and simmer, covered, for 1-3/4 hours. Remove pork hocks or ham bone; set aside boiling. Reduce heat and simmer, covered, about 15 minutes or until vegetables are tender. Meanwhile, cut meat off bones and coarsely chop. Discard

bones. Stir meat and spinach into saucepan. Cook until heated through.
- Make-ahead tip: Prepare soup; cool slightly. Transfer to 1- to 4-serving size freezer containers. Seal, label, and freeze up to 1 month. To reheat, transfer frozen soup to saucepan. Cook, covered, over medium heat until heated through, stirring occasionally to break apart.

155. Harira Soup Recipe

Serving: 8 | Prep: | Cook: 80mins | Ready in:

Ingredients

- 1.5 lbs skinless chicken wings thighs or drumsticks.
- 5 celery sticks chopped
- 1 red onion peeled and chopped
- 1.5 cup red lentil soaked in water
- 3 tablespoons virgin oil oil
- 1 can 28oz chopped tomaotoes
- 1 can cooked garbanzo beans
- 3/4 cup chopped flatleaf parsely
- 1 cup chopped cilantro
- 1/2 teaspoon each blackpepper and cayenne pepper
- 3/4 teaspoon ground cinnamon
- 1,25 teaspoons ground ginger
- 1 lemon
- 1 heaping teaspoon tumeric
- sea salt to taste
- 2 cups vermicelli pasta
- 5-6 cups water

Direction

- Place chicken, onions, celery, all the spices and olive oil, stir frequently for 5 minutes. Save the juice of the crushed can of tomatoes and add the crushed parts only, cover pot simmer for 15 minutes
- Add tomato juice and 5 cups water and lentils. Bring to boil and simmer for 35 minutes. Drain

garbanzo beans and add to the cooking mixture, bring to boil and cook for 3 minutes, add vermicelli and lemon juice.
- Turn heat to low and cook till vermicelli is done, about 10 minutes.
- Ladle into soup dishes and garnish with chopped cilantro leaves and little drizzle of extra virgin olive oil

156. Hassenpfeffer German Rabbit Stew Recipe

Serving: 8 | Prep: | Cook: 60mins | Ready in:

Ingredients

- 1 large or 2 small rabbits, cleaned, skinned, and cut into pieces
- Marinade:
- 1/2 c. red-wine vinegar
- 1 1/2 c. water
- 1 c. dry red wine (I prefer a beaujolais to a heavier burgundy)
- 1 large or 2 medium onions, thinly sliced
- 1 t. salt
- 1 t. dry mustard
- 1 t. ground pepper
- 1 T. pickling spices
- 4 whole cloves
- 2 bay leaves
- flour, seasoned with salt and pepper
- 4 T. clarified butter
- sugar (start with 1 T.)
- 3 T. flour
- 1/2 c. sour cream
- 1/2 c. heavy cream

Direction

- Mix the marinade, bring to a boil, then simmer for an hour. Cool to room temperature. Marinate the rabbit for at least a day (two is better).
- Remove the rabbit pieces and dry them. Dredge them in the seasoned flour and brown

in the butter on all sides. Strain the marinade and add it to the rabbit, cover tightly, and simmer for an hour. Remove the rabbit and place on a serving platter.
- Add 1 T. sugar to the broth and taste. Add additional sugar if necessary to get the balance of sweet and sour you prefer. Blend the 3 T. flour with the cream and sour cream and add it, stirring constantly, cooking for a couple of minutes to thicken and remove the flour taste. Add salt and pepper to taste, pour over the rabbit, and serve.

157. Hawaiian Crock Pot Recipe

Serving: 4 | Prep: | Cook: 360mins |Ready in:

Ingredients

- 3 boneless skinless chicken breasts, split
- 1 lb. kielbasa, cut into pieces
- 3 medium baking potatoes, halved lengthwise and thinly sliced
- 20 ounces of pineapple tidbits, drained
- 1/2 inch piece of ginger, grated
- 1 garlic clove, minced
- 2 tbs. Dijon mustard
- soy sauce
- pepper
- paprika

Direction

- Slightly brown the chicken in a skillet (this will lock in the flavor)
- Place all ingredients in the order listed inside the crock-pot and let cook for 6 hours on low.
- * There is no need to open the crock-pot to stir during the cooking time. A crock-pot will distribute heat evenly through all the food. Just opening a crock-pot for 10 seconds can greatly alter the temperature inside.

158. Heart Healthy Pumpkin And Black Bean Soup Recipe

Serving: 4 | Prep: | Cook: 30mins |Ready in:

Ingredients

- Heart Healthy pumpkin and black bean Soup
- 1- 1/2 tablespoon extra-virgin olive oil
- 1 medium onion, finely chopped
- 4 cups canned or fresh low-sodium
- Swanson's 98% fat free chicken stock
- 1 can (14 1/2 ounces) diced tomatoes in juice
- 1 can (15 ounces) black beans, drained
- 2 cans (15 ounces) pumpkin puree
- 1/2 cup light cream
- 1 teaspoon curry powder
- 1/2 teaspoons ground cumin
- 1/4 teaspoon cayenne pepper
- coarse salt
- fresh chives for garnish

Direction

- Heat soup pot over medium heat. Add oil.
- When oil is hot, add onion.
- Sauté onions 5 minutes.
- Add broth, tomatoes, black beans and pumpkin puree.
- Stir to combine ingredients and bring soup to a boil.
- Reduce heat to medium low and stir in cream, curry, cumin, cayenne and salt, to taste.
- Simmer 5 minutes, adjust seasonings and serve garnished with chives.

159. Hearty Broccoli Soup Recipe

Serving: 2 | Prep: | Cook: 10mins |Ready in:

Ingredients

- 1 small box of frozen chopped broccoli. You can usually get the krasdale or white rose brand for $1 or less.
- 1 regular can of Campbell's cream of broccoli soup
- 2 Tbspns Butter
- 1/4 Cup Whole Milk
- 1 tspn of each: Onion, garlic and chili powder, white pepper, dill weed and basil.
- 1 pinch of cayenne pepper

Direction

- Put the frozen block of broccoli right into the pot with a little bit of water to cover the bottom, over a medium to high flame.
- As it cooks, you'll have to smoosh the block around inside the pot with your fork and turn it over a few times so it can properly break apart.
- Once it's all defrosted, let it cook a few minutes so the water reduces a bit.
- Add the contents of the soup can right into the pot. It will be thick which is why you still need some of the water in there. Put the milk into the can and use it to get out the remainder of the soup, pouring it all right into the pot.
- Stir well until hot, then add the butter and spices, stirring often. Let it cook for a few more minutes until properly blended. Remove from heat, pour into a bowl and enjoy. It's that simple!

160. Hearty Flemish Beef Stew Recipe

Serving: 8 | Prep: | Cook: 150mins | Ready in:

Ingredients

- 4 lbs. of best quality stew beef (buy a whole roast, and cut it in 2 inch cubes yourself and save the money by doing the work)
- seasoned flour for dredging (salt and pepper mixed in flour)
- 4 large onions sliced (one onion per lb of beef cubes)
- 2 large garlic cloves minced
- 8 rashers of thick cut bacon, diced
- 2 cups of dark ale-actually use 2 bottles
- 1 cup of beef broth
- 1 tsp of thyme
- 2 tbsp of red wine vinegar
- 3 tbsp of brown sugar
- red skin potatoes, roasted after being rolled in oil and coarse salt

Direction

- Heat Dutch oven and render the bacon fat from the diced bacon.
- Remove the crisply cooked bacon; reserve for garnish later.
- Leave the renderings in hot pan.
- Add 2 tbsp. of canola oil to bacon drippings
- Dredge the beef in the seasoned flour.
- Brown very well in hot fat, do not crowd the pan, do in batches.
- After all the beef is browned, in the drippings left behind, cook the onions and garlic over low heat until softened and cooked but not browned.
- Remove from Dutch oven and add to the beef that is resting.
- Pour the ale and broth in the oven and bring to a boil, stirring up from the bottom to get up all the goodies stuck to the bottom of the pan.
- Reduce liquid by 1/3 on high simmer
- Add beef cubes, onion and garlic back into the liquid.
- Stir in thyme, red wine vinegar and brown sugar.
- Cover tightly with lid and bake in 350 degree oven for 2 hours. Don't peek.
- Bake the tiny red skin potatoes on a lipped oiled cookie sheet for the last hour of baking of the Flemish stew.
- Often roast whole small carrots with the salted small red potatoes. Sometimes I crumble dried rosemary over the veggies while they roast.

- Serve in large shallow soup bowls topped with the reserved crumbled bacon, with lots of crusty bread and good cold ale.

161. Hearty Mexican Stew Recipe

Serving: 6 | Prep: | Cook: 60mins | Ready in:

Ingredients

- 1 pound lean boneless pork, cut into 1 inch cubes
- 1 small onion, chopped
- 1/2 pound zucchini
- 1 16-ounce can of diced tomatoes
- 1 8-ounce can whole kernel corn, drained (try the mexi corn)
- 1 teaspoon sugar
- 1/2 teaspoon salt (optional)
- 1/4 teaspoon ground cumin
- 1/4 teaspoon chili powder
- 1/4 teaspoon garlic powder
- 1/4 teaspoon pepper

Direction

- In a 2 quart microwavable casserole combine pork and onion.
- Microwave, covered, on high 5 to 7 minutes, stir.
- Reduce power to medium; microwave 5 to 7 minutes or until meat losses its pink color, stirring once after 4 minutes.
- Slice zucchini; halve large slices.
- Stir zucchini, un-drained tomatoes, corn, sugar, salt, cumin, chili powder, garlic powder, and pepper into pork mixture.
- Microwave, covered, on medium (50%) 25 to 35 minutes or until meat and vegetables are tender; stirring every 10 minutes.
- Let stand, covered, 10 minutes.
- Makes 4 servings.

162. Hearty Reuben Soup Recipe

Serving: 8 | Prep: | Cook: 25mins | Ready in:

Ingredients

- 1/2 cup canned low-sodium beef broth
- 1/2 cup canned low-sodium chicken broth
- 1/4 cup chopped celery
- 1/4 cup chopped onion
- 1/4 cup chopped green bell pepper 1 tablespoon cornstarch
- 2 cups fat-free evaporated milk or half-and-half cream
- 1 cup shredded corned beef
- 3/4 cup canned sauerkraut
- 1 cup shredded swiss cheese
- Freshly ground black pepper, to taste

Direction

- Preparation Time: Approximately 10 minutes
- Cook Time: Approximately 15 minutes
- Preparation:
- Bring beef and chicken broths, celery, onion and green pepper to a boil in a heavy saucepan; reduce heat. Simmer until the vegetables are tender, about 5 minutes. Dissolve the cornstarch in the milk. Stir into soup and simmer until soup thickens. Add corned beef and sauerkraut; heat through. Stir in cheese just until melted. Do not allow to boil; season with pepper.
- Servings: 8
- Nutritional Information Per Serving: Calories 190; Total fat 9g; Saturated fat 4.5g; Cholesterol 40mg; Sodium 500mg; Carbohydrate 11g; Fiber 1g; Protein 17g; Vitamin A 8%DV; Vitamin C 10% DV; Calcium 30%DV; Iron 6%DV *Daily Value

163. Hearty Vegetable Gumbo Recipe

Serving: 4 | Prep: | Cook: 25mins | Ready in:

Ingredients

- 1/2 cup chopped onion
- 1/2 cup chopped green bell pepper
- 1/4 cup chopped celery
- 2 cloves garlic, minced
- 2 cans (14 1/2 oz each) stewed tomatoes (you can use no-salt-added stewed tomatoes)
- 2 cups tomato juice (you can use no-salt-added juice)
- 1 can (15 oz) red beans, rinsed and drained
- 1 tablespoon chopped fresh parsley
- 1/4 teaspoon dried oregano leaves
- 1/4 teaspoon hot pepper sauce or more if you like it spicier
- 2 bay leaves
- 1 1/2 cups uncooked quick-cooking brown rice
- 1 pckage (10oz) frozen chopped okra, thawed

Direction

- Spray a 4-quart Dutch oven with cooking spray; heat over medium heat until hot.
- Add onion, bell pepper, celery and garlic. Cook and stir 3 minutes or until crisp-tender.
- Add stewed tomatoes, tomato juice, beans, parsley, oregano, pepper sauce and bay leaves.
- Bring to a boil over high heat. Add rice. Cover; reduce heat to medium-low. Simmer 15 minutes or until rice is tender.
- Add okra; cook, covered, 5 minutes more or until okra is tender.
- Remove and discard bay leaves.

164. Homemade Chicken Noodle Soup Recipe

Serving: 6 | Prep: | Cook: 70mins | Ready in:

Ingredients

- 1 pound chicken breast fillets
- 1 pound chicken thigh fillets
- vegetable oil
- 2 tablespoons butter
- 1 cup chopped onion
- 1/2 cup diced celery
- 4 cups chicken stock
- 2 cups water
- 1 cup sliced carrot
- 1 teaspoon salt
- 1/2 teaspoon cracked black pepper
- 1/2 teaspoon minced fresh parsley
- 2 cups egg noodles
- Garnish
- minced fresh parsley

Direction

- 1. Preheat oven to 375 degrees.
- 2. Rub a little vegetable oil over the surface of each piece of chicken and arrange them on a baking sheet. Bake for 25 minutes. Remove the chicken from the oven when it's done and set it aside to cool.
- 3. Melt the butter in a large saucepan or Dutch oven over medium heat. Sauté the onion and celery in the saucepan for just 4 to 5 minutes. You don't want to brown the veggies.
- 4. Dice the chicken and add it to the pot along with the remaining ingredients, except the noodles.
- 5. Bring the soup to a boil, reduce the heat and simmer for 30 minutes or until the carrots are soft.
- 6. Add the noodles and simmer for an additional 15 minutes, or until the noodles are tender. Serve with a pinch of minced fresh parsley sprinkled on top.

165. Homemade Chicken Stock Recipe

Serving: 8 | Prep: | Cook: 160mins | Ready in:

Ingredients

- 3 tablespoons unsalted butter
- 1 tablespoon virgin olive oil
- 3 large carrots, peeled and roughly chopped
- 1 large yellow onion, cut in half (with skin!)
- 3 large stalks celery, roughly chopped
- 2 parsnips, chopped
- 1 head garlic, cut horizontally in half
- 8 ounces mushrooms, roughly chopped
- 1 cup dry white wine
- 6 sprigs thyme
- 6 sprigs Italian parsley
- 6 basil leaves
- 2 bay leaves, broken in half
- 1 tablespoon black peppercorns, toasted
- 3 to 4 pounds chicken bones, wings, backs, and/or necks
- 10 to 12 cups water, or enough to cover

Direction

- Heat the butter and olive oil in a large stockpot over medium heat. When the butter begins to foam, add the carrots, onion, celery, garlic, and mushrooms. Sauté the vegetables, stirring occasionally, until golden brown, about 10 minutes.
- Add the white wine and stir, then add the herbs, peppercorns, chicken bones, and water and bring just to a simmer. Turn the heat to low, skim off any impurities that have risen to the surface (don't stir or the stock will be cloudy), and simmer, uncovered for 2 1/2 hours.
- Strain the stock first through a colander, then through a fine-mesh strainer (or cheesecloth-lined colander) into a stainless steel bowl or container. Chill the stock in an ice-water bath. (This not only kills harmful bacteria, it prevents you from having to put steaming-hot stock into your refrigerator — and inadvertently heating it and its contents.) Then refrigerate until chilled, or, preferably, overnight.
- Skim any fat from the top of the stock, and transfer to airtight containers. The stock will keep for 3 days in the refrigerator, or you can freeze it for up to 6 months.

166. Homestyle Polish Pickel Soup Recipe

Serving: 8 | Prep: | Cook: 20mins | Ready in:

Ingredients

- fresh carrots cut up
- fresh potatoes cut up
- water or chicken broth to cover
- 3 large polish pickes, shredded
- water or broth to cover
- Vegeta seasoning (Vegeta.com)
- salt and pepper to taste
- flour and cream to thicken only slightly

Direction

- Cover potatoes and carrots with broth or water and cook tender.
- Drain and reserve both vegetables and cooking liquid
- Do the same for the pickles (which require much less cooking time)
- Combine the pickles and vegetables together and set aside
- Combine the vegetable broth and pickle broth and thicken only slightly with a bit of cream and flour stirred together in the hot liquid
- Season to taste with salt and pepper and Vegeta seasoning
- Add the shredded pickles and vegetables to the soup and heat through
- Garnish is optional of sour cream and chopped fresh dill- which she did not use
- Yield depends on many veggies and liquid is used

167. Honey Chili Shrimp Over Noodles Recipe

Serving: 2 | Prep: | Cook: 10mins | Ready in:

Ingredients

- 2 T vegetable oil
- 2 cloves garlic, chopped
- 1 inch fresh ginger,, grated
- 1-2 red or green chillies, deseeded and chopped
- 1 pound shelled raw shrimp
- 1 medium onion, chopped fine
- 2 T honey
- juice of 1 lemon
- 1 T soy sauce
- 8 ounces Chinese egg noodles
- chopped fresh coriander (optional)

Direction

- Heat the oil in a wok and stir-fry the garlic, ginger and chilli over a high heat for about 1 minutes.
- Add the 8 ounces of egg noodles and stir-fry with the spices.
- Make sure you keep stirring well for about 2-3 minutes.
- Add the shrimp and onions and stir-fry for 1-2 minutes until the shrimp turn pink.
- Don't overcook or the shrimp will become rubbery.
- Add the honey, lemon juice and soy sauce.
- Allow to bubble up.
- Serve immediately.
- Sprinkled with fresh coriander if you have some handy.

168. Hot And Sour Cabbage Soup Recipe

Serving: 4 | Prep: | Cook: 15mins | Ready in:

Ingredients

- ¾ teaspoon Thai red curry paste
- 5 cups vegetable broth
- 1 teaspoon finely grated lime peel
- 1 tablespoon minced peeled fresh ginger
- 4 ounces shiitake mushrooms, stemmed and sliced
- 8 ounces napa cabbage, cut crosswise
- 4 (4-oz) cans small shrimp, drained and rinsed (or 1 lb salad shrimp)
- ¼ cup fresh lime juice

Direction

- Heat a heavy large pot over medium heat.
- Add curry paste and stir until it begins to stick to pan, about 4 minutes.
- Stir in broth, lime zest, and minced ginger.
- Bring to boil; reduce heat to medium and simmer 5 minutes.
- Add mushrooms. Cook 3 minutes.
- Add cabbage and shrimp; cook until cabbage begins to wilt, about 30 seconds
- Stir in lime juice and serve.

169. Hot And Sour Soup Recipe

Serving: 4 | Prep: | Cook: 90mins | Ready in:

Ingredients

- 1 cake tofu (fresh, if possible)
- 2 ounces pork tenderloin
- Marinade:
- 1 teaspoon soy sauce
- 1/2 teaspoon sesame oil
- 1 teaspoon tapioca starch (or cornstarch)
- Other:

- 1/2 cup bamboo shoots
- 2 tablespoons black fungus (Wood Ear) or Cloud Ear fungus(or 3 - 4 Chinese dried black mushrooms or fresh mushrooms)
- 1 small handful dried lily buds
- 6 cups water (or 6 cups water and 1 cup Swansons chicken broth)
- 1 teaspoon salt, or to taste
- 1 teaspoon granulated sugar
- 2 tablespoons soy sauce
- 2 tablespoons red rice vinegar, white rice vinegar, or red wine vinegar
- 1 teaspoon sesame oil
- 1 Tbsp cornstarch dissolved in 1/4 cup water
- 1 egg, beaten
- 1 green onion, finely chopped
- white pepper to taste (no more than 1 tablespoon)
- hot chili oil, to taste, optional

Direction

- Shred pork. Mix marinade ingredients and marinate pork for 20 minutes.
- Cut tofu into small squares. Cut bamboo shoots into thin strips and then into fine slices. To reconstitute the fungus, soak in warm water for 20 minutes. Rinse, and cut into thin pieces. (If substituting Chinese dried mushrooms, soak to soften, then cut off the stems and cut into thin strips. If using fresh mushrooms, wipe clean with a damp cloth and slice.)
- To reconstitute the dried lily buds, soak in hot water for 20 minutes or until softened. Cut off the hard ends.
- Bring the water to a boil. When it is boiling, add the bamboo shoots, fungus or mushrooms, and the lily buds. Stir. Add the tofu. Bring back to a boil and add the marinated pork.
- Stir in the salt, sugar, soy sauce and vinegar and sesame oil.
- Test the broth and adjust the taste if desired. (If using chicken broth, you may want to add a bit more rice vinegar).
- Mix the cornstarch and water. Slowly pour the cornstarch mixture into the soup, stirring while it is being added. Let the broth come back to a boil. As soon as it is boiling, remove the broth from the stove.
- Slowly drop in the beaten egg, stirring in one direction at the same time. Add the green onion and the white pepper to taste. Drizzle with chili oil if desired. Serve hot.
- (Hot and Sour Soup can be prepared ahead of time and frozen. When making the soup, leave out the tofu. When ready to serve, thaw, add the tofu and bring to boiling. When the soup is boiling, add the egg.)
- Adjust the ratio of water to chicken stock as desired.

170. Hot Chili Cheese Appetizer Recipe

Serving: 8 | Prep: | Cook: 4mins | Ready in:

Ingredients

- 5 oz. cream cheese, softened.
- 3/4 cup sour cream.
- 1 cup picante sauce.
- 1 (7 oz.)can green chiles drained and chopped.
- 1 4oz. jar diced pimento, drained.
- 3 cups shredded chedder cheese.
- 2 coves garlic, minced.
- Dash red-hot sauce.
- 1 tsp. chili powder.

Direction

- Put cream cheese and sour cream in a blender.
- Mix until smooth.
- Add remaining ingredients, mix well.
- Taste to adjust seasonings to your taste.
- Serve cold or microwave a few minutes if you like a hot dip.
- Serve with chips or fruit or bread cubed.

171. Hungarian Beef Stew Recipe

Serving: 6 | Prep: | Cook: 3mins | Ready in:

Ingredients

- 1 1/4pounds beef chuck in 3/4" pieces
- 1 pound carrots, sliced
- 2 medium onions, thinly sliced
- 3 cups thinly sliced cabbage
- 2 cups water OR 1 1/2 cups water and 1/2 cup red wine
- 6 ounce can tomato paste
- 1 envelope onion-mushroom soup mix
- 1 tablespoon paprika
- 1 teaspoon caraway seeds
- 8 ounces reduced-fat sour cream
- egg noodles

Direction

- Mix all ingredients EXCEPT sour cream in slow cooker.
- Cover and cook for 8 to10 hours on low until meat is tender.
- Turn off cooker.
- Stir in sour cream until well blended.
- Makes 8 cups stew.

172. Hungarian Goulash Recipe

Serving: 6 | Prep: | Cook: 90mins | Ready in:

Ingredients

- 2 tablespoons vegetable oil or bacon fat
- 1 1/2 pounds beef boneless chuck, tip or round, cut into 3/4-inch cubes
- 2 cups water
- 1 (8 ounce) can tomatoes (with liquid)
- 3 medium onions, chopped
- 1 clove garlic, chopped
- 2 teaspoons paprika
- 2 teaspoons salt
- 1 teaspoon instant beef bouillon
- 1/2 teaspoon caraway seed
- 1/4 teaspoon pepper
- 2 medium potatoes, cut into1 1/2-inch pieces
- 2 medium green bell peppers, cut into 1-inch pieces
- French bread or rolls

Direction

- Heat oil in Dutch oven or skillet until hot. Cook and stir beef in hot oil until brown, about 15 minutes; drain. Add water, tomatoes, onions, garlic, paprika, salt, bouillon, caraway seed and pepper. Break up tomatoes with fork. Heat to boiling; reduce heat. Cover and simmer 1 hour.
- Add potatoes; cover and simmer until beef and potatoes are tender, about 30 minutes. Add green peppers; cover and simmer until tender, 8 to 10 minutes. Serve in soup bowls with French bread for dipping into hot broth.

173. Hungarian Paprika Stew Recipe

Serving: 12 | Prep: | Cook: 480mins | Ready in:

Ingredients

- 4 pounds of boneless beef chuck roast, cut into 1/2-3/4" pieces (I cut off the fat from the sides and put that in the pot for flavor)
- 1 small package of baby carrots, cut in half
- 2-3 large red peppers, slices
- 2 large onions sliced thin
- 2 (8 oz) pkgs sliced mushrooms (I used portabello)
- 2/3 cup flour
- 3 tbsp sweet paprika
- 3 tbsp (hot) or smoked paprika (used smoked)
- 1 tsp salt

- 1 tsp thyme
- 1 tsp pepper
- 1 cup chili or seafood Sauce (yes, seafood sauce) Heinze I used
- 1 (32 oz) container of beef broth
- 1/2 cup red wine
- 1 pkg dry onion soup mix
- 1 (8 oz) sour cream
- 1 (16 oz) wide noodles

Direction

- In a 6-8 quart slow cooker, put beef, carrots, onion & red pepper
- Add flour, paprika, salt, thyme and pepper, toss over beef and vegetables till coated
- Add chili sauce, broth & wine and mix well, pour over meat/veggies
- Cover and cook on high setting for the first 4 hours till hot and bubbly
- Lower temp to "low" and continue cooking for another 4 hours till meat is tender and veggies are cooked to your likings
- Add mushrooms in the 7th hours and continue cooking with them in the pot
- Add sour cream 1/2 hour before serving on low and mix thoroughly
- Cook noodles and serve with stew
- Nice warm buttered rolls or bread for dipping is recommended

174. Indian Chili Chicken Recipe

Serving: 4 | Prep: | Cook: 20mins | Ready in:

Ingredients

- 6-8 large fresh red chilies
- 4 T corn oil
- 2 onions chopped
- 1 tsp chili powder
- 1 tsp grated fresh gingerroot
- 2 garlic cloves, finely chopped
- 1/2 tsp cumin seeds
- 2 curry leaves, available at gourmet shops and some markets
- salt, to taste
- 1 1/2 lbs skinless, boneless chicken breasts, cut into cubes
- 2 T chopped fresh cilantro
- 1 T fresh lime juice
- 4 tomatoes, quartered
- naan bread or steamed rice

Direction

- Make a slit along the side of each chili
- Heat the oil in a large, heavy bottom skillet
- Add the chilies and cook over low heat, turning occasionally, for 4-5 minutes or until starting to caramelize
- Remove with a slotted spoon and set aside
- Turn up heat on pan to medium high
- Add the onions, chili powder, ginger, garlic, cumin, curry leaves, and salt to the skillet and fry for 2-3 minutes
- Add the chicken and continue to fry for 8-10 minutes, or until tender and cooked through
- Stir in the chopped cilantro and lime juice, return the chilies to the skillet, and add the tomatoes
- Stir briefly, then serve at once atop naan bread or rice

175. Irish Stew Recipe

Serving: 4 | Prep: | Cook: 40mins | Ready in:

Ingredients

- 8 lamb chops
- salt and freshly ground pepper to taste
- 1 tablespoon vegetable oil
- 1 Bouquet Garni* (instructions under directions section)
- 1 pound potatoes, (3 to 4 medium)
- 2 cups finely shredded cabbage
- 1 medium onion, chopped

- 1 cup chopped carrots
- 1 large leek white, thinly sliced
- 12 small white onions
- 1 1/2 cups celery, diced
- 1 1/2 cups frozen peas
- 1 cup chicken stock
- Freshly chopped parsley for garnish

Direction

- Season chops with salt and pepper.
- Heat oil in saucepan wide enough to hold all chops in a single layer.
- Brown on both sides.
- Spoon off fat and add the chicken stock.
- Cut chops into bite-sized pieces.
- Next, add enough water to cover chops.
- Bring to a boil and add the Bouquet Garni.
- Lower heat and simmer.
- Meanwhile, peel potatoes and shape into bite sized rounds.
- Chop trimmings from potatoes into small pieces.
- Add potatoes, trimmings, cabbage, onion, well-rinsed leek, white onions and celery to chops and liquid.
- Simmer 20 minutes and then add peas.
- Add a little more water if needed during cooking, or more chicken stock.
- Simmer 10 minutes more or until potatoes are tender.
- Season with more salt and pepper, if desired.
- Garnish with parsley and serve.
- ==================================
- To make the Bouquet Garni:
- * Enclose 2 teaspoons dried parsley, 2 bay leaves, 1 teaspoon peppercorns, 1/2 teaspoon thyme and 1/2 teaspoon rosemary in cheesecloth, tied tightly.
- Drop into the pot and cook with the meat and vegetables.
- Remove before serving.

176. Italian Beef Soup Recipe

Serving: 6 | Prep: | Cook: 45mins | Ready in:

Ingredients

- 1 pound lean ground beef
- 1 tablespoon olive oil
- 1 small onion, chopped
- 1 cup chopped celery
- 1 cup chopped carrot
- 1 clove garlic, minced
- 1/8 teaspoon fresh ground pepper
- 28 ounces diced tomato
- 28 ounces beef broth
- 1/2 cup fresh basil leaves, chopped
- 2 tablespoons tomato paste
- 1/2 tablespoon fresh thyme, chopped
- 15 ounces kidney beans, rinsed and drained
- 1 cup fresh mushroom, sliced

Direction

- Cook ground beef in a large Dutch oven about 5 minutes or until brown. Drain and set aside.
- Remove excess oil but leave the pan bits in there.
- Heat olive oil in the same Dutch oven over medium-high heat and add onion, celery, carrot and garlic. Sauté about 5 minutes or until vegetables are tender; add pepper
- Stir in tomatoes, broth, basil, tomato paste and thyme. Simmer uncovered over medium-low heat for 20 minutes, stirring occasionally.
- Add kidney beans, mushrooms and beef. Simmer 10 more minutes.
- It doesn't get any done than that. Serve it up with your favorite soup accessories. Crackers of choice, hard crusted bread, rolls, etc.

177. Italian Sausage And Bean Soup Recipe

Serving: 4 | Prep: | Cook: 3mins | Ready in:

Ingredients

- 1-1/4 cups dry great northern beans
- 1-3/4 cups beef broth
- 1/2 cup chopped onion
- 1 clove garlic, minced
- 1/2 teaspoon dried Italian seasoning, crushed
- 12 ounces fresh italian sausage links, cut into 1/2-inch slices
- 1 medium yellow summer squash or zucchini, sliced (2 cups)
- 1 14-1/2-ounce can Italian-style tomatoes, cut up
- 1/3 cup dry red wine or water
- 1/2 of a 10-ounce package frozen chopped spinach, thawed and well drained
- Grated parmesan cheese (optional)

Direction

- Rinse beans. In a large saucepan or Dutch oven combine beans and 4 cups cold water. Boil, uncovered, for 10 minutes; drain.
- Meanwhile, in a medium skillet cook Italian sausage until brown. Drain well on paper towels. In a 3-1/2- or 4-quart crockery cooker combine the drained beans, 4 cups fresh water, beef broth, onion, garlic, Italian seasoning, cooked and drained Italian sausage, squash or zucchini, undrained tomatoes, and red wine or water. Cook, covered, on low heat setting for 11 to 12 hours or until beans are tender.
- Just before serving, stir spinach into soup. If desired, sprinkle each serving with Parmesan cheese.

178. Italian Wedding Soup Recipe

Serving: 10 | Prep: | Cook: 60mins | Ready in:

Ingredients

- 3 garlic cloves minced
- 1 medium onion diced
- 3/4 cup finely diced carrot
- 1 10 oz package chopped spinach (frozen)
- 12 cups of chicken stock (homemade or college inn)
- 1/2 tsp oregano
- 1/2 tsp basil
- 1 tsp italian spice
- 2 cups un cooked pastini (small pearl like pasta)
- Meatballs:
- 2 lbs extra lean beef (I used ground chicken or turkey at times)
- 1/2 cup onion grated
- 2 eggs
- 1 1/2 cups Italian bread crumbs
- 3/4 cup grated parmasan cheese
- salt and pepper to taste

Direction

- Prepare your meatballs first, mixing all the ingredients listed under meatballs - form into small meatballs - less than 1/2" in diameter.
- Place into a frying pan and cook till 3/4 done or a nice brown coating is developed.
- Place on paper towels to drain any fats. Remove all fats from the pan and deglaze the frying pan with 1 cup of chicken stock. Reserve this stock.
- In a large soup pot add 1 tbsp. olive oil, add onions, garlic and carrot. Sauté till tender. Approximately 5 to 10 minutes.
- Add your chicken stock, basil, Italian spice and oregano. Allow 10 minutes of simmer time.
- Add frozen spinach and allow to melt into soup. Cook for 5 - 10 minutes.
- Add meatballs, and reserved stock from deglazing the fry pan.
- Cook your pastina to el dente. Add to soup.
- Serve with fresh grated Parmigiano Reggiano cheese.

179. Jamies Chili Recipe Courtesy Jamie Deen Paula Deens Son Recipe

Serving: 10 | Prep: | Cook: 240mins | Ready in:

Ingredients

- Jamie's chili Recipe courtesy Jamie Deen
- 1 pound ground beef and sausage, browned and drained
- 1 medium onion, diced
- 1 small green pepper diced
- 2 cans diced tomatoes
- 1 can whole, peeled tomatoes
- cumin (to taste)
- 1 tablespoon chili powder
- 1 can chili beans
- 1 can black beans
- 1 can kidney beans
- 1 package chili seasoning mix
- 2 cups chopped celery
- Shredded Cheddar
- sour cream
- Chopped green onions

Direction

- Brown ground beef in skillet and drain. Set aside.
- Spray large pot with nonstick cooking spray and heat over medium heat. Add the onion, green pepper, diced tomatoes, and whole tomatoes. Add cumin and chili powder, to taste, and cook for about 8 minutes or until vegetables are tender.
- Add the beans, the ground beef, chili seasoning and chopped celery. Let simmer and slow cook for 4 hours.
- Serve with Cheddar cheese, sour cream, and green onion as garnishes.

180. Jims Super Bowl Gumbo Recipe

Serving: 10 | Prep: | Cook: 180mins | Ready in:

Ingredients

- 1 ½ cups canola oil
- 2 cups bleached all-purpose flour
- **********
- 4 – 6 cloves garlic, crushed and chopped
- 2 cups onions, chopped
- 1 cup bell peppers (I like mixed colors)
- 1 cup celery, chopped
- 1 Tsp dried thyme
- 1 Tbls creole seasoning (plus more for dusting seafood.)
- 1 Tsp cayenne pepper
- salt & fresh ground black pepper to taste.
- 2 bay leaves
- ************
- 1 whole duck, cut up. (Reserve back portion)
- ½ lbs Andouille sausage, finely chopped
- 1 lbs Andouille sausage cut into ½ inch slices
- 1 lbs shrimp, peeled and deveined
- 2 lbs crawfish tails, (fresh frozen is fine)
- 1 dozen shucked oysters (From a seafood market not canned)
- 1 lbs Lump crab meat (From a seafood market not canned)
- 3 ½ quarts shrimp, fish or chicken stock (Room Temp)
- 2 Bottles Dark or Amber beer (Room Temp)
- 1 bunch scallions chopped
- ½ bunch parsley chopped
- Gumbo file powder
- 6 cups cooked long grain white rice

Direction

- Season the duck pieces with Salt & Pepper.
- Put a small amount of oil into a large Dutch oven. Wipe the oil all around the bottom and sides of pan with a paper towel. Heat over medium heat until hot. Start the duck pieces skin side down and sear until golden brown,

- (About 8 – 10 minutes per side). Remove from the pan and set aside.
- MAKE THE ROUX
- Add the Canola Oil to the remaining fat in the Dutch oven. Stir in the flour
- Stir slowly and constantly until the roux is the color of chocolate, 20 to 45 minutes. Season with Salt and Black Pepper
- Add the Onions, Bell Peppers, Celery, chopped Andouille, Garlic, Thyme, Bay Leaves, Creole seasoning and Cayenne Pepper. Cook, stirring, until the vegetables are very soft, 8 to 10 minutes.
- **************
- Whisk the beer into the roux mixture until both are well combined. Whisk in the Stock. Bring to a boil, reduce the heat to medium-low and cook, uncovered at a slow simmer, for 30 minutes. Add the duck pieces back to the pot. Including the back. Simmer slowly for 1 ½ - 2 hours stirring occasionally.
- Remove all the duck pieces from the pot. Let cool slightly and remove the meat from the bones. Discard the bones and return the meat to the pot.
- Lightly dust the Crawfish, Shrimp and Andouille Sausage slices with Creole seasoning. Add to the pot. Cook 10 minutes. Add Oysters and Lump Crab. Cook 2 minutes. Taste for seasonings and adjust. Stir in Green Onions and Parsley reserving some for garnish.
- Remove from heat, let sit 5 minutes. Skim as much fat as you can off the surface.
- Serve in individual bowls over cooked rice. Garnish with a little chopped Green Onion and Parsley and a sprinkle of Gumbo File' Powder. Pass the file' powder at the table for those who want more.

181. Julia Childs French Onion Soup Grantineed With Cheese Recipe

Serving: 6 | Prep: | Cook: 75mins | Ready in:

Ingredients

- 1 1/2 lbs (about 5 cups or a little more) thinly sliced yellow onions
- 3 T. butter... See More
- 1 T. vegetable oil
- A heavy-bottomed, 4-quart covered saucepan
- 1 t. salt
- 1/4 t. sugar (helps the onions to brown)
- 3 T. flour
- 2 quarts boiling brown stock, purchased beef stock, or 1 quart of water and 1 quart of stock
- 1/2 c. dry white wine or dry white vermouth
- salt and pepper to taste
- 2 oz. (about 3/4 c.) shredded swiss cheese
- 1 T. grated raw onion
- 8 to 10 rounds of hard toasted French bread (toast bread rounds in oven at 225 for 25 min.)
- For bread Rounds:
- 1 1/2 c. grated Swiss, or Swiss and parmesan cheese
- 1 T. olive oil or melted butter

Direction

- Cook the onions slowly with the butter and oil in the covered saucepan for 15 minutes.
- Uncover, raise heat to moderate, and stir in the salt and sugar. Cook for 30 to 40 minutes stirring frequently, until the onions have turned an even, deep, golden brown.
- Sprinkle in the flour and stir for 3 minutes.
- Off heat, blend in the boiling liquid. Add the wine, and season to taste. Simmer partially covered for 30 to 40 minutes or more, skimming occasionally. Correct seasoning.
- Preheat the oven to 325 degrees.
- Bring the soup to the boil and pour into a tureen or soup pots. Stir in the 3/4 c. shredded Swiss cheese and grated onion. Float the rounds of toast on top of the soup, and spread

the grated cheese over it. Sprinkle with the oil or butter.
- Bake for 20 minutes in the oven, then set for a minute or two under a preheated broiler to brown the top lightly. Serve immediately.

182. Kapousta Recipe

Serving: 15 | Prep: | Cook: 120mins | Ready in:

Ingredients

- 2 8" heads of cabbage, roughly chopped
- 1 medium sized rutabega or 3 large baking potatoes, peeled, washed, cut into bite sized chunks
- 8 medium sized carrots, washed and sliced
- 2 large yellow onions, chopped
- 2-3 lbs. precooked ham
- 3 c. water
- 4 links of polska kielbasa
- salt and pepper to taste
- 8-10 quart stockpot

Direction

- Chop cabbage, place 1 head in the bottom of the pot
- Chop rutabaga or potatoes (I use potatoes)
- Put half of them on top of the cabbage
- Slice the carrots, place half of them on the taters/rutabaga
- Chop ham into bite sized pieces, place it on top of the taters/R
- Then, repeat layers again with the remaining portions of ingredients
- Slice the sausage, set aside
- Add 3 c. of water and bring to a simmer, reduce heat to low, or if on the campfire, keep to one side of the fire(not on the fire), have fresh coals ready to place under the kettle, as this will take some time and the coals won't last forever
- Cook and stir about 2 hours or until the potatoes are done, always maintaining at least an inch of water in the bottom to prevent scorching, add water if you have to!
- Last- about 30 min. from being done (the potatoes will just start to be tender, check with a fork), add the sliced sausage.
- Enjoy....

183. Kartoffelsuppe Potato Soup Recipe

Serving: 6 | Prep: | Cook: 60mins | Ready in:

Ingredients

- 2 T. butter
- 2 large yellow onions, thinly sliced
- 1 stalk celery, thinly sliced
- 8 slices bacon
- 1 t. each: marjoram and thyme
- 1/4 t. grated nutmeg
- 1 lb. potatoes, peeled and thinly sliced
- 1 quart chicken stock
- 1 t. salt
- 1/2 t. white pepper
- chives or flat-leaf parsley (for garnish)

Direction

- First, fry the bacon. Reserving the drippings, drain bacon slices on paper towels, and crumble. Reserve the bacon for garnish, with the chives (or parsley).
- Add the butter to the bacon drippings, and over medium heat, cook the onions, celery, herbs, and nutmeg until well mixed. Cover, turn heat down to low, and cook slowly about fifteen minutes, until the onions are very soft.
- Add the potatoes and stock. Simmer 45 minutes, until the potatoes are falling apart.
- Purée the soup in batches, return to the pan and season to taste with salt and white pepper. Garnish with snipped chives and crumbled bacon.

184. LOBSTER BISQUE Recipe

Serving: 68 | Prep: | Cook: 40mins | Ready in:

Ingredients

- 2 lbs lobsters, Boiled
- 2 cups chicken broth, Cold
- 3 tablespoons butter
- 3 tablespoons flour
- 1 1/2 teaspoons salt
- 1 pinch cayenne
- 2 cups milk
- 1 cup cream (scalded)

Direction

- Remove the meat from lobster shell. Dice body meat. Chop claw and tail meat fine.
- Add broth to body bones and tough ends of claws, cut in pieces; bring slowly to boiling point and cook 20 minutes.
- Drain, reserve liquid. Heat butter, add flour and seasoning, and gradually the liquid.
- Scald milk and stir in gradually. Add lobster meat and cook slowly for 5 minutes.
- Add cream and serve at once.

185. Lamb Shank Stew Recipe

Serving: 6 | Prep: | Cook: 150mins | Ready in:

Ingredients

- 6 Tbsp of peanut or vegetable oil
- 8 lamb shanks
- 2 onions
- 4 cloves of garlic
- Sprinkling of salt
- 1 Tbsp turmeric
- 1 tsp ground ginger
- 1 dried red chili pepper, crumbled, or 1/4 tsp dried red-pepper flakes
- 2 tsp of cinnamon
- 1/4 tsp of freshly grated nutmeg
- black pepper
- 3 Tbsp of honey
- 1 Tbsp of soy sauce
- 3 Tbsp of marsala wine
- 6 Tbsp of red lentils

Direction

- Put 3 Tbsp. of the oil into a very large, wide, heavy-bottomed pan and warm over medium heat. Brown the lamb shanks--in batches--in the pan and then remove to a roasting pan or whatever else you've got at hand to sit them in.
- Peel the onions and garlic and process in a food processor or chop them finely by hand. Add the remaining oil to the pan and fry the onion-garlic mush until soft, sprinkling salt over to stop it from sticking.
- Stir in the turmeric, ground ginger, chili, cinnamon and nutmeg and season with some freshly ground pepper. Stir again, adding the honey, soy sauce and Marsala. Put the shanks back in the pan, add cold water almost to cover, bring to the boil and then put a lid on the pan, lower the heat and simmer very gently for 1-1 1/2 hours, or until the meat is tender. Add the red lentils and cook for about 20 minutes longer without the lid, until the lentils have softened into the sauce, and the juices have reduced and thickened slightly. Check for seasoning.
- This aromatic, sauce-rich stew can be served with plain rice or a bowl of butter-mashed potatoes, half potatoes and half parsnips, well-seasoned and spiced with mace.

186. Lamb With Minted Lime Salsa And Chili Roasted Vegetables Recipe

Serving: 4 | Prep: | Cook: 30mins | Ready in:

Ingredients

- 2 sweet potatoes, peeled and cut into chunks
- 4 small yukon gold potatoes, peeled and halved
- 2 parsnips, cut into chunks
- 1 red onion, sliced into wedges
- 1 garlic bulb, cut horizontally in half
- 5 tbsp olive oil
- 1 mild red chili, de-seeded and chopped
- 1 mild green chili, de-seeded and chopped
- 8 lamb loin chops
- salt and freshly ground black pepper
- FOR THE mintED lime SALSA
- 2 tbsp olive oil
- 2 shallots, finely diced
- 2 tsp grated fresh ginger
- 2 tbsp fine-cut lime marmalade
- 1 lime, juice and grated zest only
- 2 tbsp chopped mint
- 1 tbsp chopped coriander

Direction

- Preheat the oven to 425F
- Put the potatoes, parsnips, red onion and garlic in a shallow baking dish.
- Drizzle three tablespoons of the olive oil over the vegetables and season with salt and pepper.
- Place in the oven and roast for 30 minutes.
- Stir in the chilies five minutes before the end of cooking.
- For the salsa, mix all the ingredients together and set aside.
- Heat the remaining olive oil in a heavy-based frying pan.
- Season the lamb chops, add to the pan and sear for 5-6 minutes on each side (you will need to cook them in batches).
- Cover and keep warm.
- Arrange the roasted vegetables and lamb chops in a serving dish.
- Spoon the minted lime salsa over the chops and serve.

187. Lammas Harvest Holiday Soup Aka, Harvest Pepper Soup Recipe

Serving: 1 | Prep: | Cook: 2hours | Ready in:

Ingredients

- 2 TB butter
- 5 skinless chicken breasts diced
- 2 Med onions diced
- 10 cups waters
- ½ cup celery diced (a little more if you like)
- ½ cup carrots diced (a little more if you like)
- 1 sweet red pepper diced
- 1 sweet green pepper diced
- 1 sweet yellow pepper diced
- 2 cans sliced potatoes diced (or 2 cups diced potatoes)
- Fresh cup basil leaf, about 5 in all
- 8 teaspoons chicken bouillon
- 2 teaspoons beef bouillon
- ¼ cup ground sage
- ½ teaspoon dried basil
- 2 tablespoons cajun seasoning
- 1-2 teaspoons garlic
- 1 teaspoon fresh ground black pepper
- 3 teaspoons sea salt

Direction

- Melt butter and add onions to tender. Add in chicken and sauté until done.
- Poor in water, vegetables and spices.
- Cook for 10 minutes until boiling and turn off heat.
- Allow soup to rest for 1 hour then you may reheat and serve.

- This spicy but not overly hot soup is wonderful with fresh baked wheat bread and salad.
- Healthy, low fat and complete. Enjoy.

188. Lebanese Green Bean Meat Stew Recipe

Serving: 6 | Prep: | Cook: 120mins | Ready in:

Ingredients

- 1 lb beef or lamb stew meat, chopped to smaller bite-size pieces
- 1 lb frozen green beans
- 3 Tablespoons olive oil
- 3-4 cloves garlic, finely chopped
- 1 medium onion, finely chopped
- 1 – 14 oz cans crushed tomatoes
- 1 - 4 oz can tomato paste
- 2 cubes beef bouillon or 1 teaspoon beef base paste
- ½ teaspoon salt
- ¼ teaspoon pepper
- 1/2 teaspoon cumin
- 1 teaspoon coriander
- 1/8 teaspoon allspice
- 4 cups water (you can add more to your liking)

Direction

- Sauté meat in olive oil until lightly brown. Add onion and garlic to meat and continue to sauté over medium heat until onion is translucent.
- Add crushed tomatoes to meat mixture and stir until combined. Add spices, then add tomato paste and water. Add green beans and bring to a boil. You can add more green beans to make this heavier on the veggies.
- Once it comes to a boil, reduce to a simmer on low heat for about 2 hours, or until meat is tender and tomatoes have broken down into sauce. Serve over rice. Makes 4-6 servings. Sahtein (double your health)
- Variation - you can add some cubed potatoes which you start simmering the meat and tomatoes together. You also can replace green beans with peas. This recipe can easily be converted to vegetarian dish.

189. Lebanese Lamb And Bean Stew Recipe

Serving: 8 | Prep: | Cook: 155mins | Ready in:

Ingredients

- 1 lb dried navy beans, picked over and rinsed
- 2 lb boneless lamb shoulder or boneless leg of lamb, trimmed of excess fat and cut into 1 1/2-inch cubes
- 1 tablespoon plus 1 teaspoon baharat* (see below) or 1 (3-inch) cinnamon stick
- 9 cups water
- 2 tablespoons olive oil
- 2 medium onions, chopped
- 4 garlic cloves, finely chopped
- 2 teaspoons salt
- 3/4 teaspoon black pepper
- 3 tablespoons tomato paste
- ~~~~
- *A Middle Eastern and African ground-spice mixture that typically contains allspice, cinnamon, clove, cumin, Maras chile, and black pepper.

Direction

- Cover beans with cold water by 3 inches in a bowl and soak at room temperature at least 8 hours. Drain well in a colander.
- Bring lamb, Baharat, and water (9 cups) to a boil in a 6- to 8-quart heavy pot, then vigorously simmer mixture, covered, until meat is almost tender, 1 1/4 to 1 1/2 hours.
- Add beans and cook, uncovered, until beans are tender, about 1 hour more.

- Meanwhile, heat oil over moderate heat in a 12-inch heavy skillet until hot but not smoking, then cook onions, garlic, 1/2 teaspoon salt, and 1/4 teaspoon pepper, stirring, until onions are pale golden and tender, 8 to 10 minutes.
- Stir in tomato paste and cook, stirring, 2 minutes.
- When beans are tender, stir in tomato-onion mixture and simmer until just heated through, about 5 minutes.
- Stir in remaining 1 1/2 teaspoons salt and 1/2 teaspoon black pepper.
- *Note: Stew can be made 3 days ahead and cooled completely, uncovered, then chilled in an airtight container.
- Reheat in a 5- to 6-quart pot over moderate heat.

190. Leek And Cauliflower Creamy Soup Recipe

Serving: 8 | Prep: | Cook: 20mins | Ready in:

Ingredients

- 3 leeks, sliced
- 2 garlic cloves, chopped
- 1 medium cauliflower head, or one 2 pound pkg frozen cauliflower florets
- 3 medium carrots, sliced
- 1 big or 2 medium potatoes, in chunks
- 4 Tbsp olive oil
- 4 to 6 cups chicken broth, or use bouillon and water
- salt and pepper
- 1/2 cup goat, Cheddar or feta cheese

Direction

- In a medium pan heat oil on medium, add leeks and garlic. Cook until leek is transparent.
- Add cauliflower, carrots and potatoes. Stir well. Add broth just to cover veggies and season with salt and pepper. Cover and bring to a boil. Reduce heat until just simmering. Cook for about 20 minutes or until vegetables are tender.
- Mix in a blender, working in batches if necessary, until soup becomes a cream. Add cheese, Mix again and season to taste.
- When ready to serve, garnish with some sweet pimentón (Spanish paprika) on top and drizzle a little extra virgin olive oil for extra flavor.
- Serve hot.

191. Lemon Chicken In A Crockpot Recipe

Serving: 4 | Prep: | Cook: 360mins | Ready in:

Ingredients

- 1 (3 lb) cut up broiler-fryer chicken
- 1/4 c. of sherry wine or chicken broth
- 1/4 c. of lemon juice
- 1 tsp. of crumbled dry oregano
- 1/2 tsp. of crumbled dried rosemary
- 3 minced garlic cloves
- 2 tbsp. of butter
- salt and pepper

Direction

- First wash chicken; pat dry.
- Then season chicken generously with salt and pepper.
- Next you want to sprinkle half of oregano, rosemary and garlic inside cavity of chicken.
- Now you can melt butter in frying pan and brown chicken; transfer to slow cooker or crockpot.
- Then sprinkle with remaining oregano, rosemary and garlic.
- Add your sherry to frying pan and stir to loosen brown bits; pour into slow cooker.
- Finally, cook on LOW flame for approx. 7 hours; adding in the lemon juice and cook approx. 1 more hour (total of 8); transfer your

chicken to cutting board; skim fat from juices and serve over chicken.
- Yummy!

192. Lemon Chicken Velvet Soup For Two Recipe

Serving: 2 | Prep: | Cook: 15mins | Ready in:

Ingredients

- 2 tablespoons butter
- 2 tablespoons all-purpose flour
- 1 can (14-1/2 ounces) chicken broth
- 3 tablespoons lemon juice
- 1-1/2 cups cubed cooked chicken breast
- 1 Cup fresh or frozen sugar snap peas
- 2 tablespoons minced fresh parsley
- 1 teaspoon grated lemon peel
- 3 tablespoons heavy whipping cream (or half n half)

Direction

- In a small saucepan, melt butter. Stir in flour until smooth; gradually add broth and lemon juice. Bring to a boil; cook and stir for 1-2 minutes or until thickened.
- Stir in the chicken, peas, parsley and lemon peel; cook 2-3 minutes longer or until chicken is heated through and peas are crisp-tender. Stir in cream; heat through (do not boil). Yield: 2 servings.

193. Lemon Lentil Soup Recipe

Serving: 3 | Prep: | Cook: 50mins | Ready in:

Ingredients

- 100g lentils (green or brown)
- 1tbsp olive oil
- 2 sticks celery, chopped
- 1 onion, diced
- 1 litre vegie stock
- 1-2 cloves garlic, crushed
- 1/4 tsp cumin
- 1 green capsicum, diced
- 1/2 bunch baby spinach leaves
- salt and pepper to season
- 1 lemon, juice and zest
- fresh coriander and/or coriander salt
- natural yoghurt to serve

Direction

- Heat oil in a large pot, sauté onion, garlic and celery for approx. 4 minutes. Add stock, lemon juice and zest, lentils, cumin and seasoning. Bring to the boil, then lower heat and simmer covered for about 30 minutes.
- Add capsicum, spinach and more stock if needed. Recover and simmer a further 15-20 minutes.
- Serve garnished with coriander and/or coriander salt and yoghurt.

194. Lemon Ginger Chicken Soup With Cilantro Recipe

Serving: 4 | Prep: | Cook: 15mins | Ready in:

Ingredients

- Small amount of raw chicken breast (about 1/2 cup in volume)
- 1 1/2 cups chicken broth and 1/2 cup white wine (or, 2 cups broth)
- 2-4 cloves of garlic, to taste, roughly crushed
- About 1 T ginger, roughly chopped
- 1 dried hot pepper, crumbled, or other hot pepper, chopped
- 3 scallions, minced, white and green parts
- 1 head baby bok choy, chopped white and green parts

- About 1/3 cup sprouts -- I like mung bean sprouts, the big ones
- 3 T cilantro, minced
- 1/2 lemon (zest and juice)

Direction

- Combine the broth, wine or sherry, chicken, garlic, ginger and hot pepper in a pot. (Lemongrass would probably be excellent here, too.)
- Bring to a boil for a few minutes to cook away some of the alcohol (skip the "for a few minutes" if you aren't adding wine), then turn down and simmer on medium-low till chicken's done.
- At this point, strain everything to remove some of the chicken fat. This results in a nice, clear, but still flavorful and rich broth.
- Shred the chicken roughly with a fork, then return it and the strained broth to the pot.
- Add the sprouts and the whites of the bok choy and scallions.
- Cook until those are soft, then add all the green stuff: bok choy leaves, scallion greens, and cilantro.
- Add the lemon juice and zest, turn off the heat, and serve.

195. Lentil Soup Recipe

Serving: 4 | Prep: | Cook: 50mins | Ready in:

Ingredients

- 1/2 pound lentils
- 1-1/2 quarts water
- 3 stalks celery and leaves chopped fine
- 2 small carrots chopped
- 1 white onion chopped
- 1 clove garlic chopped
- 1 tablespoon vegetable oil
- 3 fresh ripe tomatoes diced
- 1 bay leaf
- 1 teaspoon salt
- 2 teaspoons freshly ground black pepper
- 1 pound elbow pasta

Direction

- Combine all ingredients except pasta in a heavy saucepan and cook until mixture comes to a boil.
- Let simmer for 45 minutes.
- Cook pasta according to package directions
- Add pasta to soup and cook 5 minutes longer.

196. Lentil Soup With Swiss Chard And Noodles Recipe

Serving: 6 | Prep: | Cook: 45mins | Ready in:

Ingredients

- 1 1/2 cups Green or brown lentils
- 6 cups broth (chicken or vegetable)
- 2 1/2 cups chopped swiss chard Leaves or an equal amoun of spinach leaves.)
- 2 medium onions sliced into thin crescents
- 6 cloves garlic, crushed
- 2 Tsp cumin seeds, toasted and ground
- 2 Tsp coriander seeds toasted and ground
- 1/3 cup cilantro Chopped
- 1 Tbls Fresh lemon juice or to taste
- 1 cup broken vermicelli, large Orzo, or other small pasta.
- 1/4 cup olive oil
- salt and fresh cracked pepper
- Garnish:
- lemon wedges
- Chopped green onions

Direction

- Wash Lentils well and pick through. Place in Large saucepan with the cold Broth. Bring to boil, skimming if necessary, Cover, lower heat, simmer gently 15 - 20 minutes.
- As Lentils are cooking, heat Olive Oil in a separate pan. Add onions, cook on med heat

- until well caramelized. (Dark brown, not Burnt)
- Crush Garlic into a past with salt. Add to Onions during last minute of cooking. Drain mixture, reserving oil in pan. Transfer to a blender and puree'.
- Add puree' to the cooking Lentils.
- Wash thoroughly and drain Swiss chard. Slit leaves in half lengthwise. Remove large center stalk and coarsely chop the greens. If using Spinach, remove large stems and coarsely chop.
- Heat the remaining oil (Med High) in the Onion cooking skillet. Toast the pasta until it reaches a deep golden brown.
- Add Chard or Spinach, Pasta, Cilantro, Cumin, Coriander, Lemon juice and Rhubarb (if adding). (If adding Rhubarb, test for tartness before adding lemon.) Season with Salt & Pepper. Cover and simmer gently until pasta is tender. (15-20 mins.)
- Garnish with chopped Green Onions. Serve with Lemon Wedges & Bread

197. Lentil And Pea Soup With Bourbon Recipe

Serving: 6 | Prep: | Cook: 45mins | Ready in:

Ingredients

- 1 onion, chopped
- 1 bell pepper, chopped
- 3 cloves of garlic, sliced
- 2 carrots, cut in rounds
- 1/2 cup green split peas
- 1/2 cup red lentils (or yellow split peas)
- 2 tsp fresh rosemary, chopped (or dried)
- 1 tsp crushed red pepper/ pepper flakes
- 1/2 tsp black pepper
- 1/2 tsp paprika or red chili powder
- salt
- 2 tbsp olive oil or butter
- 6 cups of vegetable stock or beef broth/ or if you prefer, just water
- THE most important ingredient 1/2 cup bourbon (use a good quality)
- **When using a regular pot, boil peas and lentils for an hour or soak in water overnight.**

Direction

- -Heat the oil in a big pot and add onion, garlic, and pepper. Stir until onions are cooked
- -Add carrots and 1 tsp. rosemary, and cook for 4-5 minutes
- -Add paprika and stir for a minute
- -Put in split peas, lentils, bourbon, broth, black pepper, crushed pepper, and salt.
- With a regular pot, cook for 45 minutes on medium heat
- -I used a hand blender to puree the soup and garnished it with the rest of the rosemary. If you want to have it chunky, you may want to cut everything into smaller pieces, especially the carrots.
- Serve with crusty bread and can be stretched to 8 mugs if serving for a crowd (Tailgate).

198. Little Bowl Fins Recipe

Serving: 5 | Prep: | Cook: 20mins | Ready in:

Ingredients

- 1 packet or 40g Glass noodles, soaked to soften
- 1/2 chicken breast or Drumstick, more if you like
- 8 Dried Chinese mushroom, soaked to soften
- 4 Crabsticks, shredded
- 2 egg whites
- 750ml chicken broth
- cornflour Mixture (Thickener)
- Seasonings:
- 1 teaspoon sugar
- 1 teaspoon salt
- 1 teaspoon light soy sauce

- 1/2 tablespoon Chinese cooking wine
- 1/2 tablespoon oyster sauce
- 1 teaspoon sesame seed oil

Direction

- Drain glass noodle, cut them into 2 inch length and set aside.
- Drain mushroom, slice thinly and set aside.
- Boil chicken till cook, retain water to be used together with broth.
- Shred chicken and set aside.
- Add mushroom to the broth and bring to a boil.
- Add in seasonings.
- When it begin to simmer, add in chicken, crabstick and glass noodles.
- Gradually add in thickener, when the soup begins to boil.
- Stir in egg whites slowly.
- Serve with pepper and vinegar.

199. Loaded Baked Potato Soup Recipe

Serving: 8 | Prep: | Cook: 60mins | Ready in:

Ingredients

- 3 lbs red potatoes, unpeeled, cut into large chunks (I have used russets and Idahoes as well, they work equally well)
- 2 c. water
- 1 carton chicken stock
- 1 white onion, chopped
- 1/4 - 1/2 stick margarine or butter
- 2 T parsely
- seasoned salt
- garlic pepper
- 2 T.chopped garlic
- 1 large can cream of mushroom soup (Family size - or use 2 cans. I have also used 1 cream of mushroom and 1 cream of celery, even cream of chicken)
- 1/2 c. sour cream
- 1/2 c. milk
- 1/2 c. cream (or use 1 c milk, or 1 c cream)
- 2 T margarine or butter
- 3 cups shredded cheese, divided into 2 and 1 (I use a colby jack blend and a rough shred cheddar)
- chives
- bacon bits (OR, fry a few strips of bacon until crisp, then crumble)

Direction

- Put potatoes in large stove top pot, cover with water and chicken stock. (May need more liquid)
- Boil with onion, seasoned salt, garlic pepper, margarine, garlic, and parsley - uncovered, to allow liquid to reduce
- When potatoes are just tender add the mushroom soup, sour cream, milk, cream, additional margarine and one c. cheese
- Cook another 10 minutes or longer
- Top each serving with more cheese, chives, and bacon bits
- ** This really is a guessing, so be prepared to add some more milk and allow it to reduce a little more to get it thick and creamy **

200. Lobster Stock Recipe

Serving: 6 | Prep: | Cook: 60mins | Ready in:

Ingredients

- 4 uncooked lobster shells (or 6 cooked lobster shells)
- 3 tablespoon unsalted butter
- 1 onion, coarsely chopped
- 2 carrots, peeled and chopped
- 2 stalks celery, peeled and chopped
- 3 garlic cloves, coarsely chopped
- 3 tablespoons tomato paste
- 2 cups tomato juice
- 1 1/2 gallons water

- 1 cup Madeira
- 1 tablespoon black peppercorns
- 1/2 bunch fresh parsley, with stems
- 2 small bay leaf

Direction

- Crush shells, which will be the base for the stock, using a mallet or hammer, then grind as fine as possible with reserved drippings in a food processor.
- Heat butter in stock pot and add lobster shells and sauté for 5 minutes.
- Add the onion, carrots, garlic, celery peppercorns parsley and sauté for 5 more minutes
- Add everything else and simmer partially covered for over an hour.
- Strain through a colander getting as much liquid out as possible.
- Put back into pot and simmer for another 1/2 an hour. Cool; use within 2 days or freeze.
- This one is for you SHEPHARDRESCUE

201. Louisiana Chicken And Sausage Gumbo Recipe

Serving: 10 | Prep: | Cook: 120mins | Ready in:

Ingredients

- 5 lbs chicken thighs (COUNT THEM AND WRITE NUMBER DOWN ON SHEET OF paper)
- 2 large onions, chopped fine
- 2 bell peppers, chopped fine
- 4 celery ribs, chopped fine
- 1 gallon chicken stock
- 2 lbs good quality rope pork sausage, sliced 1/2 inch thick
- 1 cup green onions, chopped
- 1 cup fresh parsley, chopped
- 5 or six shakes louisiana hot sauce
- 1 tbs salt
- 1 1/2 tsp red pepper
- 1 tsp black pepper
- 1 tsp white pepper
- 1 cup flour (approximate)
- 2/3 cup vegetable oil (approximate)

Direction

- Mix salt and peppers and set aside. Remove all fat and skin from chicken. Reserve some of the skin and fat.
- In large heavy skillet or Dutch oven (cast iron works great) render about 1/4 of reserved skin and fat. Discard remainder. Render chicken skin and fat, remove skin and discard and then lightly brown chicken pieces.
- Remove and set aside.
- Drain and measure oil. Add additional vegetable oil to make one cup, if you do not have enough.
- Bring heat to medium-high and when oil is hot slowly stir in flour and make a roux, stirring constantly with wooden spoon. You want a peanut butter colored roux. DO NOT BURN!
- Immediately add half onions, celery, bell pepper to stop roux from cooking. Remove from heat, stir well,
- Place stock and remaining onions, peppers and celery in large (6 - 8 quart) pot and bring to boil. Slowly stir in roux and add salt and pepper mixture. Simmer for 45 minutes.
- Add chicken (remember to count pieces) and sausage and continue to simmer for at least 90 minutes, or until chicken is falling off bone.
- If gumbo is too thick add water in small amounts
- Remember, this is gumbo, not soup.
- Remove from heat and fish out chicken pieces. You counted them to assure you get them all out. Shred chicken and discard bones.
- Place shredded chicken back in gumbo
- Stir in green onions, parsley and add Louisiana Hot Sauce.
- Serve in large bowls over rice.
- Note: With a salad and French bread, this is a complete meal.
- Freezes well.

- Note (2) This can actually all be done one-pot in a cast iron Dutch oven at least 8 quarts.
- Note (3) Amount of flour in roux is approximate since different flours absorb at different rates. Roux should be like a thin paste. If too thick add more oil, if too thin, add more flour. All in small amounts.

202. Louisiana Chicken Gumbo Recipe

Serving: 4 | Prep: | Cook: 55mins | Ready in:

Ingredients

- 1/4 cup flour
- 1 tsp salt
- 1 3 lb chicken cut into 8 pieces
- 1/4 cup vegetable oil
- 1 1/2 cup Chopped onion
- 1 cup Chopped celery
- 1 cup Chopped green onion
- 3 cloves garlic; mashed
- 1 quart chicken broth
- 2 cup canned whole tomatoes in juice; undrained, crushed
- 1 Bay leaf
- 1 tsp TABASCO pepper sauce
- 1 10 oz package frozen; whole okra
- 3 cup Cooked rice; divided

Direction

- Combine flour and salt in plastic or paper bag; dredge chicken pieces in flour mixture to coat.
- In large heavy Dutch oven or saucepot, heat oil; brown chicken on all sides, remove and reserve. Add onion, celery, onion and garlic; sauté, 5 minutes, stirring often.
- Return chicken to pot. Stir in chicken broth, tomatoes in juice, bay leaf and Tabasco pepper sauce. Bring to a boil; reduce heat and simmer, uncovered, 45 minutes. Add okra; cook 10 minutes longer.
- Serve each portion in bowl topped with 1/2 cup cooked rice.

203. Louisiana Jambalaya For A Crowd Recipe

Serving: 10 | Prep: | Cook: 60mins | Ready in:

Ingredients

- 1 pound andouille sausage or spicy italian sausage, cut into 1/2-inch pieces
- 1 pound cubed ham
- 1 pound chicken thighs, cut into 1" pieces
- 1 pound medium shrimp, precooked
- 1/2 cup (1 stick) butter
- 2 yellow onions, chopped
- 8 green onions, chopped
- 4 large celery stalks, sliced
- 1 large green bell pepper, chopped
- 6 garlic cloves, finely chopped
- 8 oz. frozen chopped okra
- 2 bay leaves
- 2 jalapeño chilis, finely chopped with seeds
- 2 tablespoons creole seasoning
- 1 teaspoon ground cayenne pepper
- 2 teaspoons dried thyme
- 4 14 1/2-ounce cans chicken broth
- 3 14-ounce cans diced tomatoes with chili peppers, with liquid
- 3 cups long-grain rice, cooked

Direction

- Melt butter in heavy large Dutch oven or extra large stock pot over medium-high heat. Add cut-up chicken thighs, brown chicken for about 3 minutes, stirring occasionally. Remove chicken from pot and set aside. Add yellow onions, green onion, bell pepper, garlic, bay leaves, jalapeño, Creole Seasoning, cayenne pepper and thyme. Cover and cook until vegetables are very tender, stirring occasionally, about 20 minutes. Mix in diced tomatoes, okra and chicken broth. Add chicken, sausage and ham. Bring mixture to simmer. Reduce heat to low, cover and cook, stirring occasionally, about 1 hour. Meanwhile, cook the rice in a separate pan. Add shrimp and cooked rice, stir and simmer for another 5 minutes.

204. Make It Yourself Condensed Cream Of Soups Recipe

Serving: 0 | Prep: | Cook: 10mins | Ready in:

Ingredients

- 2T butter
- 1/4 cup flour(sub your desired thickener, as appropriate, for allergies or intolerances)
- 1/2 cup stock(low sodium broth can probably be used)--veggie or chicken is usually best, I think
- 1/2 cup milk(lowfat is okay)
- salt and pepper
- ***1/4 cup of whatever your "of" is needed to be...(ie mushroom, celery, chicken, onion, potato, broccoli, cauliflower, etc) finely chopped***

Direction

- In small saucepan, put butter and the "of" ingredient and cook until soft, not just tender. (If using chicken, just make sure it's cooked through)
- Add flour and stir together. It will be thick and gooey, and that's okay.
- Slowly add stock while stirring or whisking to avoid lumps.
- Bring to a boil and cook a few minutes until thickened. (If seems too thick, you can add a tsp or so more broth, just don't forget, you've still got milk to add :)
- Add milk and salt and pepper and stir until combined and thick. Taste to know your seasonings prior to using it in a recipe so you can adjust salt and pepper as needed.
- ***The main is cream of celery using veggie stock, and the other is mushroom using chicken stock. Please remember, you can combine ingredients to make blend, or add garlic, etc., to make a cream of mushroom with garlic, etc. Just play around and make it to suit your needs and taste! **
- PS Please note, this is a CONDENSED version of the soup...it's meant to be thick and not intended to eat straight! ;)

205. Markys Broccoli Cheese Soup Recipe

Serving: 4 | Prep: | Cook: 40mins | Ready in:

Ingredients

- 1 tablespoon butter, melted
- 1/2 medium onion, chopped
- 1/4 cup flour
- 1/4 cup melted butter
- 2 cups half-and-half
- 2 cups chicken stock
- 1/2 pound fresh broccoli, chopped.
- 1 cup carrots, julienned.
- 1/4 teaspoon nutmeg (secret)
- salt & pepper, to taste
- 12 ounces grated sharp cheddar

Direction

- Sauté onion in butter. Set aside.
- Cook melted butter and flour using a whisk over medium heat for about 4 minutes. Be sure to stir frequently.
- Slowly add the half-and-half, continue stirring.
- Add the chicken stock whisking all the time.
- Simmer for 20 minutes.
- Add the broccoli, carrots and onions. Cook over low heat until the veggies are tender, about 20 minutes.
- Add salt and pepper.

- By now the soup should be thickened.
- Pour in batches into blender and puree.
- Return the puree to the pot and place over low heat, add the grated cheese; stir until well blended.
- Stir in the nutmeg.
- Serve!!

206. Marrow Balls For Beef Soup Recipe

Serving: 8 | Prep: | Cook: 20mins | Ready in:

Ingredients

- beef soup made from beef shank
- large knuckle bone
- 8 -10 marrow bones
- 1 egg white beaten
- seasoned bread crumbs
- kosher or grey salt and pepper to taste
- juice from 2 or 3 pressed cloves of garlic
- optional :
- 2 hot peppers chopped super super fine and mixed into balls

Direction

- Strain your soup using a large colander and big bowl or another soup pot
- So that bones remain in colander
- Allow bones to cool while you complete your soup (barley veggies or whatever
- Small pot covered with a small strainer on stove
- Tap each marrow bone on strainer until you have all marrow out of bones
- Gently use a spoon and push marrow thru
- You only want to keep out small hard tiny bony pieces
- Bring soup to rolling boil
- Meanwhile place marrow with its juice in bowl, egg white, garlic juice, salt, and add breadcrumbs slowly until you have a mixture which will easily roll into tight knit balls
- Drop balls carefully one at a time into soup....they will rise immediately and be cooked in about 5 minutes
- Turn off soup
- Leave on burner for about 10 more minutes.

207. Mediterranean Pumpkin Soup Recipe

Serving: 4 | Prep: | Cook: 35mins | Ready in:

Ingredients

- 4 cups pumpkin
- 2 Tbsp olive oil
- 1 red onion, finely chopped
- 1/4 cup leeks, chopped
- 2 garlic cloves, finely chopped
- 2 cups vegetable stock
- salt and freshly ground pepper to taste
- freshly ground nutmeg, to taste
- 1/2 cup cream or plain yogurt (NOT fat free!)
- 1 tsp cumin
- 1 tsp ground ginger
- cilantro or parsley for Garnish

Direction

- You can use squash such as a butternut or acorn in this recipe if you don't have pumpkin.
- Cut fresh pumpkin up into chunks.
- Fresh:
- On the stovetop, heat a pan to medium heat
- Put 1-2 tbsp. cooking oil into the pan
- Add the pumpkin/squash chunks also add any onion or leeks at this time and allow to sweat for 20 - 30 minutes or until fork- tender
- Let it all caramelize together, then mash or puree...
- In a pot, cook the onion and garlic with a little olive oil.
- When softened and beginning to caramelize, add the pumpkin and the stock.
- Stir and allow to simmer for about 30 minutes.

- Using an immersion blender, a blender or a food processor, puree the soup until it's smooth and creamy.
- Taste and season, adjust the seasoning by, adding more
- Freshly ground nutmeg, ginger and/or cumin if desired.
- Stir in the cream/yogurt and let it gently come back to hot serving temperature.
- Garnish with cilantro or parsley.

208. Mexican Pumpkin Soup Recipe

Serving: 4 | Prep: | Cook: 35mins | Ready in:

Ingredients

- 4 cups pumpkin pulp canned or fresh cooked
- 1 large onion, halved
- 1/4 cup butter or corn oil
- 1/2 tsp cumin
- 1 1/2 tsp salt or to taste
- 1 cup heavy cream
- 1 cup half and half cream
- 2 1/2 cups chicken stock
- 3/4 tsp of chili pepper, ground
- 2 tsp lemon juice
- 1/2 tsp lemon zest
- 1 tsp dill
- 1/2 cup crema or creme fraiche (optional)
- 1/2 cup chopped cilantro (leaves and fine stems only, Optional)

Direction

- Chop the onion,
- Melt the butter/oil in a skillet
- Add the onion and sauté until soft.
- Sprinkle the onion with the cumin and sauté another minute or two.
- Add the cooked onion, pumpkin, and salt to the food processor bowl fitted with the metal blade.
- Process just until the ingredients are blended, about 10-15 seconds.
- Add the cream and half and half with the processor running and blend (again using an immersion blender, a blender or a food processor, puree the squash) until fully incorporated.
- Transfer the mixture to a large heavy saucepan.
- Add the chicken stock and remainder of herbs specified in above ingredients, and cook over medium-low heat until the soup is steaming but not boiling.
- Garnish with a dollop of crema and cilantro
- Options:
- I recommend adding 1/2 lb. cooked Chorizo and some Pipian for garnish (toasted hulled pumpkin seed) with the cilantro and crema.

209. Mexican Seafood Cocktail Recipe

Serving: 6 | Prep: | Cook: | Ready in:

Ingredients

- 2 cups chilled clamato juice, or 1 1/3 cup tomato juice and 2/3 cup bottled clam juice
- 1/3 cup ketchup
- 1/3 cup fresh lime juice
- 1 teaspoon hot sauce such as Tabasco, or to taste
- 1 teaspoon salt, or to taste
- 1/2 cup finely chopped red onion
- 1/3 cup chopped fresh cilantro
- 2 firm-ripe California avocado, peeled, pitted, and cut into small chunks
- 1/2 lb fresh lump crabmeat (1 cup), picked over
- 1/2 lb cooked shrimp, loosely chopped - or can use baby shrimp and leave whole
- ~~~~
- Accompaniment: oyster crackers or saltines (optional)

Direction

- Stir together Clamato juice, ketchup, lime juice, hot sauce, salt, onion, and cilantro in a large bowl, then gently stir in avocado, crabmeat, and shrimp.
- Spoon into 6- or 8-ounce glasses or cups.

210. Mi Nanas Albondigas Con Aros Mexicano Mexican Meatball Soup With Mexican Red Rice Recipe

Serving: 6 | Prep: | Cook: 120mins | Ready in:

Ingredients

- 3 lbs of ground beef
- 2 cups white rice
- 1 half sliced onion
- 2 cans of mexican stewed tomatoes
- water
- 1/2 cup of oil (use what you have on hand)
- pepper, salt, garlic powder, onion powder and cumin (optional) for seasoning the meat balls
- 6 cups of chopped carrots
- 6 cups of chopped potatoes
- 6 cups of chopped celery.
- * you can add more veggies to the soup*
- Mexican red rice
- 2 cups of white rice
- 4 cups of hot water
- 2 tbs of oil
- 2 slices of onion
- salt, pepper, garlic powder, onion powder, and chicken bouillon.

Direction

- Meatball Soup:
- Preheat pot on medium high fire, drizzle the bottom of the pot with oil
- When oil is hot, add onion and stewed tomatoes. Sauté the onion and tomatoes for 15 min or until the onions are brown.
- Add warm water to the pot (half way) and put on high flame until boil
- While waiting for water to boil, put ground beef into big mixing bowl, add your seasonings and (uncooked) rice. Be sure to mix well.
- Start rolling in your palm the meat (it's up to you how big you want your meatballs) but I use about 3 tbsp. spoons of meat and roll them into balls.
- Once your water start boiling, carefully add your meatballs and cook for 45 min.
- Once meatballs are done cooking add your veggies (carefully) and lower the flame to medium low and cook soup for about 1 hr. or until the veggies are soft.
- Mexican red rice:
- In a medium pot, preheat on a medium high flame and drizzle the bottom of pot with oil
- When oil is hot add onion and rice. Sauté the onion and rice until both are brown (usually takes 15-20 mins)
- Lower flame to a medium low and add hot water, tomato sauce, and all the seasonings.
- Bring to a boil and then put on low flame and cover and cook until there is no liquid and the rice is firm and dry.
- When rice is done you can put rice on top of soup or eat on the side. Enjoy!

211. Microwave Bean And Pasta Chowder Recipe

Serving: 4 | Prep: | Cook: 15mins | Ready in:

Ingredients

- 2 cups chicken stock
- 1/4 cup dried pasta
- 1 can (19 oz size) tomatoes, chopped

- 1 can (19 oz size) chick peas, rinsed and drained
- 1/4 tsp dried oregano
- 1/4 tsp chili powder
- salt and ground balck pepper
- mozzarella cheese, shredded

Direction

- In a 2 quart casserole, microwave chicken stock at high for 4 minutes or until boiling.
- Add pasta and microwave covered at high for 4 minutes.
- Add tomatoes including juice, chick peas, oregano and chili powder. Microwave, covered, at high for 6 to 8 minutes more or until piping hot.
- Adjust seasoning with salt and pepper.
- Serve in heated bowls and sprinkle with cheese.

212. Microwave Spaghetti Soup Recipe

Serving: 4 | Prep: | Cook: 30mins | Ready in:

Ingredients

- 1/2 pound ground beef crumbled
- 1 medium white onion
- 1 clove garlic mined
- 4 cups beef stock
- 1 teaspoon olive oil
- 1 can sliced mushrooms
- 1 can tomato sauce
- 1 cup frozen cut green beans
- 1-1/2 cups broken spaghetti uncooked
- 1 teaspoon parsley flakes
- 1 teaspoon salt
- 1 teaspoon freshly ground black pepper
- 1 bay leaf
- 1/2 teaspoon oregano

Direction

- In large casserole combine ground beef, onion, garlic and oil then microwave on high for 10 minutes stirring once during cooking.
- Drain well then add remaining ingredient sand cover and microwave on high for 25 minutes.
- Stir occasionally.

213. Monkey Stew Recipe

Serving: 6 | Prep: | Cook: 120mins | Ready in:

Ingredients

- 2-Tablespoons onion powder
- 4- Cups potatoes (cut into medium pieces)
- 2- Small (8 oz.) cans of tomato sauce
- 2- Small (6 oz.) cans of tomato paste
- 2- Lbs. ground chuck
- 2- Teaspoons salt
- 4- Cups water

Direction

- In a 5 qt. Dutch oven (or larger stock pot), brown ground beef then drain off grease.
- In the same pot, add back the ground beef and the tomato sauce, tomato paste, salt, onion powder and 4 cups of water.
- Heat to a simmer boil. (Using medium heat)
- Add the potatoes and cook covered on low-med for 1 ½ to 2 hours until the potatoes are done (stirring occasionally).

214. Moqueca Brazilian Fish Stew Recipe

Serving: 4 | Prep: | Cook: 1hours | Ready in:

Ingredients

- Soup Ingredients

- - 1 1/2 to 2 lbs of cod, cut into large portions (2-3")
  - 3 cloves garlic, minced
  - 4 Tbsp lemon juice
  - Salt, Pepper
  - Olive oil
  - 1 large yellow onion, chopped
  - 1 medium red onion
  - 1/4 cup scallions, chopped
  - 1 red bell pepper, seeded and chopped
  - 2 cups seeded and chopped tomatoes
  - 1 Tbsp paprika
  - Pinch red pepper flakes
  - 1 large bunch of cilantro, chopped with some set aside for garnish
  - 1 14-ounce can coconut milk
  - Rice Ingredients
  - 1 Tbsp olive oil
  - 1/2 yellow onion, chopped
  - 1 clove garlic, minced
  - 1 cup white rice
  - 1 3/4 cups boiling water (or the appropriate ratio of liquid to rice according to rice package)
  - 1 teaspoon salt

Direction

- Marinate Fish
- Place fish pieces in a bowl, add garlic and lemon juice so that the pieces are well coated. Sprinkle generously all over with salt and pepper. Keep chilled while preparing the rest of the soup.
- Start Rice
- If you are planning on serving the soup with rice, start with the rice. Heat one Tbsp. of olive oil in a medium saucepan on medium high heat. Add the chopped 1/2 onion and cook, stirring, until the onion is soft. Add the garlic and cook for 30 seconds more, until the garlic is fragrant. Add the raw white rice and stir to coat completely with the oil, onions, and garlic. Add the boiling water. (The amount depends on your brand of rice). Stir in 1 teaspoon of salt. Bring to a simmer, then lower the heat, cover, and let cook for 15 minutes, after which, remove from heat until ready to serve with the soup.
- Prepare Soup
- In a large pot, coat the bottom with about 2 Tbsp. of olive oil and heat on medium heat. Add the chopped onions and cook a few minutes until softened. Add the bell pepper, paprika, and red pepper flakes. Sprinkle generously with salt and pepper. (At least a teaspoon of salt.) Cook for a few minutes longer, until the bell pepper begins to soften. Stir in the chopped tomatoes and scallions. Bring to a simmer and cook for 5 minutes, uncovered. Stir in the chopped cilantro.
- Use a large spoon to remove about half of the vegetables (you'll put them right back in). Spread the remaining vegetables over the bottom of the pan to create a bed for the fish. Arrange the fish pieces on the vegetables. Sprinkle with salt and pepper. Then add back the previously removed vegetables, covering the fish. Pour coconut milk over the fish and vegetables.
- Bring soup to a simmer, reduce the heat, cover, and let simmer for approximately 20 minutes (depends on fish thickness). Taste and adjust seasonings to the desired seasoning for your taste.
- Garnish with cilantro. Serve with rice.

215. Moroccan Beef Soup Recipe

Serving: 6 | Prep: | Cook: 120mins | Ready in:

Ingredients

- 500g beef, diced
- 2 tbspns flour
- 1 onion, chopped
- 4 cloves garlic, diced
- 2 cm piece of ginger, peeled and chopped
- 1 tbspn smoky paprika
- 2 tspn cumin

- 1 tspn cumin seeds
- 1 litre stock- vegetable or meat based
- 2 400g cans peeled and diced tomatoes
- 1 400g can chickpeas (at least)
- 2 tspn caster sugar
- To serve- lemon zest, greek yoghurt, coriander

Direction

- Dust beef with flour. Heat oil and brown the beef well.
- Add onion, garlic and ginger and turn the heat down to a simmer.
- Add the rest of the oil and spices and fry gently for 5 mins.
- Turn up the heat and add the stock and tinned tomatoes. Bring to the boil and season with salt and pepper and sugar.
- Cover and simmer gently for about 2 hours, till beef is soft and tender.
- If you like, pop in a hand blender (the stick variety) and do a quick blitz in the mixture, but not too much as you want the chunks in the soup.
- Add the chickpeas.
- Serve in large bowls with yoghurt, sprinkled with lemon zest and fresh coriander.

216. Moroccan Beef Stew With Dried Fruit Recipe

Serving: 6 | Prep: | Cook: 120mins | Ready in:

Ingredients

- 3 lb lean beef stew cubes
- olive oil to saute
- 1 large onion chopped
- 1 cup dry white wine
- 1 cup water or beef broth
- 1/4 cup dark raisins
- 1/2 cup chopped pitted prunes
- 1/2 cup chopped dried apricots
- 1/4 cup chopped pitted dates
- 1/4 cup pitted green olives
- 1/4 cup pitted black olives
- parsley, sage, rosemary, thyme to taste (fresh or less if dried)
- salt and pepper to taste
- honey to taste
- paprika to taste
- 1 to 2 Tbs. fine granulated tapioca or flour to thicken
- 1/4 cup sliced almonds or as desired

Direction

- In pot heat some olive oil and brown meat and then onions.
- Add wine and water plus remaining fruits and seasoning to taste.
- Bring to a boil and then cover and simmer until meat is tender (1 1/2 to 2 hours).
- Correct seasoning and add some honey (to taste).
- Stir in tapioca or flour and cook and stir to thicken mixture.
- If you want more of a spicy taste, add the paprika.
- Stir in almonds just before serving.
- Note: tastes best when allowed to cool and be reheated.
- Serves 6 to 8

217. Moroccan Chicken & Couscous Soup Recipe

Serving: 0 | Prep: | Cook: 30mins | Ready in:

Ingredients

- 3 tbsp cooking oil
- 1 onion, chopped
- 1 lb boneless skinless chicken (original recipe called for thighs but I was only able to buy breasts)
- 1/4 tsp cayenne pepper
- 1 tsp ground cumin
- 1 3/4 tsp salt

- 1/4 tsp black pepper (fresh ground)
- 1 sweet potato, peeled and cut into 3/4-inch cubes (about 1/2 pound)
- 2 zucchinis (medium), quartered lengthwise & cut crosswise into 1-inch pieces
- 3/4 cup tomato puree
- 4 cups chicken stock (canned or homemade)
- 2 cups water
- 1/2 cup cousous
- 1/3 cup fresh parsley, chopped
- 1 can garbanzo beans a.k.a chickpeas, drained

Direction

- In a large pot, heat the oil over moderate heat. Add the onion and cook, stirring occasionally until translucent, about 5 minutes.
- Increase heat to moderately high. Add the chicken, cayenne, cumin, salt and pepper. Cook, stirring occasionally for about 2 minutes.
- Stir in the sweet potato, zucchini, tomato puree, water and broth. Bring to a boil. Reduce the heat and simmer, stirring occasionally until the vegetables are tender, about 10-15 minutes.
- Add the couscous to the soup. Simmer for 5 minutes, stirring occasionally. Add the garbanzo beans, stir and cook for another minute. Remove pot from heat and let soup stand, covered for 2 minutes. Add parsley & serve.

218. Moroccan Chickpea Stew Recipe

Serving: 0 | Prep: | Cook: 30mins | Ready in:

Ingredients

- 2 tbsp olive oil
- 1 onion, diced
- 1 clove garlic, minced
- 1 large sweet potato, peel and chopped
- 2 cups of cabbage, shredded
- 1 red pepper, diced
- 1 can chickpeas
- 1 can diced tomatoes
- 1 tsp ginger
- 1 tsp turmeric
- 1 tsp cumin
- 1 tsp cinnamon
- 1/2 tsp salt
- 1/2 tsp pepper
- 2 cups vegetable broth
- 1/4 cup raisins

Direction

- In a large pot, heat oil and add onions, garlic and sweet potato.
- Cook until tender, then add cabbage, red pepper, chickpeas, tomatoes, and spices. Cook for another 5 minutes.
- Add broth and bring to boil.
- Reduce heat and simmer covered for 20 minutes. Add raisins and simmer for another 5 minutes. Serve on top of cooked couscous.

219. Moroccan Harira Soup Recipe

Serving: 12 | Prep: | Cook: 45mins | Ready in:

Ingredients

- 12 oz lentils (red, brown or green, up to you)
- carrots, as many as you like, cut into 1/4 inch coins (I use 10 or 12)
- 1 small onion, chopped
- 2 large tomatoes, chopped
- 1 small jar tomato paste or tomato puree (4 to 6 oz)
- 1 clove garlic, chopped or 1 tsp garlic powder
- Dash of ground cumin
- Dash of ground coriander
- 2 tsp iodized salt (or more or less to suit your taste)
- 1 quart cold water

Direction

- Rinse lentils gently to remove extra dust and skins from processing.
- In a large kettle or stew pot pour in lentils and water.
- Let the lentils soak for a few minutes while you peel and slice carrots.
- Place pot on medium heat and while the lentils come to a boil add the onion, tomato paste, tomatoes, garlic, cumin, coriander and salt.
- Stir gently until ingredients are mixed.
- Add carrot coins and bring soup to a boil.
- Turn down heat to a very slight simmer and cover with lid, but set the lid so some steam can escape.
- If you need to, you may add more water to make the soup the desired consistency you like.
- Simmer gently until carrots and lentils are tender.
- This soup freezes beautifully.
- I've made it over 100 times and it is always delicious!

220. Moroccan Inspired Vegetable Soup Recipe

Serving: 10 | Prep: | Cook: 90mins | Ready in:

Ingredients

- 1 tbsp olive oil
- 1/2 large onion, diced
- 5 medium carrots, chopped
- 1 large red pepper, chopped
- 1 stalk celery, diced
- 1 clove garlic, grated
- 1 tsp grated fresh ginger
- 1/2 tbsp orange zest
- 6 cups vegetable broth
- 1/3 cup orange juice
- 1 19 oz. can diced tomatoes
- 2 tbsp tomato paste
- 1 tsp curry powder
- 1 tsp cumin
- 1/2 tsp saffron threads, crushed
- 1/2 tsp black pepper
- 1 19 oz. can chickpeas, drained
- 1 cup Golden Jewel grains blend (a mixture of Israeli couscous, tri-colored orzo, split garbanzo beans and quinoa - feel free to substitute your favourite mix)
- 5 oz green beans, chopped
- Salt, to taste

Direction

- Heat olive oil in a large stockpot over medium-high flame.
- Add onion, carrots, pepper and celery. Cook 7-8 minutes.
- Stir in garlic, ginger and orange zest, cook until fragrant, about 1 minute.
- Stir in broth, orange juice, tomatoes, tomato paste, curry, cumin, saffron, and pepper.
- Bring to a boil, then reduce heat and simmer 30 minutes.
- Stir in chickpeas, grain blend and green beans, cover and simmer 15 minutes, until beans are tender.

221. Moroccan Lentil Soup Recipe

Serving: 6 | Prep: | Cook: 145mins | Ready in:

Ingredients

- 2 onions, chopped
- 2 cloves garlic, minced
- 1 teaspoon grated fresh ginger
- 6 cups water
- 1 cup red lentils
- 1 (15 ounce) can garbanzo beans, drained
- 1 (19 ounce) can cannellini beans
- 1 (14.5 ounce) can diced tomatoes
- 1/2 cup diced carrots

- 1/2 cup chopped celery
- 1 teaspoon garam masala
- 1 1/2 teaspoons ground cardamom
- 1/2 teaspoon ground cayenne pepper
- 1/2 teaspoon ground cumin
- 1 tablespoon olive oil

Direction

- In large pot sauté; the onions, garlic, and ginger in a little olive oil for about 5 minutes.
- Add the water, lentils, chick peas, white kidney beans, diced tomatoes, carrots, celery, garam masala, cardamom, cayenne pepper and cumin. Bring to a boil for a few minutes then simmer for 1 to 1 1/2 hours or longer, until the lentils are soft.
- Puree half the soup in a food processor or blender. Return the pureed soup to the pot, stir and enjoy! :)

222. Moroccan Meatball Stew Recipe

Serving: 4 | Prep: | Cook: 45mins | Ready in:

Ingredients

- 1/2 lb lean ground beef
- 1/2 lb lean ground pork
- 2 tbsp. minced cilantro
- 2 1/2 tsp. paprika
- 2 tsp. cumin
- 1 tsp. salt
- 1/4 tsp. pepper
- 1 tsp. olive oil
- 1 onion, finely chopped
- 1 garlic clove, minced
- 1 ripe tomato, seeded and chopped
- 1/2 of a 6-ounce can of tomato paste
- 3/4 cup water
- 1 tbsp. chopped parsley to garnish, if desired

Direction

- Combine the meat, 1 tbsp. of cilantro, 1 1/2 tsp. of paprika, 1 tsp of cumin, half of the salt and pepper in a large bowl. Shape into 24 one-inch balls.
- Heat a large nonstick skillet. Swirl in the oil, then add the onion and garlic. Sauté until softened. Stir in the tomato, tomato paste, water, remaining 1 tbsp. cilantro, 1 tsp. paprika, 1 tsp. cumin, remaining salt and pepper, bring to a boil. Add the meatballs, reduce the heat and simmer, covered, until the meatballs are cooked and the sauce thickens, 30 to 45 minutes. Garnish with parsley just before serving if desired.
- One serving = 6 meatballs = 204 calories/4 points.

223. Moroccan Spiced Chickpea And Lentil Soup Recipe

Serving: 8 | Prep: | Cook: 60mins | Ready in:

Ingredients

- 4 tablespoons extra virgin olive oil
- 1 medium white onion, chopped (about 1 cup)
- 1 medium red onion, chopped (about 1 cup)
- 1 fennel bulb, peeled, cored and chopped (about 1 cup)
- 1/2 teaspoon ground ginger
- 1/2 teaspoon ground turmeric
- 1/2 teaspoon ground cinnamon
- Pinch of saffron threads (optional)
- 2 cans (14 ounces each) chopped tomatoes with their juice
- 2 cloves of garlic, minced
- 2 tablespoons sugar or to taste
- 4 cups gluten-free low sodium vegetable broth
- 1 cup dried lentils (green, brown, red or yellow), picked through and rinsed
- 3 cups canned chickpeas or garbanzo beans, drained and rinsed
- 4 sprigs cilantro

- 4 sprigs parsley
- 2 dried bay leaves
- sea salt, to taste
- pepper, to taste
- CHARMOULA
- 1 garlic clove
- 1 teaspoon cumin seeds, toasted and ground
- 4 to 5 tablespoons extra virgin olive oil
- juice of 1 lemon, plus zest
- 1 jalapeño pepper, seeded and deveined
- 1 bunch cilantro
- salt to taste
- pepper to taste

Direction

- For the Chermoula
- Mix the garlic, cumin, four tablespoons of the olive oil, lemon juice and jalapeño in a food processor. Pick cilantro leaves from their stems. Add the lemon zest and cilantro and season lightly with salt and pepper. Pulse mixture a couple of times, scraping mixture down from side of the bowl in between pulses. Add the remaining olive oil if needed. The mixture should resemble a rustic pesto. Place in tightly closed container and refrigerate for up to two days.
- For the Soup
- In a medium sized pot (about 4 quart capacity) with a lid, heat the olive oil at medium heat and add fennel, gently cooking for a couple of minutes while the fennel releases its natural juices.
- Add the red and white onions, cook until soft and translucent, but without turning brown, stirring mixture from time to time, about 12 minutes.
- Add tomatoes and increase heat to high until the mixture comes to a simmer (about 5 minutes). Add the ginger, turmeric, cinnamon, garlic and saffron if using, letting them infuse the mixture with their flavors for a few more minutes.
- Add the lentils, vegetable stock, sprigs of cilantro and parsley and bay leaves and bring to a boil, then reduce heat to a simmer.
- Season with salt, pepper and sugar, stirring the mixture a couple of times. Cover pot and let simmer for about 25 minutes or until the lentils are tender. Add the cooked chickpeas and cook uncovered for another 5 to 7 minutes until heated through. Mix well, season again with salt, pepper and sugar to taste. Remove bay leafs and sprigs of cilantro and parsley.
- For a thicker soup, remove about one cup of the cooked lentils and chickpeas from the soup and process them in blender, adding some extra liquid if needed. Add the blended mixture back to the soup.
- For a thinner soup. Add extra vegetable stock.
- Serve hot with 1 tablespoon of Chermoula sauce on the top of the soup, if desired.

224. Moroccan Style Lamb And Chickpea Soup For Two Recipe

Serving: 2 | Prep: | Cook: 80mins | Ready in:

Ingredients

- 200 grams (7 oz) cubed lamb pieces
- 1 litre (1.75 pints) water or lamb stock
- 1 onion chopped finely
- 75 grams (2.5oz) red lentils
- 200 grams (7 oz) diced very ripe tomatoes
- 1 tbsn tomato paste
- 1/2 tsp ground turmeric
- 1/2 tsp ground cinnamon
- 1 cinnamon stick
- 1/2 tsp ground ginger
- 1/2 tsp salt
- 1/4 tsp freshly ground black pepper
- 200 grams (7 oz) re-hydrated (cooked) chickpeas
- 1 large celery stalk with leaves, finely chopped
- 2 cannelloni pasta tubes, smashed so that you get odd size shapes (but if you don't have that a very small handful of any pasta smashed or

crunched up a bit to add interesting texture to the soup will work
- juice of 1 lemon
- 1 small bunch of coriander (cilantro), chopped coarsely

Direction

- Put lamb cubes in medium sized pot along with the water or stock (lamb stock is best if you can make it or buy it). Bring the water to boil and skim off the little bit of froth that forms.
- Add the onion, lentils, tomatoes, tomato paste, turmeric, ground cinnamon, cinnamon stick, ginger, salt and pepper and allow the pot to simmer very gently for about 60 minutes (lamb will become very tender).
- Add the chickpeas, celery and smashed pasta and allow to simmer for another 15 minutes. Add the lemon juice and coriander (cilantro) and stir through then turn off heat and let soup stand to cool slightly before serving.
- Enjoy.

225. My Baked Potato Soup Recipe

Serving: 68 | Prep: | Cook: 15mins | Ready in:

Ingredients

- Shirley's Baked potato Soup
- Ingredients
- 8 slices bacon with drippings retained.
- 1 cup yellow onion, diced
- 2/3 cup flour
- 6 cups hot chicken broth
- 5 largepotatoes, baked, peeled, and diced
- 2 cups half & half
- 1/4 cup fresh parsley, chopped
- 1 1/2 tsp. garlic
- 1 1/2 tsp. basil (dried)
- 1 tsp. salt
- 1 tsp. black pepper
- 1 tsp. Cholula sauce or Tabasco or favorite hot sauce
- 1 cup grated cheddar cheese (I use sharp)
- 1/4 cup scallions, diced

Direction

- Cook bacon and set aside.
- Cook onions in bacon drippings until transparent.
- Add flour, whisking, and cook 3 to 5 minutes until it starts to turn golden.
- Add chicken broth, gradually whisking until mixture thickens.
- Reduce heat to simmer and add potatoes, cream, bacon, parsley, and seasonings. Simmer for 10 minutes. Don't boil.
- Add grated cheese and scallions. Heat until cheese melts completely. Garnish with bacon, cheese, and parsley.

226. My Cioppino Italian Seafood Stew Recipe

Serving: 12 | Prep: | Cook: 120mins | Ready in:

Ingredients

- 3 tablespoons olive oil
- 2 to 3 flat fillets of anchovies, drained (in olive oil, preferred)
- 1 teaspoon dried crushed red pepper flakes, plus more to taste
- 1 large fennel bulb, thinly sliced (the anise flavor totally mellows out as it cooks and adds such a depth of background flavor - essential)
- 1 medium onion, chopped
- 3 large shallots, chopped
- 2 celery ribs, chopped
- 2 teaspoons salt
- 1 teaspoon ground black pepper
- 4 large garlic cloves, finely chopped
- 1/3 cup tomato paste (if you want more, add ½ cup)
- 1 (28-ounce) can diced tomatoes in juice

- 1 1/2 cups dry white wine (if I don't have white wine, I add beer)
- 5 cups fish stock (can use clam juice or chicken broth or any combination)
- 4 sprigs fresh thyme, leaves removed (about 1 tablespoon fresh - or you could use 1 teaspoon dried thyme if you can't get the fresh)
- 1 bay leaf
- 1 pound clams, scrubbed
- 1 pound mussels, scrubbed, debearded
- 1 pound oysters, shucked and in their liquor
- 1 pound uncooked large shrimp, peeled and deveined
- 1/2 pound sea scallops (or can use bay scallops for a little sweeter taste)
- ¼ pound squid
- ¼ pound octopus
- ¼ pound cuttlefish (optional – but delicious!)
- 1 1/2 pounds assorted firm-fleshed fish fillets such as halibut or cod, cut into 1-inch chunks
- 1 handful flat-leaf parsley, chopped
- Optional: Sub in lobster and/or crab - your faves...yummm!
- crusty bread for sopping the juice…so good…a must have, peeps.

Direction

- Heat the oil in a very large pot over medium heat.
- Add anchovies - let melt into oil.
- Add the fennel, onion, shallots, celery, salt and black pepper and sauté until the onion is translucent, about 10 minutes.
- Stir tomato paste into veggies and let cook out for about 3-5 minutes (the tomato paste will start to caramelize, turning from red to a brownish colour).
- Add the garlic and 1 teaspoon of red pepper flakes, and cook 2 minutes.
- Add tomatoes with their juices, wine, fish stock, thyme and bay leaf.
- Cover and bring to a simmer.
- Reduce the heat to medium-low. Cover and simmer on medium-low until the flavours blend - at least an hour...but I like to let it go for a couple of hours.
- Add the clams, mussels and oysters to the cooking liquid. Cover and cook until the clams and mussels begin to open, about 5 minutes.
- Add the shrimp, scallops, squid, octopus, cuttlefish and fish. Simmer gently until the fish and shrimp are just cooked through, and the clams are completely open, stirring gently, about 5 minutes longer (discard any clams and mussels that do not open).
- Remove bay leaf. Season the soup, to taste, with more salt, black pepper and red pepper flakes.
- Ladle the soup into bowls, sprinkle with chopped parsley and serve with crusty bread.

227. My Grandmothers Hungarian Goulash Recipe

Serving: 6 | Prep: | Cook: 25mins | Ready in:

Ingredients

- 8 oz elbow macaroni (or pasta of your choice)
- 1 can chopped tomatoes
- 1 small can tomato puree
- 1 small onion, chopped
- 8 oz ground beef
- 1 tsp paprika
- 1/2 tsp salt
- 1/2 tsp white pepper

Direction

- Brown ground beef and onion.
- Cook pasta according to package directions.
- Drain pasta and in the same pot add beef and onion, chopped tomatoes, tomato puree, paprika, pepper and salt.
- Mix well and heat thoroughly.
- Serve with a salad and rolls.

228. Navy Bean Soup Recipe

Serving: 8 | Prep: | Cook: 75mins | Ready in:

Ingredients

- 1 (16 ounce) bag of dried navy beans
- 7 c. water
- 1 ham bone for flavor
- 2 c. diced ham
- 1/4 c. minced onion
- 1/2 tsp. salt
- 1/ tsp. ground black pepper
- 1 bay leaf
- 1/2 c. sliced carrots
- 1/2 c. sliced celery

Direction

- Add water to large pot and add beans.
- Bring to boil, let boil for 2 min, take off from heat.
- Cover with lid and let simmer for at least an hour.
- Place pot back on medium heat. Add the ham bone, the cubed ham, onion salt, pepper and the bay leaf. You will reduce the heat, and let it gently simmer for about an hour and a half. The beans will be soft to touch.
- It is recommended to skim the soup during the cooking process.
- Add carrots and celery, letting the cook until tender.
- Once the veggies are tender, remover the ham bone, getting any excess meat from bone.
- Add the meat back to soup and serve!

229. Neighbors Potato Soup Recipe

Serving: 16 | Prep: | Cook: 45mins | Ready in:

Ingredients

- 5 lbs peeled and diced potatoes
- 1 stick butter
- 1 large yellow onion
- 2 Cups milk
- 8 oz sour cream
- 1 can cream of celery soup
- 1 can cream of chicken soup
- 1 lb cubed Velveeta
- 1 8 oz pkg chopped ham pieces or cooked bacon

Direction

- In large pot melt butter, cook onions about 5 mins till soft.
- Add potatoes and enough water to cover. Boil until fork tender.
- Drain 1/2 water.
- Add milk, sour cream, soups, Velveeta, ham or bacon.
- Cook till yummy, about 20 min.
- Good with crusty bread.

230. North African Chickpea And Kale Soup Recipe

Serving: 6 | Prep: | Cook: 40mins | Ready in:

Ingredients

- 1 large onion, chopped
- 2 carrots, sliced or diced
- 4 cloves garlic, minced or pressed
- 1 1/2 teaspoon ground cumin
- 1/2 teaspoon paprika
- 1/8-1/4 teaspoon chilli powder or cayenne
- 1/4 teaspoon allspice
- 1/2 teaspoon ground ginger
- generous pinch saffron, lightly crushed
- 2 bay leaves
- 1 3-inch cinnamon stick
- 3 cups cooked chickpeas (or 2 cans, drained and rinsed)
- 8 cups vegetable broth (or water plus bouillon

- 1 large bunch kale, thick center ribs removed and chopped (at least 8 cups)
- about 2 cups water
- salt to taste

Direction

- Spray a large saucepan with olive oil spray and heat it.
- Add the onion and carrot and cook over medium-high heat until the onion begins to brown (about 5 minutes). Add the garlic and cook for 1 more minute.
- Add the spices, including bay leaves and cinnamon stick, and cook, stirring, for another minute.
- Add the chickpeas and stir to coat them with the spices.
- Pour in the 8 cups of vegetable stock, bring to a boil, and reduce heat to a simmer for 20 minutes.
- Add the chopped kale and stir. If necessary add water to cover the kale and cook until it is tender, about 10-25 minutes, depending on how cooked you like your kale. Check frequently to see if it is becoming dry and add water as needed.
- Add salt to taste and serve.

231. North African Fish Stew Recipe

Serving: 2 | Prep: | Cook: 50mins | Ready in:

Ingredients

- 1 1/2 tbsp cumin
- 1 tsp ground coriander
- 2 tsp sweet paprika
- 1/2 teaspoon pepper
- 1 lemon, juiced and zested
- 2 tablespoons olive oil
- 1/2 pound cod, cut in 2" pieces
- 1/2 cup whole-wheat couscous
- 1 cup water
- 1 medium red pepper, chopped
- 1 medium white onion, chopped
- 1 medium carrot, chopped
- 1 jalapeno, seeded and diced
- 4 cups water
- 1/2 cup tomato paste

Direction

- Combine 2 teaspoons of the cumin with the coriander, paprika, pepper, lemon juice, zest and 1 1/2 tbsp. water.
- Toss fish with the marinade. Refrigerate 1 hour.
- Put the couscous in a large heatproof bowl, and bring 2 cups of water to a boil.
- When the water boils, pour it over the couscous and cover the bowl tightly with plastic wrap. Let the couscous sit 10 minutes.
- Over medium heat in a large pot, stir in all of the vegetables, the remaining cumin and a sprinkling of salt and pepper with 1/4 cup of water.
- Cook, stirring often, until the vegetables are soft, 5-7 minutes.
- Add the stock and tomato paste.
- Bring the stew to a boil, then reduce the heat and simmer gently for 25 minutes.
- Add the fish and simmer the stew until the fish is just cooked through, another 10-15 minutes.
- To serve, add some couscous to each bowl and top with the stew.

232. Not Another Pasta E Fagioli Recipe

Serving: 8 | Prep: | Cook: 70mins | Ready in:

Ingredients

- 1 lb ground beef
- 1 small onion, chopped
- 1 large carrot, julienned (1 cup)
- 3 stalks celery, chopped (1 cup)

- 3 cloves garlic, minced
- 2 14.5 oz cans diced tomatoes
- 1 15oz can red kidney beans, with liquid
- 1 15 oz can canelli beans
- 1 15 oz can tomato sauce
- 1 12 oz can V-8 juice
- 1 T white vinegar
- 1 1/2 t salt
- 1 t oregano
- 1 t basil
- 1/2 t pepper
- pinch red pepper flakes
- 1/2 t thyme
- 1/2 lb ditali pasta, cooked, al dente

Direction

- Brown ground beef in large pot over med heat. Drain off fat. Add onion, carrot, celery and garlic and sauté for 10 minutes.
- Add remaining ingredients except pasta and simmer for 1 hour.
- Add the pasta to the soup. Simmer an additional 5 to 10 minutes and serve.
- Grate fresh parmesan over individual bowls, serve with hot garlic bread and a green salad.
- Fantastic!!

233. Olla Gitana Gypsy Pot Recipe

Serving: 6 | Prep: | Cook: 30mins | Ready in:

Ingredients

- 2 14-oz cans chickpeas, drained
- 1 fat carrot, peeled and thickly sliced
- 9-10 cups rich chicken or vegetable stock
- 1 lb. pumpkin or butternut squash, peeled and cut into 1-inch chunks
- 10 oz. green beans, trimmed and cut into 1-inch lengths
- 2 small slightly underripe pears (such as Anjou), peeled, cored and cut into 1-inch chunks
- coarse salt and freshly ground pepper
- 3 tablespoons olive oil
- 3 large garlic cloves, chopped
- a handful of blanched almonds
- 1 medium onion, chopped
- 1 teaspoon sweet paprika (not smoked)
- 2 medium ripe tomatoes, finely chopped
- 1 pinch saffron threads, crumbled and steeped in a few spoonfuls of hot stock for fifteen minutes
- 2 teaspoons red wine vinegar, or more to taste
- 2 tablespoons slivered fresh mint
- crusty bread and butter for serving (you can also easily serve this over rice or couscous)

Direction

- Combine the chickpeas, carrots and enough stock to come about 1 1/2 inches above the top in a large heavy pot and bring to a boil over medium heat.
- Add the pumpkin, green beans and pears and season with salt to taste. Bring to a simmer and cook uncovered until the vegetables have softened, about 15-20 minutes.
- Meanwhile, heat the olive oil in a medium skillet over medium heat. Add the almonds and garlic and cook, stirring, until golden, about 2 minutes. Using a slotted spoon, transfer to a bowl, leaving behind as much oil as possible, and set aside.
- Add the onion to the skillet and cook until softened, about 5 minutes. Add the paprika and stir for a few seconds, add the tomatoes and a few tablespoons of the cooking liquid and cook until the tomatoes soften and reduce, about 7 minutes.
- Gently stir the tomato mixture and the saffron into the pot with the chickpeas.

234. Omg Italian Sausage And Potato Soup Recipe

Serving: 8 | Prep: | Cook: 50mins | Ready in:

Ingredients

- 1 Cup spicy italian sausage links
- 2 medium potatoes, cut in half lengthwise, and then cut into ¼" slices
- ¾ Cup onions, diced
- 6 slices bacon
- ½ teaspoon minced garlic
- 2 Cup kale leaves, cut in half, then sliced
- 2 tablespoons chicken base
- 1 qt. water
- ⅓ Cup heavy whipping cream

Direction

- Preheat oven to 300°F.
- Place sausage links onto a sheet pan and bake for 25 minutes, or until done; cut in half length-wise, then cut at an angle into ½ inch slices.
- Place onions and bacon in a large saucepan and cook over medium heat until onions are almost clear.
- Remove bacon and crumble.
- Add garlic to the onions and cook an additional 1-minute.
- Add chicken base, water, and potatoes, simmer 15 minutes.
- Add crumbled bacon, sausage, kale and cream.
- Simmer 4 minutes and serve.
- Optional: You may wish to add a half teaspoon of fennel seed to this.
- Makes 8

235. Oyster Stew With Leeks Recipe

Serving: 6 | Prep: | Cook: 15mins | Ready in:

Ingredients

- 1/2 cup sliced leek or chopped onion
- 1 medium potato, diced
- 1 cup water
- 1/2 teaspoon instant chicken bouillon granules
- 1/4 teaspoon white pepper
- 2 12-ounce cans evaporated skim milk
- 1 pint shucked oysters
- 1 tablespoon snipped fresh parsley
- 2 teaspoons butter-flavored sprinkles (optional)

Direction

- In 3-quart saucepan combine leek or onion, potato, water, bouillon granules, and white pepper. Bring to boiling. Reduce heat; cover and simmer for 7 minutes or until potatoes are done. Do not drain.
- Stir in evaporated skim milk. Cook over medium heat for 5 minutes. Add undrained oysters. Cook about 5 minutes more or until edges of oysters curl, stirring frequently. Stir in parsley. Stir in butter-flavored sprinkles, if desired. Makes 6 servings.

236. Oyster Stew Recipe

Serving: 8 | Prep: | Cook: 30mins | Ready in:

Ingredients

- 2 slices bacon, diced
- 1/2 cup butter
- 1 medium onion, diced
- 2 stalks celery, diced
- 1 garlic clove, crushed
- 3 tablespoons flour
- salt
- fresh ground black pepper
- 1 pinch cayenne
- 1/2 teaspoon dried thyme
- 1 (8 ounce) bottle clam juice

- 1/4 cup dry sherry or a dry white wine
- 1 1/2 cups heavy cream
- 1 (12 ounce) can evaporated milk
- 1 pint shucked oysters, with their liquor
- few dashes of worcestershire sauce
- 1/2 cup parsley, finely chopped

Direction

- Sauté diced bacon in a non-stick soup pot over low heat until rendered.
- Add butter and heat until melted.
- Add onions, celery and garlic and continue to cook over low heat, stirring occasionally, until translucent.
- Add salt and pepper to taste, pinch of cayenne, thyme and flour, whisking steadily to make a roux. You want this to be light so don't cook to long as it will get darker.
- Slowly whisk in clam juice, whisking until smooth, then sherry, whisking until smooth.
- Whisk in cream, whisking until smooth, then whisk in evaporated milk, whisking until smooth.
- Raise heat slightly, stir while bringing just until it starts to boil, then lower heat and whisk until slightly thickened, about 5 minutes. Note: you never know how thick a roux makes a dish until it comes to a boil.
- Stir in oysters with their liquor, several dashes of Worcestershire sauce and the chopped parsley.
- Continue to heat, stirring occasionally, until oysters curl at the edges indicating they are heated through.

237. Pasta Fazool Recipe

Serving: 2 | Prep: | Cook: 30mins | Ready in:

Ingredients

- 3 cups canned great northern beans (drained and rinsed)
- 1/2 cup diced celery,
- 2 cloves garlic (lightly crushed)
- 1/4 cup olive oil,
- pinch of crushed red pepper,
- 1 tsp tomato paste,
- 1/2 cup water,
- 1 cup peeled, seeded, chopped fresh tomatoes,
- pinch salt,
- 1/2 lb small pasta noodles (cooked and drained)
- *Options* You can even add a half cup diced ham to this recipe.

Direction

- Cook celery and garlic in olive oil in a large saucepan over medium heat. When garlic is golden brown, remove garlic.
- Add tomatoes, tomato paste, crushed red pepper, salt and water.
- Simmer for 12 minutes, or until thickened.
- Add beans and pasta.
- Simmer another 5 minutes.
- Serve immediately.

238. Paula Deen's Baked Potato Soup Recipe

Serving: 8 | Prep: | Cook: 2hours | Ready in:

Ingredients

- 8 slices bacon
- 1 onion, diced
- 1/2 cup flour
- 3 (14.5 oz.) cans chicken broth
- 5 potatoes, baked, peeled and diced
- 1 teaspoon dried parsley flakes
- 2 cups half & half
- 1 cup sharp cheddar cheese, grated
- 1 cup sour cream
- salt & pepper to taste
- Garnish
- cheddar cheese
- sour cream

- chives

Direction

- In a Dutch oven cook bacon until crisp
- Remove and crumble, reserving drippings
- Sauté onion in bacon drippings until tender
- Add salt and pepper
- Stir in flour and cook for one minute, stirring constantly
- Slowly add chicken broth; cook, stirring constantly until thick and bubbly Add potatoes, parsley and half & half; cook for 10 minutes
- Stir in cheese and sour cream.
- Garnish with cheese, bacon, chives and sour cream.

239. Pea Soup With Shiitake Mushrooms Recipe

Serving: 3 | Prep: | Cook: 25mins | Ready in:

Ingredients

- 250 grams frozen peas
- 20 grams margarine
- 100 grams dried shiitakes, reconstituted
- 1 liter vegetable bouillon
- 1 tbs. curry powder
- 2 tbs. almonds, ground
- 1 tbs. flour
- salt
- mint leaves for garnish

Direction

- Cook your frozen peas 5 minutes in 1 liter of water.
- Add in 1 liter of vegetable bouillon and cook for 15 mins.
- Puree the mixture.
- Meanwhile, go soak the dried Shiitakes (or clean fresh ones) and cut them into cross-sectional slices.
- Set 1 or 2 of the strips aside to garnish the soup at the end.
- Now sauté the rest of the mushrooms in margarine.
- Add in the flour and ground up almonds as well as the curry powder.
- Add all to the soup and cook soup until it is warm.
- Serve soup with a few mint leaves on top as well as float a few shiitake slices on top as a garnish with the mint leaves.

240. Peach Buttermilk Soup Recipe

Serving: 6 | Prep: | Cook: | Ready in:

Ingredients

- 2 pounds peaches, peeled, pitted and sliced
- 1/3 cup frozen orange juice concentrate, thawed
- 1 cup buttermilk
- 1 cup light cream
- 1/8 teaspoon allspice

Direction

- Drop peaches into boiling water for 10 seconds.
- Peel.
- Remove pit.
- Puree peaches in food processor/blender.
- Pour puree into a medium bowl.
- Add orange juice concentrate, buttermilk, cream and allspice.
- Mix well to blend.
- Chill at least 6 hours or overnight.
- Serve in chilled bowls.
- Garnish with shaved almonds or toasted coconut.
- **This is good using nectarines also!

241. Persian Lamb Stew With Basmati Rice Recipe

Serving: 8 | Prep: | Cook: 60mins | Ready in:

Ingredients

- 4 lamb shanks choppd into 3 inch pieces (the meat department butcher can do this for you.)
- 1 large can tomato puree or tomato sauce
- 6 ripe tomatoes, chopped
- 6 large potatoes, peeled and cut into large cubes
- 6 cups water
- 2 bay leaves
- 2 Tbsp cinnamon
- 1 tsp cumin
- 1 tsp salt
- 1 clove garlic, finely minced
- 2 cups basmati rice, rinsed and drained

Direction

- Put lamb shanks in a large stew pot and add everything except potatoes and rice.
- Bring to a boil and cook at a rolling simmer until lamb is tender and liquid has reduced and is thick (about 45 minutes). Stir occasionally.
- Add the potatoes, remove the bay leaves and simmer for another 15 minutes.
- Cook the rice while the stew is simmering for its last 15 minutes.
- Serve the lamb stew over the rice.
- You can add a sprinkling of cooked lentils on top of the rice if you wish.

242. Philly Cheese Steak Soup Recipe

Serving: 8 | Prep: | Cook: 45mins | Ready in:

Ingredients

- 1 1/2lb. your favourite steak (beef filet, ribeye, etc.), cut in THIN strips *Do not use skirt steak, or cheap cuts.
- 1 tbsp. butter
- 1 1/2 tsp. steak seasoning
- 1 onion, chopped
- 3 garlic cloves, minced
- 4 sweet bell peppers (you can use different colors), thinly sliced
- 1 small package white mushrooms, sliced
- 8 cups beef broth
- 2 cups milk
- 3 tbsp. worstershire sauce
- salt and pepper to taste
- 1 small package provolone cheese, sliced

Direction

- In a Dutch oven or a heavy pot, over medium heat brown the steak strips in 1 tbsp. of butter for about 4 minutes. Sprinkle with steak seasoning, cook and stir another minute. Remove to a plate and set aside.
- Add chopped onions and garlic to the Dutch oven. Cook and stir until lightly browned and caramelized. Stir in the bell peppers and mushrooms. Cook and stir another 7 minutes, or until peppers are starting to caramelize, but still retain color.
- Add steak back to the pot.
- Add beef broth, milk, Worcestershire sauce, salt and pepper to taste. Bring to a boil and simmer on low for another 30 minutes.
- Remove from heat. Just before serving, stir in provolone cheese, a few slices per plate. Serve hot.
- *note: you can also cook this soup in a crock pot. Follow steps 1-4, then transfer everything to the crock pot for a couple of hours.

243. Pizza Soupreme With Garlic Parmesan Puffs Recipe

Serving: 6 | Prep: | Cook: 60mins | Ready in:

Ingredients

- 1lb italian sausage
- 8oz pepperoni, cubed
- 1 large or 2 small bell peppers, diced
- 1 large red onion, diced
- 2cloves garlic
- 16oz mushrooms, chopped fine(reserve about 4oz sliced)
- 2 28oz cans crushed tomatoes
- 32oz chicken or pork stock
- 1tsp red pepper flakes
- 2-3T fresh mixed Italian herbs(or 2t dried)
- kosher or sea salt and fresh ground pepper
- For serving:
- 12oz mozzarella cheese, grated
- 1 can black olives, sliced
- garlic Parmesan Puffs
- 2 sheets puff pastry, thawed
- 2T butter, melted and cooled slightly
- 1 egg, beaten
- 1t garlic powder
- 1/2t dried Italian herbs
- 1/2 cup fresh parmesan cheese, finely grated

Direction

- Cook sausage in large soup pot or Dutch oven until no longer pink.
- Add peppers, onion and garlic, and cook through, but try not to over brown the sausage.
- Add tomatoes, stock, mushrooms, herbs, salt and peppers
- Simmer for 45 minutes, stirring occasionally.
- Serve with slices of fresh mushrooms, olives, Mozzarella cheese, and puffs, as desired.
- To prepare Puffs
- Carefully unfold pastry sheets onto lightly sprayed cookie sheets.
- Combine cooled butter, egg, garlic and herbs and brush across top of pastry.
- Sprinkle with Parmesan cheese.
- With sharp knife, cut pastry into 1/2 inch squares. No need to separate, just get the indentation, there, they will break apart after baking.
- Bake at 400 until golden brown, puffed, and crisp. (Check package directions, but probably around 15 minutes)
- Let cool slightly, then remove from sheet.

244.   Plain Ole Beef Stew Recipe

Serving: 6 | Prep: | Cook: 60mins | Ready in:

Ingredients

- 3 medium potatoes, peeled and chopped
- 1/2 medium onion, sliced thin
- 1 1/2 pounds beef roast
- 1 cup baby carrot, cut 1" thick
- 1 cup water
- 3 tablespoons cornstarch
- 1 teaspoon garlic powder

Direction

- Place roast in a small stock pot with just enough water to cover it. Cook until tender. Or cook in a pressure cooker for 1/2 hour. Remove meat to a plate. Strain the broth and return it to the pot.
- Carefully cut up the meat into 1-2 inch pieces while removing fat and gristle. This is the ugly part. :-]
- Add the meat, potatoes, onions, carrots and garlic powder to the broth and cook until vegetables are fork tender. If more water needed for cooking just add it.
- Mix together 1 cup of water and cornstarch until smooth. Pour slowly into boiling stew, stirring constantly, so the mixture remains at a boil. Only add enough to reach the desired consistency. Cook for an additional 3-5 minutes on medium heat.

245. Poblano Potato Soup Recipe

Serving: 6 | Prep: | Cook: 40mins | Ready in:

Ingredients

- 8 large yukon gold potatoes Peeled, cut into large cubes (10 Med)
- 4 Strips bacon chopped
- 4 - 6 Medium Sized poblano peppers. (roasted, Peeled, Chopped)
- 1 Large onion chopped
- 3 cloves garlic chopped
- 1 Cup creme fraiche
- 1 Cup heavy cream, Half & Half, or milk
- 1 Qt chicken or vegetable stock
- 1/2 Cup dry sherry (Chardonay works fine.)
- salt & Pepper to taste

Direction

- On a Grill, Broiler, or Gas Stove, Roast Poblanos until the Skins are blistered and black all around. Place in a paper bag or lidded container to steam. (15 Min.) Peel, remove seeds and roughly chop. If you want to make your soup less piquant, cut out all the white inside veins.
- In a Dutch oven or large Stock Pot, render chopped bacon on medium heat until crisp. Remove to drain in a paper towel lined bowl.
- Increase heat to medium high, add Onion, cook until transparent and tender (4 - 5 Min). Add 1/2 the Poblano 1/2 the bacon and Garlic, cook for another 2 min.
- Deglaze with Sherry and cook 1 - 2 Min. Add Potatoes and Chicken Stock. Cook Approx. 25 - 30 min until potatoes are fork tender.
- Puree' in batches in a blender and return to pot. (Pulse only enough to make the mixture smooth. Over blending will make the soup "Gluey"
- Reheat soup until hot
- In a large measuring cup or bowl, whisk the Crème Fraiche with Cream, Half & Half or Milk until smooth. Wisk mixture into soup.
- Stir in remaining bacon and chopped Poblano. Heat gently until hot, Remove from heat and serv.
- Garnishes I have used: Crisp Bacon, Chopped Roasted Poblano Peppers, Fried Cheese slice, 2 Seared Shrimp per bowl, 1 Seared Portobello slice per bowl w/ a drizzle of Truffle oil. Parsley, Cilantro. Shredded Anejo Cheese.

246. Polish Beetroot Soup Barszcz Recipe

Serving: 8 | Prep: | Cook: 60mins | Ready in:

Ingredients

- 2 litres beef stock or vegetable stock
- 1 large onion, peeled and chopped
- 1 bouquet garni (your choice of herbs)
- 1 can mushrooms, or fresh or as my Mother-in-law did, she took a small handful of dehydrated mushrooms from Poland and soaked them overnight.
- 3 uncooked medium-sized beetroots, peeled and sliced thickly
- 300 ml kwas - ascorbic acid
- 1 tsp. sugar
- sour cream and homemade croutons to garnish

Direction

- Heat beef stock in a large saucepan.
- Add onion, bouquet garni, mushrooms and sliced beetroot.
- Boil on medium high heat for 1 hour.
- Strain the soup and stir the kvass into the clear soup.
- Add sugar to taste and reheat if necessary without boiling.
- Serves 8.
- Note: My Mother-in-law always added small little meat ravioli's or tortellini to the Barszcz.
- You can add vegetables such as celery, carrot, potato or parsnip - roughly chopped.

247. Polish Sauerkraut Stew Recipe

Serving: 8 | Prep: | Cook: 120mins | Ready in:

Ingredients

- 1/4 cup dried mushrooms (preferably porcini), chopped
- 1 cup dried prunes
- 8 oz. lean boneless pork, cubed
- 8 oz. lean chuck steak, cubed
- 8 oz. kielbasa, cubed
- 1/4 cup flour
- 2 onions, sliced
- 3 tbsp. olive oil
- 4 tbsp. sherry wine
- 2 lb. can or package sauerkraut, well rinsed
- 14 oz. can fire roasted tomatoes
- 1/4 tsp. cloves
- 1/2 tsp. cinnamon
- 1 tsp. dried dill
- 2 1/2 cups of beef stock (low sodium)
- black pepper to taste
- 2 tbsp. fresh parsely, chopped, for garnish

Direction

- Pour boiling water to completely cover the dried mushrooms and prunes in a bowl. Leave for 30 minutes, then drain well.
- Toss the cubed pieces of beef, pork and kielbasa in the flour. Set aside.
- Gently fry the onions in the oil in a Dutch oven or a heavy pot, for about 10 minutes. Remove from pot and set aside.
- In the same pot, brown the meat in batches for about 5 minutes, or until browned. Remove from pan and set aside.
- Add the Sherry wine to the pan and simmer, scraping the bottom of the pan, for about 2 minutes.
- Add the meat and onions back to the pan. Stir in tomatoes, cloves, cinnamon, dill, mushrooms, prunes and a well rinsed sauerkraut. Make sure the sauerkraut is well rinsed, otherwise the stew could come out too salty. Season with black pepper.
- Add the beef stock to the pot and bring to the boil. Reduce the heat, cover and simmer for about 2 hours, or until the meat is very tender. Remove the lid during the last 30 minutes of cooking to let the liquid evaporate, as the stew should be thick.
- Serve hot, sprinkled with chopped parsley and accompanied by baby boiled potatoes, if desired.

248. Polish Sausage And Bean Soup Recipe

Serving: 6 | Prep: | Cook: 22mins | Ready in:

Ingredients

- 12 ounces dry mixed beans
- 1-1/2 pounds turkey sausage links
- 1 (29 ounce) can diced tomatoes
- 2 (14 ounce) cans chicken broth
- Note: I also like to add vegetable stock
- 1 cup white wine
- 1 red bell pepper, chopped
- 1 large onion, chopped
- 3-4 cloves of garlic, minced or chopped
- 2-3 stalks celery, peeled and chopped
- 2 large carrots, peeled and chopped
- 2 cups frozen green peas, thawed

Direction

- Pick through and rinse beans.
- Place in a 4 quart pot, and cover with at least 3-4 inches of water.
- Bring to a boil for 2 to 3 minutes.
- Cover, and let stand in the refrigerator overnight.
- Drain and rinse beans.
- Place beans in crockpot with canned tomatoes, broth, white wine, and vegetables.

- Cover, and cook on low for 7 to 8 hours.
- In a skillet, cook the sausage over medium heat until done.
- Slice links into 1/2 inch pieces.
- Add meat to crockpot, and cook soup another 30 to 60 minutes.

249. Polish Sausage Stew Recipe

Serving: 6 | Prep: | Cook: 480mins | Ready in:

Ingredients

- 10 3/4oz can of cream of celery soup
- 1/3c packed brown sugar
- 27oz can sauerkraut, drained
- 1 1/2lbs Polish sausage, cut into 2 inch pieces and browned
- 4 medium potatoes, cubed
- 1c chopped onions
- 1c shredded monterey jack cheese

Direction

- Combine soup, sugar, and sauerkraut.
- Stir in sausage, potatoes, and onions.
- Cover and cook on low for 8 hours, or on high 4 hours.
- Stir in cheese and serve.

250. Polish Sausage Stew Bigosz Recipe

Serving: 6 | Prep: | Cook: 120mins | Ready in:

Ingredients

- 4 Tbs butter or oil
- 1 lg onion thick sliced
- 1 head of cabbage, cut in 8th lenthwise
- 2 lbs quality Polish sausage cut into 1/4 inch thick slices
- 2 to 3 tart green apples, washed and unpeeled and quartered
- 3 tomatoes ,quartered
- 2 bay leaves
- 1 Tbs white vinegar
- pinch of sugar if apples not overly sweet

Direction

- Sauté onion in butter till soft in a Dutch oven
- Add cabbage slices and sausage
- Add tomatoes and apples with bay leaf and vinegar
- Cover tightly and simmer for about 2 hours
- Before serving, skim off fat, remove bay leaf and correct seasoning
- Serve in bowls with a good crusty bread
- If there is any left, flavor improves with age!

251. Polish White Borscht Recipe

Serving: 6 | Prep: | Cook: 20mins | Ready in:

Ingredients

- 1 or 2 rings Polish kielbasa
- water as needed
- Roux: flour and water to thicken
- hard cooked eggs
- 1 - 2 Tbs vinegar
- pepper as needed

Direction

- Cover 1 or 2 rings of kielbasa w/ water & bring to a boil.
- Simmer 30 mins or so till the sausage is thoroughly cooked.
- Remove the sausage & cool the cooking liquid.
- Once the fat has solidified, remove it and reserve

- Depending on your dietary preferences you can make this soup high or low fat.
- For high fat & the most flavor, melt the reserved fat in a sauce pan & combine w/ an equal amount of flour to make a roux.
- Bring the sausage liquid up to a boil & whisk in the roux to get a thin consistency, coating a spoon.
- For a low fat, remove a 1/2 cup of the cooking liquid & add 1 to 2 TBL flour to make a slurry.
- Bring the sausage liquid up to a boil & whisk in the slurry to get a thin consistency, coating a spoon.
- After the broth has been thickened, add the sausage that has been cut into 1/8 to 1/4" slices.
- Also add 1 or 2 hard cooked eggs that have been sliced.
- Finally, add 1 TBL vinegar, more or less to taste.
- Generally no need to add salt, but pepper to taste.
- Ladle into soup bowls with generous helping of sausage & egg slices & serve with rye or pumpernickel bread.

252. Polski Potato And Sauerkraut Soup Recipe

Serving: 4 | Prep: | Cook: 50mins | Ready in:

Ingredients

- 6-7 medium size potatoes. cut it into small chunks
- 1 (15 ounce) can/jar sauerkraut. drained
- 1 large onion, chopped
- 2 garlic cloves, finely chopped or minced
- 1 - 2 ribs of celery, peeled and chopped
- 1/2 teaspoon caraway seeds, 1 bay leaf, 5 pepper corns and a sprig of thyme or rosemary tied in a small piece of cheesecloth
- Note: If you have juniper berries in your cupboard, then add a couple to the above blend
- salt and pepper to taste
- 2 - 3 Tbsps. sour cream
- 1 lb. Polish kielbasa, cut into chunks
- 1 Tbsp. vinegar
- parsley for garnish

Direction

- Place onions, garlic and celery into the saucepan with a splash of oil and sauté over low heat until onions are light golden in colour but do not brown.
- Add enough water to cover the potatoes with salt and bouquet garni
- Allow to cook for 15 minutes then add sauerkraut and Polish kielbasa.
- Cook for at least 25-30 minutes or until potatoes are soft.
- Add sour cream, pepper and vinegar if needed.
- Garnish with chopped parsley.
- Note: If you are not familiar with the term "bouquet garni" it is a bundle of herbs tied into a piece of cheesecloth. This is done so that you taste the essence of the herbs without actually consuming the seeds, stems or leaves.

253. Pork Chile Verde Recipe

Serving: 8 | Prep: | Cook: 180mins | Ready in:

Ingredients

- 4 pounds natural pork butt/shoulder, trimmed of fat and cut into 2-inch cubes
- 2 teaspoons kosher salt
- 1 teaspoon freshly ground black pepper
- flour for dredging
- 1/4 cup oil
- 3 sweet yellow onions
- 2 green bell peppers, cut into 1-inch cubes

- 2 Anaheim or poblano chiles, cut into 1-inch cubes
- 2-3 jalapenos, seeds removed, and finely chopped
- 6 garlic cloves, peeled and finely chopped
- 1 1/2 pounds tomatillos, roasted, peeled and chopped
- 1 tablespoon dried oregano
- 2 tablespoons ground cumin
- 2 teaspoons ground coriander
- 2 dried turkish bay leaves
- 1 bunch cilantro leaves, cleaned and chopped
- 4 cups chicken stock (preferably homemade)

Direction

- Season the pork meat generously with salt and pepper, lightly flour. Heat oil in a heavy-bottomed skillet over medium high heat and brown pork chunks well in small batches, on all sides. Lift pork out of pan and place in a wide soup pot. Discard a little bit of the excess fat and place the onions and peppers in the same skillet and sweat over moderate heat, stirring occasionally until limp, about 5 minutes. Add all of the chiles and cook an additional 3-4 minutes, then add the garlic and cook 1-2 minutes more.
- Add the sautéed vegetables, chopped roasted tomatillos, dried herbs and cilantro to the meat, cover with the chicken stock and bring up to a boil and reduce to a slight simmer. Cook for 2-3 hours uncovered or until the pork is fork tender.
- Adjust the seasoning to taste with salt and pepper.
- I like to serve my pork chile verde in a fresh, warm flour tortilla: Place chunks of pork in tortilla, roll up, ladle chile verde sauce over. Homemade refried organic black beans topped with sharp white cheddar, side of sour cream and garnished with fresh cilantro sprigs :-)

254. Portugese Bean Stew Recipe

Serving: 6 | Prep: | Cook: 100mins | Ready in:

Ingredients

- 1 lb dried navy or great northern beans, picked over
- 1 lb sliced bacon
- 1 large onion, chopped
- 3 garlic cloves, minced
- 4 to 5 cups water (I add some chicken broth in place of some of the water)
- 1 (6-oz) can tomato paste
- 1 lb Portuguese chouri·o or Spanish chorizo (cured spicy pork sausage), cut into 1/4-inch-thick slices
- 1/2 teaspoon dried hot red pepper flakes, or to taste
- 1 tablespoon paprika

Direction

- Soak beans in cold water to cover by 2 inches 8 hours.
- Cook bacon in a 4- to 6-quart heavy pot until crisp. Transfer to paper towels to drain. Spoon off (and discard) all but about 3 tablespoons fat in pot. Cook onion in reserved fat over moderate heat, stirring frequently, until golden, 7 to 9 minutes. Add garlic and cook, stirring, until it begins to turn golden.
- Drain beans and add to onion mixture with remaining ingredients (except bacon). Bring to a boil, then simmer, covered, stirring occasionally, until beans are tender, about 1 1/2 hours. (Older beans will take longer to cook and require more water during cooking.) Crumble bacon into beans and season with salt and pepper before serving.

255. Portuguese Bean Soup Recipe

Serving: 10 | Prep: | Cook: 30mins | Ready in:

Ingredients

- 1/2 lb. chorizo sausage, chopped
- 1/4 c. of olive oil
- 2 chopped carrots
- 1 c. of chopped onion
- 3 qts. of chicken broth
- 1 1/2 tbsp. cayenne pepper
- 1 (15 ounce) can of drained kidney beans
- 1/2 c. tomato paste
- 5 chopped stalks of celery
- 5 chopped tomatoes
- 3 small potatoes, peeled and the chopped
- Add salt and pepper to you individual taste

Direction

- You will first add sausage to a large pan over medium flame.
- Cook the sausage until brown.
- You will need to drain the grease off the sausage then crumble the sausage with your fingers.
- Next you will sauté the carrots, onion and celery in a large pot over medium flames.
- Once the veggies are tender, add the tomatoes, potatoes, kidney beans and the broth.
- After this has come to a boil, add a dash of cayenne pepper and the tomato paste.
- You will then reduce the flame to low and let it simmer for around 20 min.
- Just before serving, add the sausage.
- Use salt and pepper according to your individual taste.

256. Portuguese Traditional Fish Soup Recipe

Serving: 4 | Prep: | Cook: 60mins | Ready in:

Ingredients

- 2 pounds fresh fish of your choice (salmon, seabass, fresh cod, monkfish...)
- 1/2 pound tiger prawns
- 5 table spoons olive oil
- 1 carrot
- 2 potatoes
- 1 onion
- 4 garlic cloves
- 1 pound good red tomatoes (peeled)
- 1 red chili (if you like it)
- 1/2 pint white wine
- coriander leaves
- salt
- pepper
- 6 pints water to boil the fish and prawn (add more later if needed)

Direction

- Boil the fish and the prawns in water seasoned with salt and bay leaf.
- Use a big pot and start cooking the chopped onion, garlic and carrot in olive oil. Let it be in low heat for 10 minutes stirring occasionally so it doesn't burn.
- Add the skinless potato in cubes, the tomato and the wine. Let it cook for 10 minutes and don't forget to stir.
- Save the boiled fish water and add to your vegetables.
- Taste it and season again if needed. It's time to add the chili pepper.
- While you let the soup cook, get rid of the fish bones.
- 45 minutes later take the chili and the bay leaf and use a hand blender to transform your veggies and water into a nice broth.
- After blended add the fish, prawns and chopped coriander leaves.
- Cook for 10 minutes more and serve.

257. Posole Rojo Recipe

Serving: 6 | Prep: | Cook: 240mins | Ready in:

Ingredients

- 1 lb. natural boneless pork shoulder
- 6 organic chicken thighs (with bone preferably)
- 1 large onion, peeled (divided)
- 4 cloves garlic, peeled and sliced (divided)
- 2 teaspoons dried oregano (divided)
- ground cumin, to taste
- 2 teaspoons kosher salt (divided)
- 24 peppercorns (divided)
- 8 Cups water (divided)
- 6 dried New Mexico chiles
- 1 12-Ounce package "Los Chileros" white corn Posole (hominy) OR
- 1 (1 lb, 13 oz) can golden hominy
- Note: if using canned hominy, drain and rinse first
- Condiments:
- homemade salsa fresca
- 1 cup diced red onion
- 2 ripe avocados, peeled and cut into small chunks
- 4 limes, quartered
- 12 fresh flour tortillas, cut in thick strips and fried until crisp
- Fresh cilantro

Direction

- If using dried pozole corn (which I highly recommend), place the pozole in a large pot covered with unsalted water, and cook for 3 to 4 hours, until the corn has softened. (Better done the night before; allow the pozole to cool in the cooking broth overnight. Important: Salt should only be added when the kernels are nearly tender.)
- Cut pork into 1-inch cubes and place in a large saucepan. Place chicken thighs in another large saucepan. Cut onion in half. In each saucepan, place each half of onion, 2 cloves garlic, cumin to taste, 1 teaspoon kosher salt, 12 peppercorns and 4 Cups water. Bring each to a boil and skim foam from surface. Cover pork and simmer for 1 hour. Cover chicken and simmer for 45 minutes.
- While meats are cooking, break open the chilies and remove the seeds and veins. Put the chilies to cook in a medium sized pot. Cover with fresh water and gently boil until chilies are very soft. Let the mixture cool then purée the chilies with a little of the cooking water in a blender to make a paste. Strain and set aside.
- Remove cooked pork and chicken from broths with a slotted spoon, shred the meats and place in a large pot or Dutch oven.
- Strain broths and discard the solids. Add both broths with drained, cooked hominy and red chili puree to pork and chicken.
- Put pot on stove top and bring to a boil; reduce heat. Cover and simmer 30 minutes.
- Taste pozole and add more salt if needed. Serve in large soup bowls and add condiments to soup as desired.

258. Potato Pinto Bean Soup Recipe

Serving: 4 | Prep: | Cook: 40mins | Ready in:

Ingredients

- 1 medium onion, chopped
- 1 cup sliced shiitake or button mushrooms
- 2 tsp olive oil or cooking oil
- 3 large potatoes, peeled and thinly sliced
- 29 fl oz canned vegetable, chicken or beef broth
- 15 oz canned pinto beans, rinsed and drained
- 1/2 cup buttermilk
- 1 tbsp cornstarch
- 1 tbsp snipped fresh basil
- 1/4 cup plain yogurt or dairy sour cream
- fresh basil sprigs
- (optional)

Direction

- In a large saucepan cook the onion and mushrooms
- In hot oil until onion is tender but not brown.
- Add the potatoes and broth.
- Bring to a boil.
- Reduce heat.
- Cover and simmer about 30 minutes or until potatoes are tender.
- Stir in beans.
- In a small bowl, stir together the buttermilk and cornstarch.
- Stir into potato mixture.
- Cook and stir till thickened and bubbly.
- Cook and stir for 2 minutes more.
- Stir in 1 tbsp. snipped basil.

259. Pressure Cooker Chili Recipe

Serving: 10 | Prep: | Cook: 30mins | Ready in:

Ingredients

- 2 lbs beef cubes
- olive oil
- 1 large onion, chopped
- 1 cubanelle pepper, chopped
- 1 long hot pepper, chopped
- 4 cloves garlic, chopped
- 2 Tablespoons chili powder, or to taste
- 1 Tablespoon ground cumin
- 1 teaspoon hot pepper flakes (optional)
- 1 bottle beer or ale
- 1 cup beef broth
- 2 14-ounce cans diced tomatoes
- 2 14-ounce cans black beans, drained and rinsed
- sour cream and shredded cheese for serving

Direction

- Heat pressure cooker over medium high heat, add oil.
- Working in batches, brown beef cubes on all sides in oil.
- Remove browned beef to a plate.
- Add more oil if necessary and cook onions over medium heat until slightly browned and softened.
- Add peppers and garlic to onions and cook, stirring for 3 minutes.
- Add chili powder, cumin, and optional hot pepper flakes.
- Cook, stirring for 2 minutes until fragrant.
- Add beer and deglaze pan.
- Put beef back in pressure cooker and add all remaining ingredients except sour cream and cheese.
- Bring up to pressure and cook for 20 minutes.
- Let sit for 10-15 minutes to release pressure and finish cooking.
- If thicker chili is desired, just simmer uncovered for another 15 minutes to thicken it up.

260. Pretty Darn Good Chili Verde Recipe

Serving: 10 | Prep: | Cook: 90mins | Ready in:

Ingredients

- 4 - 5 pounds pork shoulder or pork butt, cut into 1/2 inch cubes
- 2 whole poblano peppers
- 8 whole anaheim chili peppers*
- 2 whole jalapeno peppers
- 2 whole serrano peppers
- 1 onion, diced (preferably a white onion)
- 3 cloves garlic, minced
- 8 - 10 tomatillos, husked and cut into quarters
- 1 (14 - ounce) can tomatoes with their juice
- 1 tablespoon dried oregano (or to taste)
- 1 teaspoon cumin (or to taste)
- salt and pepper, to taste

- *LindySez: You can used canned anaheim chilies such as Ortega brand, if desired, in place of the fresh anaheim chilies.

Direction

- Roast the peppers on a broiler pan under the broiler, or over a flame until the skin blisters. Put them into a bowl covered with plastic wrap. Allow to sit for about 15 minutes. Peel the skin off, seed and dice. Set aside. (Do not run the pepper under water as this just dilutes their flavor, a little bit of skin hanging on won't hurt anything.
- Meanwhile; pour a small amount of oil in a large Dutch oven; begin browning the pork cubes, in small batches, until they are all browned. Set them aside as they brown.
- Put the tomatoes along with their juice and the tomatillos into the work bowl of a food processor or blender; pulse them until coarsely chopped. Set aside.
- Once the pork is all browned, add it back to the pan; add the onions and garlic. Sauté until the onion and garlic are soft; add the tomatillos and tomato mixture along with the peppers, oregano, cumin, salt and pepper. Bring to a boil; put on the lid and bring to pressure. Reduce heat to just maintain pressure and cook for 1 hour. Turn off the heat and allow the pressure to release naturally, about 10 minutes. Slowly open the lid allowing any remaining pressure out; taste and adjust seasonings. Serve with some good corn and/or flour tortillas or cornbread. Chopped cilantro goes well on top; as well as Cotija cheese.
- Lindy Sez: This recipe can also be cooked in a low oven (300 - 325 degrees F). Cover and allow to cook 3 hours.
- Per Serving: 598 Calories, 42g Fat (14g Sat, 18g Mono, 5g Poly); 42g Protein; 14g Carbohydrate; 3g Dietary Fiber; 161mg Cholesterol; 161mg Sodium.

261. Prize Winning Chicken Sausage Jambalaya Recipe

Serving: 10 | Prep: | Cook: 60mins | Ready in:

Ingredients

- Splash of vegetable oil
- 1 lb Andouille sausage, 1/8 inch slices
- 1 lb pork smoked sausage, 1/8 inch slices
- 1 lb ham, course chopped
- 10 - 12 chicken thighs, skin removed (count and write number down)
- 2 cups onion, chopped
- 2 cups celery, chopped
- 1 cup green bell pepper, chopped
- 1/4 cup minced garlic
- 1 can (16 oz) diced tomatoes, do not drain
- 1 cup dry white wine
- 1 tbs brown sugar
- 3 bay leaves
- 3 tbs dried basil
- 3 cups chicken stock
- 1 bottle (12 oz) dark beer + additional bottles for cook
- 1 1/2 - 2 tsp salt
- 6 or 8 or 10 shakes louisiana hot sauce
- 3 1/2 cups raw long-grain rice or converted rice
- 1 cup green onions, sliced
- 1/2 cup fresh parsley, minced

Direction

- Using heavy Dutch oven, brown sausages and ham, Remove and set aside
- In same pot, lightly brown chicken, remove and set aside.
- Wilt onions, celery, and bell pepper. Add garlic at end of cooking.
- Melt brown sugar on top of veggies. Do not burn.
- Add tomatoes, wine, chicken stock, bay leaves, hot sauce, beer, salt and basil and simmer for about 5 minutes.

- Place all meats back in pot and simmer covered for about 30 minutes or until chicken is tender and pulling from bone.
- Remove all chicken (this is the reason you counted) and pull meat from bone making sure not to get any gristle. Place pulled chicken meat back in pot.
- Adjust seasonings -- salt and hot sauce.
- Add rice, stir in and turn heat to very low. Barely simmering.
- Cover and let cook for another 30 minutes. Check halfway to stir once and make sure rice is not sticking. Stir once again in six or seven minutes. If trying to stick, turn heat lower. If rice is dry, but not tender, add additional liquid (such as a couple of slugs from the beer you are drinking)
- When rice is tender remove from heat.
- Stir in green onions and parsley and let sit to absorb liquid.
- Note: You can leave wine out, but if you do, increase chicken stock by one cup.
- Serve with French bread and green salad.

262. Pumpkin Chili Mexicana Recipe

Serving: 8 | Prep: | Cook: 45mins | Ready in:

Ingredients

- 2 tablespoons vegetable oil
- 1/2 cup chopped onion
- 1 cup (1 large) chopped red or green bell pepper
- 1 clove garlic
- 1 pound ground turkey
- 3 1/2 cups (two 14.5-ounce can diced tomatoes
- 1 3/4 cups (15-ounce can) 100% Pure pumpkin
- 1 3/4 cups (15-ounce can) tomato sauce
- 1 1/2 cups (15 1/4-ounce can) kidney beans
- 1/2 cup (4-ounce can) Diced Green Chiles
- 1/2 cup whole kernel corn
- 1 tablespoon chili powder
- 1 teaspoon ground cumin
- 1 teaspoon salt
- 1/2 teaspoon ground black pepper

Direction

- HEAT vegetable oil in large saucepan over medium-high heat.
- Add onion, bell pepper and garlic cook, stirring frequently, for 5 to 7 minutes or until tender.
- Add turkey; cook until browned. Drain.
- ADD tomatoes with juice, pumpkin, tomato sauce, beans, chiles, corn, chili powder, cumin, salt and pepper.
- Bring to a boil
- Reduce heat to low.
- Cover; cook, stirring occasionally, for 30 minutes.

263. Pumpkin Pie Soup Aka Pumpkin Soup Recipe

Serving: 8 | Prep: | Cook: 30mins | Ready in:

Ingredients

- pumpkin Pie Soup A.k.a. pumpkin Soup
- This is like a freshly baked pumpkin pie in your soup bowl. It is super easy to make and tastes great served hot or cold. I was in search of a good pumpkin Soup, only to find that they all contained ingredients that I certainly did NOT associate with a pumpkin pie. So I made this recipe up. Hope you enjoy it!

Direction

- 6-8 servings 30 min 10 min prep
- 2 cups apple cider
- 1 (14 1/2 ounce) can chicken broth (about 2 cups worth)
- 1 (29 ounce) can pumpkin puree

- 1 cup granulated sugar (you may need slightly more or less depending on how tart your cider is)
- 1 tablespoon cinnamon
- 1/2 tablespoon cloves
- 1/2 tablespoon nutmeg
- 1/2 tablespoon allspice
- 1 pint heavy whipping cream
- In large pot on LOW HEAT, combine all ingredients EXCEPT whipping cream; while stirring frequently, bring to simmer.
- Allow to simmer for 10 minutes, stirring occasionally.
- Stir in heavy cream; serve.

264. Quick Chili Cheese Dip Recipe

Serving: 8 | Prep: | Cook: 5mins | Ready in:

Ingredients

- 1 Pkg cream cheese
- 1 can of chili - spread on top of cr.cheese
- 1 1/2 - 2 cups shredded cheddar cheese

Direction

- 1 Pkg. Cream cheese softened, spread on platter.
- 1 can of Chili - spread on top of cream cheese
- 1 1/2 - 2 cups shredded cheddar cheese - sprinkle on top of chili
- Microwave for 1-2 min. Eat with Tostitos or Fritos

265. Quick N Tender Deer Stew Recipe

Serving: 12 | Prep: | Cook: 150mins | Ready in:

Ingredients

- 1-2 lbs. deer meat
- water to cover
- beef bouillon - 1 cube per cup of water, plus 1-2 extra
- 1/2 cup onion
- Dash black pepper
- 5-1/2 oz. spicy tomato juice (such as V8)
- Dash hot sauce
- 2 cans stewed tomatoes with liquid
- 3 cups chopped red potatoes
- Any fresh or canned vegetables you have on hand (except peas) such as:
- mixed vegetables, drained
- mexicorn
- mushrooms, drained
- green beans, drained

Direction

- Preparing fresh deer meat before starting stew:
- Soak for 1-2 days in salted ice (do not drain melt water, just add more ice); when finished soaking, wash meat thoroughly, making sure to get every last hair. This method works best in cold weather.
- Stew:
- Pressure cook first 5 ingredients for 25 minutes then release steam and check to see if deer is tender. If not, add a cup of water and a bouillon cube, pressure back up, cook for 15 more minutes, and then release steam again.
- Pour off about half of cooking liquid.
- Add rest of ingredients and simmer for 2 hours, or until potatoes are tender.

266. REALLY GOOD HOT AND SOUR SOUP Recipe

Serving: 4 | Prep: | Cook: 20mins | Ready in:

Ingredients

- 3Dried wood ears

- These are a dried mushroom you find in a chinese supply store along with the tiger lily buds...
- 20Dried tiger lily buds
- 3cHot water
- ¼lb.pork butt
- MARINADE:
- ½tsRice wine or dry sherry
- ½tsCornstarch1tsSesame oil
- 1tsSalt2oz.fresh mushrooms, sliced
- ¼cShredded bamboo shoots
- 3" square bean curd, sliced
- 2tbWorcestershire sauce
- 2tsWhite vinegar and adjust (U always add more)
- 5tbCornstarch
- 5tbWater1
- egg, beaten
- ½tsBlack pepper
- (I add a few shakes of crushed red pepper flakes)
- ½tsWhite pepper
- 1tbSesame oil6
- ½cChicken broth or stock
- ¼cWater chestnuts

Direction

- Soak wood ears and lily buds in 3 cups hot water 15 minutes to soften.
- Remove stems from softened wood ears.
- Shred wood ears with a cleaver.
- Slice pork into thin strips.
- Use a cleaver to chop strips into shreds.
- Combine marinade ingredients in a small bowl.
- Add pork shreds; mix well.
- Let stand 15 minutes.
- Combine chicken broth and salt in a medium saucepan.
- Bring to a boil over high heat; reduce heat to medium.
- Add mushrooms, water chestnuts, bamboo shoots, wood ears and lily buds to broth.
- Simmer 3 to 4 minutes.
- Add pork shreds with marinade and bean curd.
- Bring to a boil.
- Add Worcestershire sauce and vinegar, if desired.
- I did not think the Worcestershire belonged so I used soy sauce.
- Dissolve cornstarch in 5 tablespoons water to make a paste.
- Slowly stir into soup.
- Cook over medium heat until soup thickens slightly.
- Stir egg into soup.
- Add black pepper, white pepper and sesame oil.
- This make an incredible soup. Better than the take out or restaurants. Try it.
- Enjoy

267. Ratatouille My Way Recipe

Serving: 8 | Prep: | Cook: 60mins | Ready in:

Ingredients

- 1 medium eggplant cut in medium sized cubes (don't bother to peel)
- 2 zucchini, scrubbed and cut in medium chunks
- 2 yellow squash, scrubbed and cut in chunks
- 1 full head of garlic, most of the outer peel pulled off
- 2 large yellow or red onions cut in coarse wedges, ends removed
- 1 8 oz. box of white button mushrooms or crimini, wiped down left whole (on the small side, don't aim for huge mushrooms here, you don't want to cut them; that is more work)
- 1 green pepper, seeded and cut in medium chunks
- 1 red pepper seeded and cut in medium chunks
- 1 yellow pepper seeded and cut in medium chunks

- 2 lbs. of roma tomatoes stem ends removed and halved
- extra virgin olive oil
- sea salt
- fresh ground black pepper
- fresh marjoram if available (I mysteriously kill mine each year)
- several sprigs of fresh thyme leaves
- a handful of parsley, stemmed and coarsely chopped
- two long pieces of lemon rind, juice of one lemon
- sprinkle of crushed red pepper flakes
- few shavings of parmesan if you must gild the lily

Direction

- Line a large sheet pan with foil.
- Preheat oven to 450 degrees while you prep the veggies.
- Toss the eggplants, zucchini, yellow squash in a scant amount of oil, you don't want them drenched.
- Put on sheet pan, don't crowd and sprinkle with sea salt and ground black pepper.
- Trim the end of the garlic bulb and rub generously with oil.
- Toss peppers and onion and mushrooms with scant oil and put on the other end of the sheet pan. Again, don't crowd.
- If there is too much for your sheet pan, fix up another sheet pan and plan to rotate the pans while cooking.
- DON"T ROAST THE TOMATOES.
- Roast the veggies in hot oven for about 20 minutes. You want each to maintain their shape but to get a tiny bit of char on the surface.
- Don't cook the garlic to mush, you want to be able to just squeeze it from the bulb.
- Finally dump all the veggies into a stock pot, including the prepped tomatoes, squeeze the garlic out of the bulb into the pot, the thyme leaves, the marjoram, the lemon rind and the lemon juice and a sprinkle of red pepper flakes.
- Cook over low heat until the tomatoes give up their juice and stir only enough to combine, you don't want to break down the veggies anymore if at all possible.
- At service, fish out lemon rind and thyme branches if you left them whole. Garnish with chopped fresh parsley and long shavings of parmesan.

268. Ratatouille The Best Recipe

Serving: 4 | Prep: | Cook: 10mins | Ready in:

Ingredients

- 2 Tbsp. olive oil
- 1 large onion, chopped
- 3 cloves garlic, minced
- 3 cups eggplant, chopped
- 3 cups zucchini, chopped
- 3 tomatoes, chopped
- One half cup parsley, chopped
- 1 cup water or chicken broth
- salt and pepper
- 1 pound penne pasta
- 1 cup parmesan cheese, grated

Direction

- Heat olive oil in large pot. Cook onion and garlic in olive oil until tender. Add eggplant and simmer for 10 minutes. Add zucchini, tomatoes, parsley and about 1 cup of water or chicken stock.
- Salt and pepper to taste. Simmer on low/medium heat for about 30 minutes until vegetables are tender, stirring frequently. You may need to add just a little more water as the dish cooks down. Meanwhile cook pasta according to package directions until just al dente. Drain pasta and spoon into bowls. Spoon ratatouille over pasta and top with cheese.

269. Ratatouille Not The Movie Recipe

Serving: 6 | Prep: | Cook: 90mins | Ready in:

Ingredients

- 1 med. eggplant
- 2 lg. potatoes
- 2 lg. green peppers
- 1 lg. Spanish or red onion
- 2 med. size zucchini
- 3 lg. tomatoes, or a 28-oz. can plum tomatoes, well drained
- 8 garlic cloves, crushed, or 2 tbsp. minced garlic
- 2 tbsp. olive oil
- 2 tsp. dried basil
- 1 tsp. each of dried leaf oregano and salt
- 1/2 tsp. each of ground black pepper and cayenne
- 1 tbsp. sugar
- 2 tbsp. balsamic vinegar

Direction

- Peel eggplant and cut into 1-inch cubes.
- Put cubes in a large deep saucepan or casserole that will hold at least 16 cups.
- Cut unpeeled potatoes into 1/2-inch cubes, slice peppers into 1-inch pieces and finely chop onion.
- Add them to casserole.
- Slice zucchini lengthwise into quarters, then slice it into 1/2-inch pieces and add to other vegetables.
- Coarsely chop unpeeled tomatoes and add them along with any juices, or cut drained canned tomatoes into bite-size pieces and add.
- Preheat oven to 375 F.
- In a small bowl, stir garlic with oil and all seasonings.
- Add mixture to casserole and stir vigorously until vegetables are evenly coated.
- Place casserole in oven and bake, uncovered, for 1 1/2 hours.
- Stir at least every half hour.
- Vegetables at the top will appear to dry out but will actually take on a little roasted taste.
- Baking uncovered also allows some vegetables juices to evaporate, and concentrated vegetable juices will be soaked up by eggplant and zucchini.
- Remove hot casserole from oven.
- Sprinkle mixture with sugar. Drizzle in vinegar and stir until well mixed.
- Taste.
- You may want to add more salt, sugar or vinegar. It's wonderful sprinkled with lots of chopped fresh basil, coriander or parsley.
- GREAT ADDITION: Stir together 1/2 cup chopped parsley, 3 cloves minced fresh garlic and the finely grated peel of 1 lemon, then sprinkle over top of hot casserole just before serving.

270. Razor Clam Chowder Recipe

Serving: 6 | Prep: | Cook: 45mins | Ready in:

Ingredients

- 2 pounds razor clams
- 4 ounces meaty salt pork, rind removed and cut into 1/3-inch dice (You can substitute thick bacon if necessary)
- 4 T. unsalted butter
- 1 medium onion (7 to 8 ounces), cut into 1/4-inch dice
- 2 stalk celery, cut into 1/4-inch dice
- 2 sprigs fresh thyme, leaves removed and chopped (1 teaspoon)
- 1 1/2 pounds Yukon Gold, Maine, or other all-purpose potatoes, peeled and cut into 1/2-inch dice
- About 3 cups water

- 1 1/2 c. heavy cream (or up to 2 cups if you wish)
- Freshly ground black pepper
- Kosher or sea salt if needed
- FOR GARNISH:
- 2 T. chopped fresh Italian Parsley
- 2 T. minced fresh chives

Direction

- 1. To shuck the clams, have two small bowls ready, one for the shucked clams and one to catch the juices that drip from the clams as they are shucked. Run a teaspoon (the eating kind, not the measuring kind) lengthwise down the inside of each clam, keeping it pressed against one shell. That will loosen the first shell. Then turn the spoon over and run it back along the other side, releasing the clam and scooping it out of the shell. To dice the clams, first slice each one lengthwise in half, then cut across into about 1/4 to 1/3-inch pieces to make small dice. You will want to chop the area near the siphon (the part that sticks out of the clam shell and looks like a long, dark neck; the meat in this area is tough) a little finer than the rest of the clam, which is more tender.
- You should have about 2 cups {1 pound} diced clams. Place the clams back in the bowl and strain the juice over. Cover and refrigerate until ready to use.
- 2. Heat a 4- to 6-quart heavy pot over low heat and add the diced salt pork. Once it has rendered a few tablespoons of fat, increase the heat to medium and cook until the pork is crisp and golden brown. With a slotted spoon, transfer the cracklings to a small ovenproof dish, leaving the fat in the pot, and reserve cracklings until later.
- 3. Add the butter, onion, celery, and thyme to the pot and sauté, stirring occasionally with a wooden spoon, for about 8 minutes, until the vegetables are softened but not browned.
- 4. Add the potatoes and just enough water to barely cover them. Turn up the heat, bring to a boil, cover, and cook the potatoes vigorously for about 10 minutes, stirring every few minutes, until they are soft on the outside but still firm in the center. If the broth hasn't thickened, smash a few potatoes against the side of the pot and cook a minute or two longer to release their starch.
- 5. Reduce the heat to low and stir in the chopped razor clams. As soon as the chowder comes back to a simmer, remove it from the heat and stir in the cream. Season to taste with pepper and possibly a pinch of salt. (The clams do add their own salt, but since the chowder is made with water instead of clam broth, I have found that it usually benefits from a pinch of salt.) If you are not serving the chowder within the hour, let it cool a bit, then refrigerate; cover the chowder after it has chilled completely. Otherwise, let it sit at room temperature for up to an hour, allowing the flavors to meld.
- 6. When ready to serve, reheat the chowder over low heat; don't let it boil. Warm the cracklings in a low oven, around 200 degrees F for a few minutes.
- 7. Ladle the chowder into cups or bowls, making sure the clams, onions, and potatoes are evenly divided. Scatter the cracklings over the individual servings and sprinkle with the chopped parsley and chives.

271. Real Chinese Sweet And Sour Soup Recipe

Serving: 2 | Prep: | Cook: 20mins | Ready in:

Ingredients

- # chicken breast, ¼ lb thinly sliced
- # Fresh shitake mushrooms, 2 ozs
- # Chinese soy sauce, 1 tablespoon
- # beef broth, 8 ounces
- # rice wine vinegar, 1 tablespoon
- # sugar, 1 teaspoon
- # lemon juice, 1 teaspoon

- # corn starch, 1 and ½ teaspoons

Direction

- Ok, mix the cornstarch with twice as much water, then the soy sauce and beef broth.
- Add that all to a saucepan and heat up over medium heat to a boil.
- Add the chicken (which should be really thinly sliced and given a light sprinkle with some sea salt) and the mushrooms, vinegar, sugar, and lemon juice.
- Give that about 5 minutes on medium low, then you're done.
- Simple and easy!
- Optional: Some people have been known to add Lo Mein Noodles or Bok Choy for color to the broth.

272. Red Bell Pepper And Sweet Potato Soup Recipe

Serving: 2 | Prep: | Cook: 10mins | Ready in:

Ingredients

- 1 small onion, chopped
- 1 clove garlic, minced
- 1 red bell pepper, cut in bite sized chunks
- 1 sweet potato, pealed and cut in bite sized chunks
- 1 cup tomato juice
- 2 cups vegetable bouillon
- salt and pepper
- lemon juice
- chili powder
- tabasco to taste
- fresh basil

Direction

- Fry the garlic, onion, sweet potato and pepper over a medium heat for approximately 10 minutes.
- Add the vegetable bouillon and tomato juice. Puree the mixture to a nice smooth consistency.
- Cook the soup on a low heat.
- Season with pepper chili powder, salt, lemon juice and Tabasco.
- Allow the soup to simmer for around 15 mins.
- Garnish the soup with basil leaves cut in fine strips.

273. Red Chili Shrimp Recipe

Serving: 4 | Prep: | Cook: 15mins | Ready in:

Ingredients

- 500 gm medium shrimp-shell and devein, leave tails on and drain well
- 10 fresh large red chilies-discard seeds and stalks
- 5 shallots-peeled
- 3 cloves garlic-peeled
- 1 level tsp salt (or to taste)
- 1/2 level tsp sugar
- 1/4 cup water
- juice from 1-2 calamansi limes (cherry sized asian green limes)

Direction

- Cut up chilies, shallots and garlic and pop in the blender. Process with minimal water till you get a not too smooth paste.
- Heat 1/2 cup OR 6tbs oil in a wok or deep pan till very hot then fry shrimp only till they change colour. Remove from pan, leaving oil behind and set aside.
- Add another tbsp. oil to pan and when hot, add chili paste and fry till fragrant and glistening. Return shrimp to pan and stir for about 3 minutes.
- Season and add lime juice (to taste) and water. Stir well. Turn off heat and serve with white or coconut rice and sliced cucumbers if you like.

274. Red Lentil Soup Recipe

Serving: 4 | Prep: | Cook: 40mins | Ready in:

Ingredients

- 1 cup dry red lentils
- 1 cup butternut squash - peel and seeds removed, and cut into cubes
- 1 small onion, diced
- 1 tbsp fresh ginger root, minced
- 2 tbsp tomato paste
- 1 garlic clove, chopped
- 1 tbsp peanut oil
- 1 pinch fenugreek seeds
- 1 pinch cayenne pepper
- 1 tsp curry powder
- 1/3 cup fresh cilantro, finely chopped
- 1 pinch ground nutmeg
- 2 cups water
- salt and pepper, to taste

Direction

- In a large pot, over a medium heat, warm the oil then cook the onion, ginger, fenugreek and garlic until onion becomes tender.
- Add the lentils, squash, and cilantro, then stir in the coconut milk, tomato paste and water. Season with the cayenne pepper, curry powder, nutmeg, salt, and pepper then bring to a boil. Reduce heat to low, and simmer for 30 minutes, or until lentils and squash become tender. Serve.

275. Remys Ratatouille Recipe

Serving: 6 | Prep: | Cook: 240mins | Ready in:

Ingredients

- Piperade (bottom layer):
- ½ red bell pepper, seeds and ribs removed
- ½ yellow bell pepper, seeds and ribs removed
- ½ orange bell pepper, seeds and ribs removed
- 2 tablespoons extra-virgin olive oil
- 1 teaspoon minced garlic
- ½ cup finely diced yellow onion
- 3 tomatoes (about 12 ounces total weight), peeled, seeded and finely diced, juices reserved
- 1 sprig fresh thyme
- 1 sprig flat-leaf parsley
- ½ bay leaf
- kosher salt
- For the vegetables:
- 1 medium zucchini (4 to 5 ounces) sliced in 1/16-inch-thick rounds
- 1 Japanese eggplant (4 to 5 ounces) sliced into 1/16-inch-thick rounds
- 1 yellow (summer) squash (4 to 5 ounces) sliced into 1/16-inch-thick rounds
- 4 roma tomatoes, sliced into 1/16-inch-thick rounds
- ½ teaspoon minced garlic
- 2 teaspoons extra-virgin olive oil
- ⅛ teaspoon fresh thyme leaves
- kosher salt and freshly ground black pepper
- For the vinaigrette:
- 1 tablespoon extra-virgin olive oil
- 1 teaspoon balsamic vinegar
- Assorted fresh herbs (such as thyme flowers, chervil, thyme)
- kosher salt and freshly ground black pepper

Direction

- Make the piperade, preheat oven to 450 F. Line a baking sheet with foil.
- Place pepper halves on the baking sheet, cut side down. Roast until the skins loosen, about 15 minutes. Remove the peppers from the oven and let rest until cool enough to handle. Reduce the oven temperature to 275 F.
- Peel the peppers and discard the skins. Finely chop the peppers, then set aside.
- In medium skillet over low heat, combine oil, garlic, and onion and sauté until very soft but not browned, about eight minutes.

- Add the tomatoes, their juices, thyme, parsley, and bay leaf. Bring to a simmer over low heat and cook until very soft and little liquid remains, about 10 minutes. Do not brown. (Note: I like to place the herbs in a metal tea infuser -- that way, when it's time to discard the herbs, I simply lift out the infuser and save myself the trouble of fishing around for a soggy bay leaf.)
- Add the peppers and simmer to soften them. Discard the herbs, then season to taste with salt. Reserve a tablespoon of the mixture, then spread the remainder over the bottom of an 8-inch oven-proof skillet.
- To prepare the vegetables, arrange the sliced zucchini, eggplant, squash, and tomatoes over the piperade in the skillet.
- Begin by arranging eight alternating slices of vegetables down the center, overlapping them so that ¼ inch of each slice is exposed. This will be the center of the spiral. Around the center strip, overlap the vegetables in a close spiral that lets slices mound slightly toward center. All vegetables may not be needed. Set aside.
- In a small bowl, mix the garlic, oil and thyme, then season with salt and pepper to taste. Sprinkle this over vegetables.
- Cover the skillet with foil and crimp edges to seal well. Bake until the vegetables are tender when tested with a paring knife, about two hours. Uncover and bake for another 30 minutes. (Lightly cover with foil if it starts to brown.)
- If there is excess liquid in pan, place it over medium heat on stove until reduced. (At this point it may be cooled, covered and refrigerated for up to two days. Serve cold or reheat in 350 F oven until warm.)
- To make the vinaigrette, in a small bowl whisk together the reserved piperade, oil, vinegar, herbs, and salt and pepper to taste.
- To serve, heat the broiler and place skillet under it until lightly browned. Slice in quarters and lift very carefully onto plate with an offset spatula. Turn spatula 90 degrees as you set the food down, gently fanning the food into fan shape. Drizzle the vinaigrette around plate.
- NOTE: Can also make individual servings in small skillets.

276. Rich Cabbage Soup Recipe

Serving: 6 | Prep: | Cook: 30mins | Ready in:

Ingredients

- 2 c. of shredded cabbage
- 1 c. of sliced carrots
- 1 c. of frozen green peas
- 3/4 c. of sour cream
- 1 tbsp. of olive oil
- 3 tbsp. of bacon bits
- 1 chopped onion
- 1 tbsp. of all-purpose flour
- 3 (14.5 oz) cans of chicken broth
- 1 tsp. of salt
- 1/4 tsp. of ground black pepper
- 1 bay leaves

Direction

- Add some olive oil to a large pan over a medium flame.
- Now sauté the onion and bacon bits approx. 5 min.
- Then stir in the flour until coated.
- Add the chicken broth, stirring around 3 min. (until thickened)
- Now add to the mixture cabbage, carrots, salt, pepper, and bay leaf.
- Leave the flame on low for around 20 min.
- Just before serving, add peas and sour cream.
- Remove bay leaf just before you ladle the soup.

277. Rich Roasted Veggie Stock Recipe

Serving: 8 | Prep: | Cook: 140mins | Ready in:

Ingredients

- 2 carrots, roughly chopped
- 3 large celery stalks, roughly chopped
- 1 large onion, roughly chopped
- 2 large tomatoes, cored and quartered
- 5 whole cloves garlic
- 5 oz mushrooms, halved
- 16 cups water
- 1/2 cup parsley, chopped
- 1 tsp whole black peppercorns

Direction

- Preheat oven to 400F.
- Place carrots through mushrooms on a foil-lined baking sheet. Pour 1/4 cup water over top of the vegetables.
- Roast for 20 minutes.
- Scrape all vegetables and juices from the sheet into a large pot, add the 16 cups water, parsley and peppercorns.
- Bring stock to a boil, then reduce heat to a simmer.
- Cook, covered, 1 hour, then uncover and simmer 1 hour longer.
- Strain stock, discard solids and keep in fridge or freezer to store.

278. Roasted Butternut Squash Soup Recipe

Serving: 8 | Prep: | Cook: 70mins | Ready in:

Ingredients

- 1 halved and seeded butternut squash
- 2 large peeled and quartered onions
- 1 medium head of garlic
- 6 c. of vegetable broth
- 1 c. of plain yogurt
- 6 c. of vegetable broth
- 1 bay leaf
- 1 tsp. of brown sugar
- 1 tp. of mild curry powder
- 1/2 tsp. of dried oregano
- 1/2 tsp. of ground cinnamon
- 1/4 tsp. of ground nutmeg
- salt and pepper to taste
- 1/4 c. of chopped fresh parsley (optional

Direction

- First you need to preheat oven to 350 degrees.
- Then line a baking sheet with aluminum foil.
- Now place your squash halves and onion on the baking sheet.
- Take your garlic and cover with foil and place beside the other veggies and roast for approx. 45 to 60 min. (squash is tender)
- Let these cool.
- Now you want to squeeze garlic until they become paste into blender. Scrape squash into blender also and puree until creamy.
- Now add this mixture back to pot and add veggie broth and stir.
- Then add the bay leaf, brown sugar, curry powder, oregano, cinnamon, nutmeg, and salt and pepper.
- Let all of this simmer around 10 min.
- Take this off the heat and add in your yogurt.
- Take out the bay leaf and ladle and serve!

279. Roasted Garlic Soup Recipe

Serving: 6 | Prep: | Cook: 40mins | Ready in:

Ingredients

- About 4 bulbs of garlic
- 3 T olive oil
- 1 quart chicken or vegetable stock
- 1/2 c dry white wine

- juice of 1/2 lemon
- 3 egg yolks
- Chopped parsley
- ¾ cup of sour cream or plain yogurt
- ground almonds

Direction

- Preheat the oven to 400. Take the some of the papery outer layers of skin covering the garlic bulbs, but leave the skins on the individual cloves. With your scissors, snip off the very tips of each garlic clove. Lay a sheet of aluminum foil on a baking pan. Arrange the garlic on the foil. Brush each bulb with 1 or 2 teaspoons of the olive oil. Wrap the aluminum foil around all the garlic and pinch the seams shut. Place in the preheated oven and roast for about half an hour.
- Allow the roasted garlic to cool enough that you can handle them. Squeeze each clove out of its skin. Mash them with the tines of a fork. Combine with the stock in a pan and simmer over medium low heat for about 15 minutes. Add the wine and lemon
- Beat the egg yolks with a wire whisk. Then slowly incorporate a little bit of the garlic broth, just a spoonful at a time until you've added about a cup of the broth to the egg. Then combine the two mixtures together slowly, heat until almost boiling, and serve.
- Garnish each bowl of soup with a dollop of sour cream or yogurt, fresh chopped parsley, and ground almonds.

280. Roasted Carrot Ginger Soup With Lemon Yogurt Recipe

Serving: 4 | Prep: | Cook: 60mins | Ready in:

Ingredients

- 1 clove garlic, minced
- 1 can coconut milk
- 1 2inch ginger, peeled and grated
- 500 grams carrots, washed, peeled and sliced
- 1/2 liter water
- 1 small onion, finely chopped
- salt and pepper to taste
- 2 tsp. turmeric
- 1 tsp. ginger powder
- sugar
- for the yogurt
- 1&1/2 tsp. ground coriander
- 4 tbs. soy yogurt
- 1 tbs. corn syrup or fine sugar
- 4 tbs. lemon juice
- 1 tsp. cumin

Direction

- Preheat the oven to 250 (C).
- Put the sliced carrots and grated ginger in a baking dish and add a bit of (non-flavourful) oil.
- Roast the carrots for about 1 hour, turning with a spoon once every fifteen minutes.
- Meanwhile, make the yogurt sauce.
- When the carrots are soft, sauté the onion until glassy, add the garlic, ginger powder and turmeric.
- Add the coconut milk and then the roasted carrots and ginger.
- Puree the mixture. It will be a thick soup. If you prefer it thinner, add a bit of water.
- Season to taste with salt pepper and ginger.
- Serve the soup in a shallow bowl with a generous dollop of yogurt in the middle.

281. Rockin Morrocan Stew Recipe

Serving: 8 | Prep: | Cook: 40mins | Ready in:

Ingredients

- 2 tsp olive oil
- 1 c. chopped onions

- 1/2 c each: diced celery and chopped green pepper
- 1 cup chopped mushrooms
- 3 cloves minced garlic
- 3 c chicken or vegetable broth
- 3 cups peeled, cubed sweet potatoes
- 1 can (19 oz) diced tomatoes
- 1 can (19 oz) chickpeas, drained and rinsed
- 1 tbsp lemon juice
- 2 tsp grated gingeroot
- 1 tsp each: cumin, curry, coriander & chili powder
- 1/2 tsp salt
- 1/4 tsp pepper
- 1/4 c raisins (optional)
- 2 tbsp each: peanut butter and cilantro (optional)

Direction

- Heat olive oil in a large, saucepan over medium high heat. Add onions, celery, gr pepper, mushrooms and garlic.
- Cook and stir until veggies begin to soften about 3 minutes.
- Add remaining ingredients, except raisins, p. butter and cilantro.
- Bring to a boil. Reduce heat to low and simmer, covered for 20 minutes or until sweet potato is tender.
- Stir in raisins, p. butter and cilantro. Mix well. Simmer for 5 more minutes.
- ENJOY!

282. Root Beer Barbecue Beans Recipe

Serving: 8 | Prep: | Cook: 20mins | Ready in:

Ingredients

- 5 slices bacon, diced
- 1 medium onion, diced
- 2 (16-ounce) cans of beans, preferably Bush's baked beans
- 1 cup root beer (regular, not diet)
- 2 tablespoons dark molasses
- 1/2 teaspoon dry mustard
- 1/4 teaspoon garlic salt
- 1/4 teaspoon lemon pepper
- 2 to 3 whole ribs celery

Direction

- Cook the bacon with the onions in a medium saucepan over a grill or side burner until the bacon is brown and crisp, and the onions have become transparent and are just starting to brown.
- Add all of the remaining ingredients.
- Bring to a boil over medium-high heat; then reduce the heat and simmer, stirring often, until the mixture is slightly thickened, about 20 minutes.
- Remove the celery and serve the beans hot.

283. SLOW COOKER IRISH STEW Recipe

Serving: 6 | Prep: | Cook: 480mins | Ready in:

Ingredients

- 2 lbs. lamb, well trimmed of fat and cut into 1-1/2 inch cubes
- 1/2 cup flour
- 1/2 teaspoon ground black pepper
- 1 teaspoon minced garlic
- 3-4 potatoes, peeled and cut into 1-inch cubes (see note)
- 3 carrots, peeled and sliced (or use baby-cut carrots for convenience)
- one small onion, coarsely chopped
- 1 cup beef broth
- one 10 ounce package frozen peas (do not thaw)

Direction

- Spray a 3.5 quart crockpot with no-stick cooking spray.
- Combine flour and pepper. Toss with lamb cubes to coat well. Place meat in crockpot. Add garlic, potatoes, carrots, and onion. Pour beef broth over meat and vegetables and stir gently to combine.
- Cover and cook on LOW setting 8-10 hours. About 15 minutes before serving, stir in frozen peas. The stew should be thick enough on its own, but if the gravy is a bit on the thin side, thicken it with a flour/cold water paste and cook until nicely thickened, about 10-15 minutes.
- Note: Peeling the potatoes helps the starch in them thicken the stew without adding a thickener, so don't scrimp on the amount of potatoes. We love this served with Irish soda bread

284. STOVE TOPSKILLET TAMALE PIE Recipe

Serving: 6 | Prep: | Cook: 30mins | Ready in:

Ingredients

- 1 Pound ground beef
- 1 Package McCormick taco seasoning
- 1 can (8 ounces) tomato sauce
- 1 can (14 ounces) kidney beans, undrained
- 3/4 cup water
- 1 package (8 ounces) corn muffin mix
- 1 cup shredded cheddar cheese
- 1/4 cup sliced green onions
- 1/4 cup minced green pepper (optional)

Direction

- 1. Brown meat in large skillet on medium-high heat. Drain fat.
- 2. Stir in Seasoning Mix, tomato sauce, beans and water. Bring to boil. Reduce heat to low; cover and simmer 10 minutes.
- 3. Meanwhile prepare corn muffin mix as directed on package. Drop small spoonfuls of batter over meat. Cover. Cook on low heat 15 minutes or until corn bread is cooked through.
- 4. Sprinkle with cheese and green onions. Cover. Cook on low heat until cheese is melted.
- I cut back on the taco seasoning and add Cumin to get the taste without the heat. I also add sliced black olives to the sauce. Extra cheese is always nice!
- Enjoy!

285. Saltymikes Best Gumbo Recipe

Serving: 12 | Prep: | Cook: 120mins | Ready in:

Ingredients

- 1 lb shrimp
- 1 lb. bay scallops
- 2 qts. water
- 2 Tbls. butter
- 1/2 cup olive oil
- 1/2 cup flour
- 1 lb. lump crab meat (imitation is OK if you don't have crabmeat)
- 1 lb. smoked sausage links, diced
- 1 medium onion, chopped
- 1 bell pepper, chopped
- 2 ribs celery, chopped
- 1/4 cup parsley, chopped
- 3 cloves garlic, chopped
- 2 16 oz. cans stewed diced tomatoes
- 1 16oz. package frozen cut okra
- 2 bay leaves
- 2 Tbls. worcestershire sauce
- salt to taste
- 1/2 tsp. black pepper
- 1/2 tsp. cayenne pepper
- 6 cubes prepared fish bullion

Direction

- Boil shrimp (in shells) in 2 qts. Water. DO NOT DRAIN. Peel and devein shrimp. Set shrimp aside in refrigerator. Cook scallops in the same water. Remove scallops and set aside when done. Add Fish bullion and shrimp shells to water and continue boiling to make a fish stock.
- In a large (8 qt. or larger) heavy Dutch Oven make a very dark brown roux with the butter, olive oil and flour. Add diced smoked sausage, onions, bell pepper, celery, garlic and parsley and saute until veggies are tender. Add tomatoes and cook 15 minutes. Add okra, fish stock, bay leaves, Worcestershire sauce, black pepper and cayenne. Bring to a slow boil for 10 – 20 minutes, then reduce to simmer, stirring occasionally. Add salt to taste. Add the shrimp, scallops and crab meat. Continue cooking until the gumbo simmers for about an hour. Add additional cayenne or hot sauce to taste.
- Serve over steamed rice. This gumbo is best if cooked a day in advance, refrigerated overnight and re-heated and served the second day.

286. Saltymikes Oyster Stew Supreme Recipe

Serving: 8 | Prep: | Cook: 20mins | Ready in:

Ingredients

- 2-3 pints shucked oysters with liquor
- 3-4 large potatoes, diced
- 2 cloves garlic, minced
- 6 chicken bullion cubes
- ¼ cup chopped parsley
- 2 sticks + 2 Tbsp butter (lightly salted is OK) or
- 2 sticks butter + 2 Tbsp bacon drippings
- 1/2 cup buttermilk
- 1 quart half and half
- 1 quart whole milk
- salt and black pepper to taste

Direction

- Melt 2 Tbsp. butter or bacon drippings in heavy skillet. Separate oysters from liquor. Season oysters with salt and black pepper and sauté in butter until edges begin to curl. Remove from heat and place to side.
- Steam diced potatoes in a large Dutch oven until fork tender. Drain water from the pot.
- While potatoes are hot add buttermilk, 2 sticks butter, garlic, parsley and chicken bouillon to the pot and season with salt and black pepper. Mash as if preparing mashed potatoes.
- Add half and half to the pot. Whisk over low heat until the mixture forms a thick paste.
- Add buttered oysters, oyster liquor, approx. half of the whole milk to pot. Bring to a low boil, whisking constantly. Slowly add more milk until the broth is "stew thick."
- Reduce heat to warm. Re-season if necessary.
- Serve hot with garlic toast.
- Note: For a great twist add 1 can of tomato paste, 2 tsp. of sugar and a dash or two of cider vinegar.

287. Sauerkraut SoupPolish Style Recipe

Serving: 12 | Prep: | Cook: 150mins | Ready in:

Ingredients

- 1 cello bag of refrigerated sauerkraut, drained- not rinsed
- 1 2 oz. container of dried imported mushrooms, Polish import if possible
- 1/4 cup of dry sherry or enough to cover mushrooms
- 1 large yellow onion, minced.
- 2 or 3 smoked pork neck bones
- 1 bay leaf
- a few sprigs of fresh thyme
- 1/2 tablespoon of whole peppercorns

- handful of flat leaf parsley
- 2 tbsp. of canola oil/or mixture of one butter/one oil
- 2 tbsp. of flour
- 2 quarts of low sodium chicken stock
- 1 cup of sour cream
- chives, snipped

Direction

- Drain sauerkraut don't rinse. Reserve juice and sauerkraut.
- Chop the sauerkraut to finest shred possible.
- Soak the imported mushrooms in warm sherry for 20 minutes. Strain mushrooms through a strainer lined with a coffee filter. Reserve liquid and mushrooms.
- In a heavy sauce pot, heat butter/oil, add onion and cook till translucent.
- Add flour and cook for a few minutes more to get rid of the raw flour taste. Add the neck bones to the onion/flour/butter mixture. Heat a few minutes while you prepare your bouquet garni.
- Tie the peppercorns/bay leaf/thyme/parsley in a cheesecloth bag or alternately put them in a tea ball.
- Add stock to the pot, along with the sauerkraut, mushrooms and bouquet garni.
- Simmer on low heat for almost two hours. Taste and add sauerkraut juice if you want a stronger piquant flavor.
- Remove bouquet garni and discard/remove neck bones and discard.
- In the last five minutes, add sour cream and stir gently and heat over the lowest possible heat. You don't want the sour cream to boil and curdle.
- Adjust for seasoning, adding salt or pepper.
- Serve in shallow bowls with an extra dollop of sour cream if desired and minced chives on top for garnish

288. Sausage And Bean Soup Recipe

Serving: 6 | Prep: | Cook: 180mins | Ready in:

Ingredients

- 1 cup small white beans, rinsed and drained
- 2 cups water
- 2 tablespoons butter or margarine
- 1 medium onion, finely chopped
- 3 leeks, sliced (use part of green tops)
- 2 stalks celery, thinly sliced
- 2 carrots, thinly sliced
- 1/2 cup chopped parsley
- 1 large can (49 1/2oz) chicken broth or 3 1/2 cans(14.5oz) chicken broth
- 2 medium potatoes, diced
- 1/4 teaspoon dried thyme leaves
- 1 lb Polish sausage or smoked bratwurst, sliced about 1/4-inch thick
- salt

Direction

- Bring beans and water to boiling in a medium saucepan. Boil briskly for 2 minutes, then remove from heat. Let stand, covered, 1 hour.
- In a 5 to 6 quart kettle or Dutch oven, melt butter over medium heat. Cook onion, leeks celery and carrots, stirring, until onion is soft. Mix in parsley, broth, beans and their liquid, potatoes and thyme.
- Bring to boiling. Cover, reduce heat, and simmer until beans are tender about 2 1/2 hours.
- Add sausage slices. Cover and simmer 20 minutes.
- Taste, and add salt if needed.

289. Sausage Soup Recipe

Serving: 6 | Prep: | Cook: 15mins | Ready in:

Ingredients

- 1 lb. of italian sausage
- 2 chopped onions
- 1 c. of chopped celery
- 1 c. of chopped carrots
- 1 1/2 c.of shredded cabbage
- 1 (28 oz) can of whole peeled tomatoes with juice
- 6 c. of chicken broth
- 2 tsp.of dried basil
- 2 c. of bow tie pasta
- 1/2 tsp. of garlic salt

Direction

- First you want to take a soup pot, and then cook sausage over medium flame until no pink remains.
- Next add onions, celery, and carrots.
- Let this cook uncovered approx. 5 minutes, or until onions are tender
- Then add tomatoes, chicken broth, cabbage, and basil.
- You want to let this come to a boil.
- Next you can stir in macaroni, and cover.
- Let this cook on low for approx. 10 minutes, or until pasta is tender.
- Finally you can season with garlic salt.
- Serve.

290. Scallop And Proscuitto Wontons With Safron Broth Recipe

Serving: 8 | Prep: | Cook: 15mins | Ready in:

Ingredients

- 1 lb Bay or sea scallops
- 1/2 lb coarsely chopped ground pork or mild pork sausage, sauteed drained of fat and cooled
- 1/4 lb thick slice of proscuitto, chopped fine
- 8 fresh water chestnuts, finely chopped.
- 5 Shitake dried mushrooms, soaked in hot water for 30 minutes, drained, squeezed dry and finely minced
- 1 medium egg
- 6 tablespoons finely minced shallots
- 2 tablespoons dry Spanish Sherry
- salt and pepper
- 2 teaspoons saffron threads
- 8 cups of chicken stock
- 1 bunch greeon onions, finely chopped with some greeen left for garnish

Direction

- Note: When using wonton skins, make sure that you put the floor side down on your work surface. You will poach these first in water and when they are all poached you can then add them to the wonderful chicken stock you have prepared or purchased.
- Combine first 8 ingredients. Fry a tiny bit and adjust to taste with salt and pepper.
- Place a wonton flour-side down on your workspace and place about 1 teaspoon of the filling in the middle of the wonton. Dip your finger in a bowl of water and moisten the edges. Make sure to seal. Pinch edges and twist into wonton shape. Be careful not to overstuff or your wonton will be doo-doo.
- Fill a stock pot with water to boil. Add the wontons in batches and cook until they float to the surface about 30 -45 seconds.
- Remove and place cooked wontons on a wax-papered cookie sheet until ready to add to chicken stock.
- Dissolve saffron in 1/2 cup of hot stock. Bring remaining stock to simmer. Stir in saffron. Add the wontons, and heat slowly but thoroughly for about 10-15 minutes.
- Serve with garnish if desired.

291. Seafood Chowder Recipe

Serving: 4 | Prep: | Cook: 40mins | Ready in:

Ingredients

- 2 large potatoes (peeled and diced)
- 1 quart of stock (I use 2 cups fish stock and 2 cups chicken stock for richer flavor)
- 1 bay leaf
- 2 ounces salt pork (cut into small pieces)
- 1 large onion (peeled and diced)
- 2 cans evaporated milk, or 3 cups light cream (I use the cream, but she says that if you're going to leave this on the heat for a while, use the evap. milk, as it's more stable and won't curdle.)
- 2 TBSP butter
- salt and pepper to taste
- 3/4-1 tsp dried thyme
- 2 tsp dried parsley
- 1/2 lb shrimp (peeled and deveined)
- 1/2 lb bay scallops
- 1 7 oz can chopped clams
- 1 good size fillet of firm whitefish (haddock or cod) cut into approx 2 inch pieces

Direction

- Peel and dice potatoes and put them in the stock to boil. Add the bay leaf.
- Cook the salt pork in a skillet over medium heat until enough fat is rendered to sauté the onions in.
- Remove the salt pork from the pan and cook the onions in the rendered fat.
- When the onions are translucent, add them to the potatoes in the stock. (Potatoes are ready when you can bite into them, but they are still firm.)
- Return the salt pork to the skillet and continue to cook until they're brown and crispy. Save them for garnishing the chowder later.
- Add the butter, thyme and parsley to the stock.
- Next add all of the seafood to the chowder. It should not be boiling, just simmering lightly. You don't want to overcook the seafood.
- Add the cream or evap. milk, season with salt and pepper, and just heat until the cream is heated through, don't boil.
- Serve in warm bowls, garnished with the salt pork.

292. Seafood Chowder Recipe

Serving: 0 | Prep: | Cook: | Ready in:

Ingredients

- 1 ½ cups fat free milk
- 1 (8 ounce) container fat free cream cheese
- 2 cloves garlic, minced
- 1 (26 ounce) can fat free condensed cream of mushroom soup
- 1 cup chopped green onions
- 1 cup sliced carrots
- 1 (15.25 ounce) can whole kernel corn, undrained
- 1 ½ cups chopped potatoes
- 1 teaspoon dried parsley
- ½ teaspoon ground black pepper
- ½ teaspoon ground cayenne pepper
- ½ pound shrimp
- ½ pound bay scallops
- ½ pound crabmeat
- ½ pound calamari tubes
- 1 (6.5 ounce) can chopped clams

Direction

- Place 1/2 cup milk, cream cheese, and garlic in a large pot over low heat. Cook and stir until blended. Mix in soup, green onions, carrots, corn with liquid, potatoes, parsley, and remaining milk. Season with black pepper and cayenne pepper. Simmer 25 minutes. Do not boil.
- Mix the shrimp, scallops, crabmeat, calamari, and clams, and continue cooking 10 minutes, or until seafood is opaque.
- Nutrition Facts:
- Per Serving:
- 313.7 calories; protein 34.6g 69% DV; carbohydrates 32g 10% DV; fat 5.1g 8% DV;

cholesterol 157.8mg 53% DV; sodium 1237.4mg 50% DV.

293. Seafood Gumbo Recipe

Serving: 0 | Prep: | Cook: 40mins | Ready in:

Ingredients

- shrimp - 4 lbs
- crabmeat - 2 @ 1 lb cans (we crab so we always have some in the freezer)
- green onions chopped - 1 large bunch
- bell pepper chopped - 1
- tomatoes - 2 @ 16 oz cans
- tomato paste - 1 @ 6 oz can
- water - 12 cups
- Roux (12 oz jar) - 3/4 jar
- bay leaves - 6
- worcestershire sauce - 6 TBS
- salt - 3 1/2 TBS
- parsley Chopped - 3/4 cup
- celery Seed - 1 1/2 tsp
- tarragon - 1 tsp
- black pepper - 1 TBS
- thyme - 1 tsp
- red pepper - 1/2 TBS
- okra Cut - 2 bags @ 16 oz
- Zatarain's crab Boil - 1 tsp

Direction

- Bring 12 cups of water to a boil. Add roux and be sure to stir constantly or it will stick on the bottom and burn. After roux is melted, turn temperature down on low to medium and add all ingredients except for the meat. After the okra gets tender, smash it with two large spoons and let cook for 30 minutes. Add crab meat and let cook for 10 minutes. Add shrimp and let cook 10 minutes. Turn heat off and let gumbo stand for 30 minutes before serving.

294. Seafood Okra Gumbo Recipe

Serving: 8 | Prep: | Cook: 180mins | Ready in:

Ingredients

- 1 can tomatoes
- 2 cups chopped onions
- 6 toes chopped garlic
- 2 lbs. fresh or frozen okra cut up
- 1/4 cup oil
- 1 1/2 quarts water
- 2 lbs shrimp, peeled and deveined
- 2 lbs polish or smoked sausage
- 1 Tsp. salt or less, to taste
- 1/2 tsp. black pepper
- 1/2 tsp. red pepper (cayenne)
- 1/4 cup oil
- 1/4 cup flour
- crab Meat (if you desire - add an amount to suit your taste)

Direction

- In a 4 quart casserole dish stir into 1/4 cup oil, the tomatoes, onions, garlic and okra.
- Cook covered on HIGH for 1 hour. Stir occasionally
- In a 3 cup measuring cup make roux with 1/4 cup flour and 1/4 cup oil. (A roux is flour and oil browned. It is the basic for most Creole recipes. It colors and thickens gumbos, etc.)
- Microwave the oil and flour on HIGH for 5 to 7 minutes. Watch that it doesn't burn. It should be caramel colored when finished.
- Add Roux to okra mixture along with water and seasoning. Bring to boil on HIGH and boil for 15 minutes.
- Stir in the shrimp, sausage, and crab meat if you're using it.
- Cook on MEDIUM for 30 minutes.
- Serve hot over rice with lots of either French bread or garlic bread and a nice salad

295. Shrimp Rangoon With Chili Garlic Dipping Sauce Recipe

Serving: 30 | Prep: | Cook: 30mins | Ready in:

Ingredients

- 2 Tbsp. chopped fresh cilantro
- 2 Tbsp. scallions, chopped
- 2 tsp.. fresh ginger, chopped
- 1 tsp. sugar
- 1 pkg. cream cheese, softened (8-oz.)
- 2 tsp. fresh lime juice
- Salt to taste
- 3/4 lb. cooked shrimp, peeled and deveined, diced
- 30 wonton wrappers
- peanut oil
- CHILI-garlic DIPPING SAUCE:
- 1/2 cup sugar
- 1/4 cup water
- 1/4 cup white vinegar
- 1 Tbsp. garlic, chopped
- 1/2 tsp. kosher salt
- 2 tsp.red pepper flakes or to taste

Direction

- Pulse cilantro, scallions, ginger and sugar in a food processor until minced.
- Add cream cheese, lime juice and salt, pulse until combined.
- Transfer to a bowl and stir in shrimp.
- Arrange a few wontons on a work surface.
- Place 2 tsp. shrimp mixture in the center of each wrapper, moisten with water and fold to form a triangle, pressing to seal.
- Transfer to a parchment lined baking sheet, repeat with remaining wrappers and shrimp mixture.
- Heat 1" peanut oil in a large sauté pan over medium high heat.
- Fry Rangoon in batches until golden brown on both sides, about 1 minute.
- Drain on paper towel lined plate.
- Serve hot with dipping sauce.
- CHILI-GARLIC DIPPING SAUCE:
- Simmer 1/2 cup sugar, water, vinegar 1 Tbsp. garlic and salt in small saucepan over medium heat.
- When sugar is dissolved, reduce heat to medium low and simmer until the consistency of maple syrup, about 10 minutes.
- Off heat stir in pepper flakes.
- NOTE:
- Remember to seal really well because leakage from the Rangoons cause the hot oil to splatter.

296. Simple Cinnamon Stewed Apples Recipe

Serving: 6 | Prep: | Cook: 45mins | Ready in:

Ingredients

- 6 Cups granny smith apples, peeled and chopped. (about 1 inch in size)
- 1/2 cup packed brown sugar
- 1/4 cup apple juice (or cider)
- Dash of lemon juice
- 1 teaspoon ground cinnamon
- 1/8 teaspoon ground nutmeg
- 1/8 teaspoon salt

Direction

- Combine all ingredients in a large, heavy saucepan. Cover and cook over medium-low heat 45 minutes or until apple is tender, stirring occasionally. Let stand 5 minutes.

297. Simple Fish Gumbo Recipe

Serving: 2 | Prep: | Cook: 20mins | Ready in:

Ingredients

- 2 pieces of cod, fresh or frozen, cut into chunks
- 1 large onion, diced
- 1/4 cup of diced ham, bacon, or smoked pork jowl
- 6 cloves of garlic, diced
- 2 ribs of celery, diced
- 1 cup of fresh or frozen bell pepper strips
- 1 cup of fresh or frozen okra
- 1 large can of roma tomatoes
- 8 ounces of chicken stock or water (if needed)
- Tabasco sauce to taste
- Worchester Sauce to taste
- 2 teaspoon Gumbo Filé powder

Direction

- If you're using frozen fish get it out of the freezer.
- Add to a 4 quart pan on medium heat the pork, celery, onion, and garlic. Allow this to cook until soft.
- Add the pepper strips, tomatoes and stock or other liquid if needed. Bring the heat back up and then add the Tabasco and Worchester sauces to taste.
- Check for salt. Add the okra and bring back up to heat.
- Cut the fish into chunks and add it to the pot.
- Bring it back up to heat and then reduce to a simmer. Once the fish is cooked through add the Gumbo Filé and stir well.
- Serve with some parsley on top.

298. Slap Your Mama Texas Chili Recipe

Serving: 8 | Prep: | Cook: 90mins | Ready in:

Ingredients

- 2lbs. Course chili meat or ground beef
- 1lb. ground pork
- 1lb. ground italian sausage
- 24oz. Mexican Chorrizo sausage
- (2) 12oz bottles Shiner Bock beer (use what you like to drink) or 750ml Zinfindel
- 2 jalapeno peppers chopped (or more depending on where your are from)
- 2-4 tbsps. of chili powder
- 4 cloves crushed garlic
- 1 tbsp. finely chopped green onions
- 1 tbsp. black pepper
- 1-3 tsps. dry oregano
- 1 tbsp. cumin powder
- 1 tbsp. salt
- 1 16oz. can of tomato sauce (your choice)
- 1 tbsp. finely chopped green bell pepper

Direction

- Mix well all the meat in a large pot and brown (CUT OPEN ALL MEAT CASINGS and squeeze out)
- Mix well until done
- Add tomato sauce, beer or wine, and all the seasonings
- Cook over low - medium heat for 30 min. stirring occasionally to avoid sticking
- Then reduce heat to low and cover and cook 1 hour more
- Stirring occasionally
- Sample, sample and sample
- Add more whatever you think it needs (you make the call)
- Turn heat off and let cool
- Place in the refrigerator overnight (yep overnight)
- Reheat the next day and serve it your way!
- Eat one spoon full and slap the person next to you and say "Boy was he right"
- Enjoy!

299. Slow Cooker Asian Inspired Chicken Stew Recipe

Serving: 8 | Prep: | Cook: 5mins | Ready in:

Ingredients

- 2 pounds boneless, skinless chicken, cut into bite size pieces
- 2t Chinese 5-spice powder
- 1-1 1/2t red pepper flakes
- 1t celery salt
- 2T peanut or olive oil
- 2 leeks, sliced diagonally
- 10oz fresh mushrooms, sliced
- 6 cloves garlic, minced
- 24oz chicken stock
- 2-4T cornstarch
- 2 red or orange bell peppers, cut into 1 inch pieces
- 1/4 cup soy sauce
- 2T sesame oil
- salt and lemon pepper
- 5 cups cooked rice(optional)
- chopped cilantro(optional)

Direction

- Toss chicken pieces with 5-spice powder, red pepper flakes, salt and lemon pepper.
- Sauté chicken in peanut oil in large skillet, until just browned, about 5-7 minutes, then add mushrooms, leeks and garlic and cook until chicken is no longer pink.
- Place chicken, vegetables, soy sauce, celery salt and chicken stock in slow cooker. Cook on low about 4 hours until heated through and peppers are tender.
- Stir cornstarch into 1/4 cup water and add that and sesame oil to slow cooker. Stir and let cook about another hour for broth to thicken.
- Add cooked rice to slow cooker and combine before serving or serve stew over rice. Top each serving with cilantro.

300. Slow Cooker Beef And Black Bean Stew With Cornmeal Dumplings Recipe

Serving: 4 | Prep: | Cook: 10hours | Ready in:

Ingredients

- 1 lb. beef stew meat
- 1 14.5 oz diced tomatoes with green chili, undrained
- 1/2 cup minced onion
- 1/2 tsp chili powder
- 1/2 envelope taco seasoning mix (I always seem to have an open one of these!)
- 1 15 oz. can black beans, rinsed and drained
- 1 8.5 oz. can whole kernel corn
- For cornmeal dumplings:
- 1 cup of cornmeal
- 1/4 cup of flour
- 1 tsp baking powder
- 1/2 tsp of salt
- 2 eggs
- 1/2 cup of milk
- 1 Tbs butter, melted

Direction

- Line your slow cooker pot with a liner for easier clean up. Also, there isn't much moisture in this and I think it helps.
- Mix beef, tomatoes, onions and chili powder in the slow cooker. Cover and cook on low heat 8 to 9 hours.
- Stir in taco seasoning mix using a wire whisk. Stir in black beans and corn. Cover and turn to high.
- Make the dumplings:
- Combine dry ingredients. Whisk together the eggs and milk and add to the dry ingredients. Stir in the melted butter. Mix all together until smooth. Spoon batter onto the stew. Cover and cook for 30 to 35 minutes.

301. Slow Cooker Chicken Noodle Soup Recipe

Serving: 8 | Prep: | Cook: 195mins | Ready in:

Ingredients

- 4 c cooked chicken, chopped up
- 1 c celery, diced
- 2 tspn herbes (I used chervil, chives, parsley, and tarragon)
- 1 c carrots, diced
- 1/2 c frozen peas
- 1 c onions, diced
- 4 (14 oz) cans chicken broth
- 2 (10 3/4 oz) cans condensed cream of mushroom soup
- 2 c egg noodles, cooked
- salt, to taste
- pepper, to taste

Direction

- Pull the skin off your chicken and cut up the meat.
- Put your celery, onions, carrots, peas and chicken in the slow cooker.
- Stir in your broth, herbs, and mushroom soup.
- Season with a little salt and pepper (to your tastes).
- Cover this and cook it for 3-4 hours on *high* OR 8 hours on *low*.
- When it is finished, mix in your noodles and season a bit.
- Enjoy!

302. Slow Cooker Chicken Stock Recipe

Serving: 3 | Prep: | Cook: 3mins | Ready in:

Ingredients

- 1 chicken carcass
- 2 carrots
- 3 celery stalks
- 1 onion
- 1 bay leaf
- 1 teaspoon dried thyme, basil and/or sage
- 1 teaspoon whole peppercorns

Direction

- Break some of the chicken bones.
- Chop (no need to peel) the carrots into large chunks.
- Chop the celery and the onion as well.
- Put all the ingredients in a slow cooker. Any size will do, but preferably at least 4 quarts.
- Fill the crockpot 3/4 full with water, cover, then set for 10 hours on low.
- After 10 hours, add salt if you wish, then turn the crockpot off and let the broth cool for half an hour.
- Strain out the meat and vegetables and discard them.
- Chill the stock in the fridge overnight and skim off the fat.
- Put the stock in baggies, label with date and amount, then freeze.

303. Slow Cooker Chile Verde Recipe

Serving: 8 | Prep: | Cook: 9mins | Ready in:

Ingredients

- 3 pound pork butt, bone removed if one. meat cubed to 1 inch cubes
- 1 lb tomatillo tomatoes(i use small to med ones)
- 1 pasilla pepper
- 2 aneheim peppers
- 1 jalapeno
- 1 yellow onion, diced
- 1 cans of diced green chiles
- 1 1/2 cups of chicken broth
- salt, pepper to taste
- 1 1/4 tsp garlic powder
- rue-
- equal parts flour and water. mixed well with wisk

Direction

- On a foil lined baking sheet, add tomatillos, husks removed, pasilla's, Anaheim's, and

jalapeño pepper. Roast under a broiler on all sides until nicely browned. Put in a glass bowl, cover with lid to steam.
- Rinse pork and cube then add to slow cooker, add diced onion and salt, pepper, and garlic powder. Remove charred skins from peppers, and seeds, and dice and add to slow cooker, chop up all tomatillos, add to slow cooker, add the cans of diced green chiles, and broth. Stir to combine. Cover and cook on low for about 8 hours. After the meat is falling apart, to thicken sauce, make rue, and very quickly whisk in rue while drizzling in really slow to avoid lumps. Add enough to desired thickness. Serve hot, on top of fried quesadillas, or chimis, or burritos. YUM

304. Slow Cooker Chili Recipe

Serving: 12 | Prep: | Cook: 360mins | Ready in:

Ingredients

- 1 1/2 pound ground chuck
- 1 pound hot pork sausage
- 2 garlic cloves-minced
- 1 14 1/2oz can tomatoes-whole,crushed,stewed,or diced
- 1 8oz can tomato sauce
- 1 6oz can tomato paste
- 1 large onion-chopped
- 1 medium bell pepper-chopped
- 2 15oz cans kidney beans-drained
- 1/4 cup brown sugar-light or dark
- 1 tablespoon chili powder
- 1 teaspoon salt
- 1 teaspoon black pepper
- 1 teaspoon crushed red pepper
- 1 teaspoon cayenne pepper.

Direction

- Brown ground chuck and sausage in large skillet.
- Drain and transfer to slow cooker/crock pot (4 quart or larger).
- Add remaining ingredients and mix well.
- Cover and cook on low for 8-10 hours or high for 4-6 hours.
- If chili becomes too thick, add a little water.
- Can be served with corn bread and topped with sour cream, chopped raw onion, cheddar cheese, or whatever you like.

305. Slow Cooker Jambalaya Recipe

Serving: 6 | Prep: | Cook: 420mins | Ready in:

Ingredients

- 1 pound skinless, boneless chicken breast halves - cut into 1 inch cubes
- 1 pound andouille sausage, sliced
- 1 (28 ounce) can diced tomatoes with juice
- 1 large onion, chopped
- 1 large green bell pepper, chopped
- 1 cup chopped celery
- 1 cup chicken broth
- 2 teaspoons dried oregano
- 2 teaspoons dried parsley
- 2 teaspoons cajun seasoning
- 1 teaspoon cayenne pepper
- 1/2 teaspoon dried thyme
- 1 pound frozen cooked shrimp without tails
- cooked rice as desired

Direction

- In a slow cooker, mix the chicken, sausage, tomatoes with juice, onion, green bell pepper, celery, and broth.
- Season with oregano, parsley, Cajun seasoning, cayenne pepper, and thyme.
- Cover, and cook 7 to 8 hours on Low, or 3 to 4 hours on High.
- Stir in the shrimp during the last 30 minutes of cook time.

- Stir in some cooked rice as desired or just serve over cooked rice

306. Slow Cooker Kielbasa Stew Recipe

Serving: 5 | Prep: | Cook: 24mins | Ready in:

Ingredients

- 4 cups coarsely chopped cabbage
- 3 cups peeled, cubed potato
- 1-1/2 cups sliced carrots
- 1 pound cooked kielbasa, sliced
- 1/2 teaspoon dried basil, crushed
- 1/2 teaspoon dried thyme, crushed
- 1/2 teaspoon ground black pepper
- 2 14-ounce cans reduced-sodium chicken broth

Direction

- In a 4- to 5-quart slow cooker combine cabbage, potato, and carrots. Top with kielbasa. Sprinkle basil, thyme, and pepper over kielbasa. Pour chicken broth over all.
- Cover; cook on low-heat setting for 7 to 9 hours or on high-heat setting for 3-1/2 to 4-1/2 hours.

307. Slow Cooker Seafood Stew Recipe

Serving: 8 | Prep: | Cook: 300mins | Ready in:

Ingredients

- 1 cup chopped onion
- 1 cup chopped celery
- 5 cloves garlic, minced
- 1 - 28 oz. can diced tomatoes, undrained
- 1 - 8 oz. bottle clam juice
- 1 - 6 oz. can tomato paste
- 1/2 cup dry white wine or water
- 1 Tbs. red wine vinegar
- 1 Tbs. olive or vegetable oil
- 2-1/2 tsp. dried Italian seasoning
- 1/4 tsp. sugar
- 1/4 tsp. crushed red pepper flakes
- 1 bay leaf
- 1 lb. cod, cut into 1" pieces
- 3/4 lb. shelled and deveined medium shrimp, tails removed (uncooked)
- 1 - 6-1/2 oz. can chopped clams with juice, undrained
- 1 - 6 oz. can crabmeat, drained
- 1/4 cup chopped fresh parsley

Direction

- In 5 to 6 quart slow cooker, combine the first 13 ingredients (from onions down to bay leaf); mix well.
- Cover; cook on High setting for 4 hours.
- Stir fish, shrimp, clams with juice and crabmeat into stew. Reduce heat to Low; cover and cook an additional 30 to 45 minutes or until fish flakes easily with fork.
- Just before serving, remove and discard bay leaf. Stir in parsley.

308. Slow It Down Mediterranean Stew Recipe

Serving: 10 | Prep: | Cook: 3mins | Ready in:

Ingredients

- 1 butternut squash, cubed
- 2 cups cubed eggplant, with peel
- 2 cups cubed zucchini
- 1 (10 ounce) package frozen okra, thawed
- 1 cup tomato sauce (home-made or store-bought)
- 2 cups chopped onion
- 2 ripe tomatoes, chopped

- 3 carrots, sliced
- ½ cup vegetable broth
- 1/3 cup raisins
- 4 cloves garlic, chopped
- 1 teaspoon ground cumin
- ½ teaspoon ground turmeric
- ½ teaspoon crushed red pepper
- ¼ teaspoon ground cinnamon
- ¼ teaspoon paprika
- 2 teaspoons oregano

Direction

- Combine all ingredients in a slow cooker. Stir well.
- Cover, and cook on LOW for 8 to 10 hours, or until vegetables are tender.

309. Soothing CHICKEN SOUP Recipe

Serving: 6 | Prep: | Cook: 300mins | Ready in:

Ingredients

- 1 (5 to 6-pound) fowl, or 7 to 8-pounds of broilers, with neck and all giblets except liver
- 10 to 12 cups water, as needed
- 2 medium carrots, scraped and quartered
- 2 or 3 celery stalks with leaves, whole or cut in half
- 1 medium yellow onion, whole or cut in half, peeled or unpeeled
- 3 parsley sprigs, preferably the flat Italian type
- 8 to 10 black peppercorns
- 2 to 3 teaspoons coarse salt or 1 to 2 teaspoons table salt, or to taste

Direction

- Clean, trim and quarter the chicken.
- Place quartered chicken in a close-fitting 5-quart soup pot.
- A whole chicken should fit into a 6 to 7-quart pot.
- Add 10 cups water if you use broilers or 12 cups if you use a fowl.
- Water should cover chicken.
- Cover pot and bring to a boil.
- Reduce to a slow simmer and skim foam as it rises to the surface.
- Soup should cook at a simmer.
- When foam subsides, add all remaining ingredients with only 1 teaspoonful of salt.
- Cook chicken until it is loosened from the bone.
- ***** If chicken is quartered, allow 1 1/4 hours for cooking broilers and 2 1/2 to 3 hours for a fowl.
- *****If you cook the chickens whole, allow an extra 15 minutes for broilers and 30 minutes for the fowl.
- Add more water during cooking if chicken is not seven-eighths covered.
- Turn chicken 2 to 3 times during cooking.
- Add salt gradually, tasting as the soup progresses.
- Adjust the salt to your preference.
- Remove chicken, giblets, and bones and set aside.
- Pour soup through a sieve, rinse pot, and then return soup to pot if it is to be served immediately.
- Skim fat from surface of soup if it is to be served without being stored.
- =================================
- Soup can be prepared in advance up to this point.
- If you are going to store the soup, strain it over a bowl but do not skim.
- Cool thoroughly, uncovered, then cover and place in refrigerator.
- Store wrapped chicken separately in the refrigerator.
- Discard (or nibble on) giblets, bones, and soup vegetables.
- Chicken can be reheated in soup, either in quarters with bones and skins for a hearty dish, or trimmed of bones and skin and cut into smaller, easily spooned pieces.
- ENJOY! (And feel better real soon!)

310. Southwest Chicken Chowder Recipe

Serving: 8 | Prep: | Cook: 20mins | Ready in:

Ingredients

- 6 cups chicken stock/broth (it might've been more, I didn't measure)
- Leftover cooked chopped chicken or 2 boneless skinless chicken breasts chopped into bite size pieces (before cooking)
- I cooked my stock with 1/2 onion, 3 carrots, 3 celery stalks, fresh sage, fresh rosemary, black peppercorns, parsley, before straining, so I didn't add any veggies to the chowder, you might want to add some finely chopped onion if using canned broth (or not)
- 1 1/2 cups (approx.) cubed peeled red potatoes (my back was killing me, so I used frozen cubed potatoes cuz I didn't feel like peeling potatoes)
- 1 cup frozen corn kernels (or fresh if so inclined, I wasn't)
- 1 can hot fire roasted chiles (or use mild)
- Chipotle chile powder (I just shook in to taste)
- Ancho chile powder (ditto)
- cumin (about 1 tsp.)
- 1 tsp. Mexican oregano (ditto)
- 8 oz. cream cheese (I use Philly light)
- Big handful of shredded cheddar cheese (I used Mexican blend)
- salt to taste
- corn starch and water if you want it thicker

Direction

- Get your stock/broth to boiling, turn down to rolling simmer
- If adding onion, sauté in small pan w/butter or EVOO prior to adding to broth
- Add your chopped raw chicken to the broth (if using leftover cooked chicken, then add after potatoes are cooked)
- Add potatoes, (cooking in the stock helps thicken it up too) depending on whether you use raw or the frozen adjust cooking time
- Add corn
- Simmer until chicken and potatoes are cooked approx. 15 mins. (It doesn't hurt to let it simmer longer until you're ready to eat)
- Add canned chiles, oregano, chile powders to taste
- When ready to eat, turn down to low and incorporate cream cheese until dissolved completely
- Add cheddar and stir in till melted
- If the chowder isn't as thick as you like you can add the corn starch mixed with a little water to thicken it up, or instant mashed potatoes work well to thicken if you like them.
- Serve with extra shredded cheddar on top (of course!)

311. Southwest Chicken Soup Recipe

Serving: 6 | Prep: | Cook: 80mins | Ready in:

Ingredients

- 1 1/4 lb. of skinless, boneless chicken breast halves
- 1 c. of diced tomatoes
- 1/2 c. of chopped onions
- 1/2 c. of chopped celery
- 1 diced avocado
- 2 tbsp. of taco seasoning mix
- 1 c. of shredded cheddar cheese
- 2 tsp. of ground cumin
- 1/4 tsp. of ground black pepper
- 1 c. of water
- 3 (14 oz) cans of chicken broth
- 1 tbsp. of chopped fresh cilantro
- 1 tbsp. of vegetable oil
- 1 c. of crushed tortilla chips

Direction

- First preheat oven to 350 degrees.
- Then lay chicken pieces on baking sheet and sprinkle with taco seasonings.
- Let this cook 30-35 min.
- Cool and shred.
- Now add olive oil to a pot over medium flame.
- Sauté the onions and celery until tender.
- Now sprinkle the cumin, pepper, and rest of taco seasoning.
- Let these flavors simmer for approx. 30 min.
- Now add in the tomatoes, cilantro, and the chicken, and let cook approx. 5 more min.
- Serve this hot with sliced of avocado and shredded cheese and chips.

312. Spanish Lentil Soup Recipe

Serving: 6 | Prep: | Cook: 30mins | Ready in:

Ingredients

- 2 cups brown lentils
- 5 cups water
- 2 bay leaves
- 1 whole garlic head, unpeeled
- 1 whole onion
- 1 red bell pepper, diced
- 1 tomato, diced
- 2 medium potatoes, peeled, diced in chunks
- 2 carrots, peeled and diced
- 2 Tbsp bouillon (vegetal or beef)
- 2 Tbsp vinegar
- ½ tsp ground cumin
- 2 tsp salt
- Sofrito:
- 4 Tbsp extra virgin olive oil (Spanish if possible)
- 1 onion, diced
- 2 garlic cloves, diced
- 1 Tbsp smoked hot paprika*
- 1 Tbsp smoked sweet paprika*

Direction

- Wash lentils in cold running water and place in a casserole. Add cold water and the rest of ingredients. Take it to a boil and let it simmer on low heat for 30-40 minutes, depending on lentils.
- While lentils are cooking make the sofrito: heat the 4 Tbsp. oil in a shallow pan, add onion and cloves and cook until translucent. Add paprika and quickly stir, on very low heat as it burns easily. Turn heat off and set aside.
- When lentils are cooked and tender but still firm, take onion and garlic head out and discard.
- Add paprika mixture to the casserole, mix thoroughly and let it cook 10 more minutes. Let it rest for 1 hour and when ready to serve sprinkle with chopped fresh parsley.
- * Paprika, in Spain called Pimentón Dulce (sweet) or Pimentón Picante (hot), gives the dish its characteristic flavour and is well known as being the main ingredient, along with ground pork meat and other spices, of famous Spanish Chorizo. It is mainly produced in the province of Caceres, region of La Vera, in the mid-west side of Spain.

313. Spicy Cabbage Soup Recipe

Serving: 4 | Prep: | Cook: 50mins | Ready in:

Ingredients

- 1 medium onion, quartered and sliced thin
- 3 medium cloves garlic, chopped
- 1 tsp minced jalapeno pepper
- 2 tsp cumin
- 1 Tbsp dry mustard
- 5 cups + 1 Tbsp vegetable broth
- 2 Tbsp fresh lemon juice
- 2 medium sized red potatoes cut in ½ inch cubes, about two cups
- 1 15oz can diced tomatoes
- 3 cups thinly sliced savoy cabbage,

- black pepper to taste

Direction

- Heat 1 tbsp. of broth in a medium soup pot.
- Add onion and sauté for about 5 minutes. Stir in garlic and jalapeno. Continue to sauté for another minute.
- Stir in cumin and mustard, and add broth and rest of ingredients except cabbage, salt and pepper.
- Simmer for about 30 minutes, uncovered.
- Add cabbage, and cook for another 5 minutes.
- Season with salt and pepper to taste.

314. Spicy Chicken Jambalaya Recipe

Serving: 6 | Prep: | Cook: | Ready in:

Ingredients

- 1 pound boneless skinless chicken breasts (cut into 1 inch pieces)
- 10 ounces andouille sausage (sliced into rounds)
- 2 tablespoons peanut oil, divided
- 1 16oz can crushed Italian tomatoes
- 1 tablespoon cajun seasoning
- 3 minced cloves garlic
- 1 onion, diced
- 1/2 teaspoon ground black pepper
- 1 small green bell pepper, diced
- 2 stalks diced celery
- 1 teaspoon file powder
- 1/2 teaspoon red pepper flakes
- 1 teaspoon salt
- 2 teaspoons worcestershire sauce
- 1/2 teaspoon hot pepper sauce
- 1 1/4 cups uncooked white rice
- 2 1/2 cups chicken broth

Direction

- Heat up 1 tbspn of peanut oil in a large heavy pot (aka Dutch oven) over medium heat. Season up the chicken and sausage pieces with your Cajun seasoning. Sauté sausage until it is browned. Remove this with a slotted spoon (to drain) and set it aside. Add 1 tbspn of peanut oil and sauté the chicken pieces until slightly browned. Remove with a slotted spoon and set them aside.
- In the same pot, sauté bell peppers, onion, celery and garlic until all tender. Stir in the crushed tomatoes and kick it up with red and black pepper, salt, Worcestershire sauce, hot pepper sauce and file powder (ground sassafras leaves). Stir in the sausage and chicken. Cook it up for about 10 minutes remembering to stir every once in a while.
- Finally stir in rice and chicken broth. Bring this to a boil then turn down the heat and let simmer for 25 minutes (the liquid should be absorbed).

315. Spicy Corn Chowder Recipe

Serving: 4 | Prep: | Cook: 30mins | Ready in:

Ingredients

- 3 C chicken broth
- 1 large potato, diced
- 4 slices bacon
- 1 small onion, chopped
- 1 diced red bell pepper
- 1 can chopped green chilies
- 1 chipotle pepper, diced
- 1/2 teaspoon ground cumin
- 1/4 teaspoon cayenne pepper
- 1 can evaporated milk
- 4 C frozen corn
- 1/4 cup (1/2 stick) butter
- 2 C shrimp (optional)
- 1/4 cup all purpose flour
- 1 C diced tomatoes

310. Southwest Chicken Chowder Recipe

Serving: 8 | Prep: | Cook: 20mins | Ready in:

Ingredients

- 6 cups chicken stock/broth (it might've been more, I didn't measure)
- Leftover cooked chopped chicken or 2 boneless skinless chicken breasts chopped into bite size pieces (before cooking)
- I cooked my stock with 1/2 onion, 3 carrots, 3 celery stalks, fresh sage, fresh rosemary, black peppercorns, parsley, before straining, so I didn't add any veggies to the chowder, you might want to add some finely chopped onion if using canned broth (or not)
- 1 1/2 cups (approx.) cubed peeled red potatoes (my back was killing me, so I used frozen cubed potatoes cuz I didn't feel like peeling potatoes)
- 1 cup frozen corn kernels (or fresh if so inclined, I wasn't)
- 1 can hot fire roasted chiles (or use mild)
- Chipotle chile powder (I just shook in to taste)
- Ancho chile powder (ditto)
- cumin (about 1 tsp.)
- 1 tsp. Mexican oregano (ditto)
- 8 oz. cream cheese (I use Philly light)
- Big handful of shredded cheddar cheese (I used Mexican blend)
- salt to taste
- corn starch and water if you want it thicker

Direction

- Get your stock/broth to boiling, turn down to rolling simmer
- If adding onion, sauté in small pan w/butter or EVOO prior to adding to broth
- Add your chopped raw chicken to the broth (if using leftover cooked chicken, then add after potatoes are cooked)
- Add potatoes, (cooking in the stock helps thicken it up too) depending on whether you use raw or the frozen adjust cooking time
- Add corn
- Simmer until chicken and potatoes are cooked approx. 15 mins. (It doesn't hurt to let it simmer longer until you're ready to eat)
- Add canned chiles, oregano, chile powders to taste
- When ready to eat, turn down to low and incorporate cream cheese until dissolved completely
- Add cheddar and stir in till melted
- If the chowder isn't as thick as you like you can add the corn starch mixed with a little water to thicken it up, or instant mashed potatoes work well to thicken if you like them.
- Serve with extra shredded cheddar on top (of course!)

311. Southwest Chicken Soup Recipe

Serving: 6 | Prep: | Cook: 80mins | Ready in:

Ingredients

- 1 1/4 lb. of skinless, boneless chicken breast halves
- 1 c. of diced tomatoes
- 1/2 c. of chopped onions
- 1/2 c. of chopped celery
- 1 diced avocado
- 2 tbsp. of taco seasoning mix
- 1 c. of shredded cheddar cheese
- 2 tsp. of ground cumin
- 1/4 tsp. of ground black pepper
- 1 c. of water
- 3 (14 oz) cans of chicken broth
- 1 tbsp. of chopped fresh cilantro
- 1 tbsp. of vegetable oil
- 1 c. of crushed tortilla chips

Direction

- 3 carrots, sliced
- ½ cup vegetable broth
- 1/3 cup raisins
- 4 cloves garlic, chopped
- 1 teaspoon ground cumin
- ½ teaspoon ground turmeric
- ½ teaspoon crushed red pepper
- ¼ teaspoon ground cinnamon
- ¼ teaspoon paprika
- 2 teaspoons oregano

Direction

- Combine all ingredients in a slow cooker. Stir well.
- Cover, and cook on LOW for 8 to 10 hours, or until vegetables are tender.

309. Soothing CHICKEN SOUP Recipe

Serving: 6 | Prep: | Cook: 300mins | Ready in:

Ingredients

- 1 (5 to 6-pound) fowl, or 7 to 8-pounds of broilers, with neck and all giblets except liver
- 10 to 12 cups water, as needed
- 2 medium carrots, scraped and quartered
- 2 or 3 celery stalks with leaves, whole or cut in half
- 1 medium yellow onion, whole or cut in half, peeled or unpeeled
- 3 parsley sprigs, preferably the flat Italian type
- 8 to 10 black peppercorns
- 2 to 3 teaspoons coarse salt or 1 to 2 teaspoons table salt, or to taste

Direction

- Clean, trim and quarter the chicken.
- Place quartered chicken in a close-fitting 5-quart soup pot.
- A whole chicken should fit into a 6 to 7-quart pot.
- Add 10 cups water if you use broilers or 12 cups if you use a fowl.
- Water should cover chicken.
- Cover pot and bring to a boil.
- Reduce to a slow simmer and skim foam as it rises to the surface.
- Soup should cook at a simmer.
- When foam subsides, add all remaining ingredients with only 1 teaspoonful of salt.
- Cook chicken until it is loosened from the bone.
- ***** If chicken is quartered, allow 1 1/4 hours for cooking broilers and 2 1/2 to 3 hours for a fowl.
- *****If you cook the chickens whole, allow an extra 15 minutes for broilers and 30 minutes for the fowl.
- Add more water during cooking if chicken is not seven-eighths covered.
- Turn chicken 2 to 3 times during cooking.
- Add salt gradually, tasting as the soup progresses.
- Adjust the salt to your preference.
- Remove chicken, giblets, and bones and set aside.
- Pour soup through a sieve, rinse pot, and then return soup to pot if it is to be served immediately.
- Skim fat from surface of soup if it is to be served without being stored.
- ==================================
- Soup can be prepared in advance up to this point.
- If you are going to store the soup, strain it over a bowl but do not skim.
- Cool thoroughly, uncovered, then cover and place in refrigerator.
- Store wrapped chicken separately in the refrigerator.
- Discard (or nibble on) giblets, bones, and soup vegetables.
- Chicken can be reheated in soup, either in quarters with bones and skins for a hearty dish, or trimmed of bones and skin and cut into smaller, easily spooned pieces.
- ENJOY! (And feel better real soon!)

- Minced fresh cilantro
- 1 C Spicy cheese (optional), shredded
- salt and white pepper to taste

Direction

- Bring broth to a boil. Add potatoes and cook 10 minutes. Set aside.
- Cook the bacon until the fat renders. Transfer the bacon to the broth and potatoes. To the bacon fat, add the onion, red bell pepper, green chilies, chipotle pepper, cumin and cayenne. Sauté until vegetables are tender, about 8 minutes. Add the vegetables (including the corn) to the broth.
- Melt the butter in the saucepan and sauté the shrimp until they turn opaque. Add the shrimp to the broth mixture. To the butter add the flour (to make a roux) and stir 1 minute. Add the roux, milk and tomatoes to the broth. Bring mixture to boil. Add the shrimp. If desired, puree 1/3 of the soup. Ladle soup into bowls. Garnish with cilantro and cheese if desired and serve.
- Serves 4.

316. Spicy Gazpacho Recipe

Serving: 8 | Prep: | Cook: | Ready in:

Ingredients

- 2 cups diced seeded peeled cucumber
- 1 cup chopped celery
- 1 cup chopped green onions
- 1 4-ounce can chopped mild green chilies
- 3 14 1/2-ounce cans diced tomatoes in juice
- 1 slice white bread, torn into pieces
- 1/4 cup olive oil
- 1/4 cup drained capers
- 2 tablespoons red wine vinegar
- 1 tablespoon chili powder
- 2 garlic cloves

Direction

- Place 1 cup cucumber, 1/2 cup celery, 1/2 cup green onions and half of chilies in small bowl and reserve.
- Working in batches, coarsely puree remaining cucumber, celery, green onions, chilies and next 7 ingredients in blender. Pour into large bowl. Mix in reserved vegetables. Season with salt and pepper. Chill at least 6 hours and up to 1 day.

317. Spicy Lentil Soup Recipe

Serving: 4 | Prep: | Cook: 50mins | Ready in:

Ingredients

- 2 c red lentils, picked over and rinsed
- 1 serrano chili pepper, chopped (remove seeds for less heat)
- 1 large tomato, roughly chopped
- 1 1-1/2" piece ginger, peeled and grated
- 3 cloves garlic, finely chopped
- 1/4 tsp ground tumeric
- kosher salt
- 1/4 c roughly chopped fresh cilantro
- plus more for topping
- 1/4 c Greek yogurt
- Naan or other flatbread for serving.

Direction

- Combine lentils and 7 c warm water in a pot, cover and bring to boil. Add chili pepper, tomato, ginger, garlic, turmeric and 2 tsp salt. Partially cover and simmer over med-low heat, stirring frequently, until thickened, 18 to 20 mins.
- Stir in the cilantro. Thin soup with water, if desired, and season with salt.
- Mix the yogurt with 2 tsp water and pinch of salt in a small bowl. Ladle soup into bowls and top with the yogurt and more cilantro. Serve with naan.

318. Spicy Maryland Crab Soup Recipe

Serving: 8 | Prep: | Cook: 60mins | Ready in:

Ingredients

- 4 cups water
- 3 chicken parts (neck or wing)
- 1/2 cup onion (chopped)
- 2 stalks celery (chopped)
- 2 tablespoon hot sauce (I use Texas Pete)
- 2 tablespoon olive oil
- ¾ tablespoon Old Bay Seasoning (add more or less to taste)
- 1/4 teaspoon lemon pepper
- 1 tablespoon worcestershire sauce
- 2 cups red potatoes (cubed)
- 1/2 cup frozen lima beans
- 1 cup frozen green beans or frozen peas, thawed
- 8 ounces frozen corn, thawed
- 28 ounces canned tomatoes with juices
- 1 bay leaf
- 1 pound crab meat, fresh or pasteurized, regular or claw

Direction

- Place water and chicken in a 6-quart soup pot. Cover and simmer over low heat for at least one hour (as a short cut you could use 1 quart chicken broth and skip this step). Remove chicken parts, add vegetables and seasonings and simmer, covered, over medium-low heat from about 45 minutes, or until vegetables are almost done. Add crab meat, cover and simmer for 15 more minutes, or until hot. (For a milder soup, decrease amount of Old Bay and hot sauce).

319. Spicy Peanut Soup Recipe

Serving: 4 | Prep: | Cook: 15mins | Ready in:

Ingredients

- 1 cup peanut butter
- 100 grams fresh mung bean sprouts
- 2 tbs. oil
- 1 onion, chopped
- 1 clove garlic, minced
- 1/2 teaspoon cayenne pepper
- 1 tbs. fresh ginger, grated
- pinch salt
- 1 tbs. tomato paste
- 1 liter vegetable bouillon
- splash Tabasco
- 1 tbs. sugar

Direction

- Heat up your oil in a good sized sauce pan. Add in the onions and sauté until glassy.
- Put in the garlic and lightly brown it.
- Add the bouillon and the peanut butter. Stir this well to mix.
- Add the spices and tomato paste. Allow to simmer until warm and blended well.
- Season to taste with salt, Tabasco sauce and a pinch of sugar.
- Just prior to serving add the fresh mung bean sprouts. Do not cook the bean sprouts! Their natural crunchiness adds a contrast to the smoothness of the soup.

320. Spicy Rustic Red Lentil Soup Recipe

Serving: 6 | Prep: | Cook: 25mins | Ready in:

Ingredients

- 4 cups red lentils
- 2 Tblspn olive oil

- 2 carrots, diced finely
- 1 onion, diced finely
- 2 cloves garlic, chopped finely
- 1 tspn paprika
- 1 tspn cumin
- 1.5 tspn sweet paprika
- 1 tsp. tumeric
- 1 Tblspn tomato paste (or use home-made tomato paste)
- 8 cups vegetable stock or chicken stock
- finely grated rind of half a lemon
- sea salt and freshly ground pepper
- thick thick yoghurt (or use Greek yoghurt, creme fraiche, cream or feta)
- herbs of choice, chopped finely

Direction

- Sauté the carrot, onion and garlic in the oil over a low heat for 3 or 4 minutes.
- Add the paprika, sweet paprika and cumin, continue to cook over low heat for 6 - 8 minutes or until the vegetables begin to soften.
- Stir in the tomato paste and cook for another minute or two.
- Add the lentils and stock and bring to the boil.
- Cook for 20 - 30 minutes, until the lentils are mushy and the vegetables cooked.
- Stir from time to time.
- Beat the yoghurt with the herbs, or cut the feta into cubes and roll in the herbs.
- Serve the soup with feta cubes or a large dollop of thick yoghurt.

321. Spicy Thai Pumpkin Noodle Coconut Soup Recipe

Serving: 4 | Prep: | Cook: 40mins | Ready in:

Ingredients

- 17og (6oz) rice noodles
- 675g (1 1/2 lb) pumpkin, peeled and cut into bitesize chunks
- 4 tblspn olive oil
- 1/2-1 tspn dried chili flakes
- 400g (14oz) can unsweetened coconut milk
- 75g (2 1/2 oz) coconut cream
- 450ml (15fl oz) vegetable stock
- 2 tblsps light soy sauce
- 2 tspn soft brown sugar
- 75g (2 1/2 oz) bean sprouts
- 75g (2 1/2 oz) carrots, cut into thin strips
- salt, pepper
- coriander (cilantro) to garnish

Direction

- Preheat the oven to 220'/425'f/gas 7.
- Prepare the rice noodles according to the packet instructions. Put the pumpkin into a roasting dish, drizzle 2 tablespoons olive oil over it and season. Roast for 40 mins or until tender.
- While the pumpkin is roasting, heat remaining oil in a frying pan. Add chili flakes and sauté over a moderate heat for about 2 mins.
- Add the coconut milk, coconut cream and vegetable stock. Simmer gently, stirring, until the cream has dissolved. Stir in soy sauce and sugar. Season well. Mix in bean sprouts and carrots. Simmer for a further minute. Add the rice noodles and warm them through.
- Divide the chunks of pumpkin between 4 serving bowls and pour the soup over them.
- Scatter the coriander over the top'
- Enjoy!! :)

322. Spinach And Yogurt Soup Recipe

Serving: 4 | Prep: | Cook: 20mins | Ready in:

Ingredients

- 10 oz. frozen leaf spinach
- 1 medium onion chopped
- 3 scallions finely chopped
- 2 tbl vegetable oil

- ½ cup long-grain rice
- 3½ cups water
- 1 tsp tumeric
- salt and white pepper to taste
- 2 ¼ cups plain yogurt
- 1 really really crushed clove of garlic

Direction

- Defrost frozen spinach.
- Drain and cut into strips.
- In a large saucepan, fry the onions and scallions in the oil until soft.
- Add rice and stir to coat with oil.
- Pour in water, add turmeric, and season with salt and pepper. Bring to a boil,
- Simmer for 15 minutes.
- Add the spinach and cook for 5 minutes or until softened and rice is tender.
- Beat yogurt with garlic and beat into the soup.
- Heat through but don't let it boil

323. Split Green Pea Soup With A Zing Recipe

Serving: 4 | Prep: | Cook: 120mins | Ready in:

Ingredients

- 2 tablespoons oil
- 8 ounces chopped bacon
- 1 large onion, finely chopped
- 1 medium sized dried red chili (deseeded or not depending on heat desired), finely chopped
- 8 ounces green split peas, soaked overnight in water to cover
- 3 1/2 pints chicken stock
- 2 small sticks of celery with leaves, finely chopped
- A bunch of cilantro
- 2-3 bay leaves

Direction

- Heat the oil in a large saucepan.
- Add the bacon, onion and chili.
- Fry for 10 minutes over gentle heat until the onion is soft but not colored.
- Drain the split peas.
- Add them to the pot with the onions, bacon, stock, celery, and bay leaves.
- Add salt and pepper to taste.
- Bring to a boil and then lower the heat.
- Simmer for at least 2 hours or until the peas are very tender.
- If soup becomes too thick, add extra water or stock.
- Remove the bay leaves before serving.
- Serve the soup as is or puree in blender.

324. Stewed Beef Boat Noodle Soup Gkuay Dtiow Lauy Recipe

Serving: 8 | Prep: | Cook: 120mins | Ready in:

Ingredients

- 2 lb package of fresh or dry rice noodles
- 1/2 lb. tender cut of steak, thinly sliced in bite-size strips, set aside in refrigerator until use (optional)
- 1 1/2 lb of beef flank
- 8-10 beef meat balls, cut in half or leave whole (optional)
- 1/2 tsp. ground white pepper
- 4 cups fresh bean sprouts, Chinese broccoli long sliced or fresh spinach
- 1 cup short cilantro sprigs
- 4 green onions thinly sliced
- Fried garlic oil - 8 cloves of chopped garlic fried in 1/4 cup of peanut oil for topping
- 10 cups water
- 2 star anise or five spices
- 2 stalks lemongrass, cut in 2-inch segments and crushed
- 2-inch section fresh or frozen galangal, crushed (or use 6 dried pieces)
- 1 head garlic cloves, crushed whole for stock

- 1/2 cup cilantro roots
- 1/2 up Tbs. thick black soy sauce
- 1 tsp. sea salt
- SIDE CONDIMENTS :
- sliced hot pepper in vinegar
- sugar
- hot dried red pepper blended
- fish sauce

Direction

- Place a whole beef flank and all the herbs, spices and flavor ingredients in a large pot. Add water and bring to a boil. Reduce heat to low and simmer covered for 3+ hours. Remove beef flank from broth. Slice into bite-size chunks and return to broth.
- For noodle (If use fresh) separate the noodles as much as possible into single strands.
- For dry, soak in hot sink water for 10 minutes, removed and drained.
- When the soup is ready, Toss the beef meat balls into the pot and continue cooking for 15 minutes.
- In a serving bowl, place noodle, bean sprouts and spoon a few pieces of stewed beef and broth over the noodles.
- Next, blanch a few pieces of the sliced steak in the broth using the wire-mesh basket, just enough to cook to medium rare. Arrange beef slices over the noodles and spoon one or more pieces of meat balls into the bowl.
- Sprinkle with green onions and cilantro, dust with white pepper and top with fried garlic oil.
- Serve immediately with a side condiments if needed.

325. Stroganoff Soup Recipe

Serving: 6 | Prep: | Cook: 40mins | Ready in:

Ingredients

- 1 lb. ground beef
- 1/2 lb. mushrooms, sliced
- 1 small onion, chopped
- 4 cups chicken broth
- 2 tbls. red wine
- 2 tbls. red wine vinegar
- 1/2 tbls. brown mustard
- 1/2 tsp. garlic powder
- 1 tbls. dark soy sauce
- 1 tbls. worcestershire sauce
- salt and pepper to taste
- 1/2 sick butter
- 1/2 cup flour
- 1/2 cup sour cream
- 1/2 cup half and half
- 1 cup egg noodles, cooked

Direction

- Brown beef then drain
- In large pot add beef and next 10 ingredients
- Bring to boil then reduce heat and simmer 15 minutes
- In skillet, melt butter
- Add flour and cook for a minute or 2, stirring until blended
- Gradually add to soup and simmer another 15 minutes
- Reduce heat to low and add sour cream, half and half, and noodles
- Heat through

326. Stupid Easy Crock Pot Chili Recipe

Serving: 8 | Prep: | Cook: 240mins | Ready in:

Ingredients

- 2 lbs. lean ground beef, cooked and drained
- 1 tbsp onion powder
- 2 tsp minced garlic
- 1 16-oz jar picante sauce (mild, medium or hot)
- 2 14-1/2 oz cans diced tomatoes, undrained

- 1 1.25 oz packet taco seasoning (mild, medium or hot)
- 2 15 oz cans chili beans in sauce
- 1 15.5 oz can dark red kidney beans, undrained
- 1 15 oz can black beans, undrained
- 3 tbsp chili powder
- 2 tbsp ground cumin
- 1/2 tsp salt (optional)
- 1 tsp black pepper
- 1 tsp oregano
- ½ to 2 tsp red pepper flakes

Direction

- Mix all ingredients in Crock Pot. Cover; cook on HIGH for 3 to 4 hours.
- Note: To make on stovetop, mix all ingredients in a big soup pot; cover and simmer for about an hour or so.

327. Super Bowl Super Chili Bowls Recipe

Serving: 12 | Prep: | Cook: 120mins | Ready in:

Ingredients

- 2 pounds lean ground beef - at room temperature (or at least 30 minutes out of the fridge - don't "shock your meat kids" - sounds naughty doesn't it? lol)
- 4 fresh Italian sausages (2 sweet & 2 hot)
- 1 large onion - diced
- 1 med. bermuda onion – diced
- 4-5 fresh garlic cloves – minced
- 4 stalks of scallions – minced/sliced
- 2 large green sweet peppers
- 2 large red sweet peppers
- OR switch out 2 of the peppers for other colors if your budget can afford it - such as orange and yellow – chili looks incredibly amazing when you do this and doesn't affect the taste any.
- 4-6 tablespoons of olive oil
- 1 jalapeño pepper – minced with out seeds as they add even more heat (add more peppers if you like it hotter – keep seeds in if you are a football player)
- 1 large can of crushed tomatoes (28 oz)
- 1 large can of diced tomatoes (28 oz)
- 28oz or less water from rinsed out tomato cans (see below)
- 3 cans dark kidney beans
- 2 cans of your choice beans (I used 1 can of black beans and 1 can of roman beans for added interest this time)
- 1/3 cup balsamic vinegar
- 1-1/2 tablespoons salt
- 3/4 tablespoons pepper (freshly ground preferred)
- 4 tablespoons worcestershire sauce
- 3 tablespoons chili powder
- 2 tablespoons freshly minced cilantro
- 2 tablespoons freshly dried oregano
- 1 tablespoon dry mustard
- 1 tablespoon dried cumin
- 1 tablespoon garlic powder
- 1 teaspoon red chili flakes
- 6 good shakes of Tabasco sauce
- 3 good shakes of hot sauce
- 2 bay leaves

Direction

- Put large pot on stove and add ½ of olive oil (say about 3 tablespoons) and put heat on under pot.
- Add diced onions (both Bermuda and Spanish/white)
- Sauté on medium heat stirring occasionally and continue cooking for 5 minutes.
- Add cumin, fresh ground pepper, chili flakes to cooking onions. I like these spices to heat up, so that their flavors are enhanced before adding the meat to brown.
- Add sliced sausages and continue cooking till onions are looking translucent.
- Add freshly minced garlic and sauté for 2 minutes.
- Add room-temperature ground beef, stir frequently, and "break down" meat so you

- have no large "clumps" – some clumps ok, but not huge chunks.
- Add additional olive oil only if needed.
- While meat is browning, take colander and place in sink.
- Open up each can of beans and place into the colander that should be in the sink by now.
- Run water over beans thoroughly, so that all that surgery juice has been rinsed off.
- Check pot, if meat is completely cooked and not looking pink, add 1/3 cup of the balsamic vinegar.
- Don't have balsamic? You can substitute red wine vinegar, apple cider vinegar or heck red wine – you want the acidity here folks, or the juice of one lemon – it will add the brightness to your chili that I discussed earlier.
- When adding your acidic liquid of your choice (balsamic vinegar preferred), scrape bottom of pot with spoon to lift up those little extras what I call "flavor-enhancers" that were created from the caramelized onions and sausages browning.
- Add all the now rinsed beans from the colander to the pot.
- Next add the entire contents of the 2 large cans of tomatoes (1 crushed and 1 diced)
- Take each emptied can of tomatoes and add water to each to fill by half.
- Swirl gently around getting any last bits of those tomato juices and place this water as well into stock pot.
- Add all remaining ingredients expect for one green pepper and one red pepper.
- You will add these peppers during the last 30 minutes of cooking.
- Stir gently over medium heat till it starts to boil.
- Lower heat to a simmer or extra low and place lid on top of pot.
- Let simmer for an hour at least. I let it simmer for over 2 hours or more.
- Stirring every 20 minutes or when you're up getting yourself another beer during your super bowl party.
- 30 minutes prior to serving, or If you are reheating the next day, since you made this the day before your party, add the additional green and red peppers 30 minutes before serving. This will help brighten the colors and the peppers will have a little crunch to them.
- Serve this with tortilla chips, additional fresh minced chives on top of each bowl, grated cheese of your choice, and a dollop of sour cream. Voila, you are now a chili master – enjoy the super bowl!

328. Sweet And Spicy Black Bean Soup Recipe

Serving: 8 | Prep: | Cook: 30mins | Ready in:

Ingredients

- 1 tablespoon olive oil
- 2 medium-size red onions, chopped
- 2 medium-size red bell pepper, chopped
- 8 garlic cloves, minced
- 4 teaspoons ground cumin
- 3 cans black beans, drained
- 1 tablespoon chopped canned chipotle chilies
- 4 cups vegetable stock, 2 cups water
- 2 tablespoons fresh lime juice
- 3 T honey
- 2 teaspoons coarse kosher salt
- 1/4 teaspoon ground black pepper
- 1 T red wine vinegar
- 1 cup plain nonfat yogurt, sour cream
- 1/2 cup chopped seeded plum tomatoes
- 1/4 cup chopped fresh cilantro

Direction

- Heat olive oil in large nonstick skillet over medium-high heat. Add onions and both bell peppers and sauté until beginning to brown, about 8 minutes. Add garlic and cumin; stir 1 minute. Transfer mixture to 6-quart saucepan. Add beans and chipotles, then 6 cups liquid. Cover and cook on high 30 – 45 minutes. Transfer 3 cups bean mixture to blender (or use an immersion blender to puree some of the

beans in the pot); puree until smooth. Return puree to remaining. Stir in lime juice, honey, vinegar, salt, and pepper.
- Ladle soup into bowls. Spoon dollop of yogurt into each bowl. Sprinkle with tomatoes and cilantro and serve.
- *Chipotle chiles canned in a spicy tomato sauce, sometimes called adobo, are available at Latin American markets and many supermarkets.
- Don't leave out the vinegar as it gives a brightness to the soup that really livens it up. Substitute lemon or lime juice if desired.

329. Taco Soup Recipe

Serving: 7 | Prep: | Cook: 20mins | Ready in:

Ingredients

- 14.5 ounce canned diced tomatoes
- 14.5 ounce canned diced tomatoes with chilis
- 14.5 ounce canned Mexican corn with chilis
- 15.5 ounce can black beans
- 15.5 ounce can red kidney beans
- 1 large onion, chopped
- 1 package taco seasoning mix
- 1 package ranch salad dressing mix (dry)

Direction

- Sauté onion with vegetable oil cooking spray. When softened, combine all other ingredients and cook until heated through.
- Makes 7 cups.
- Serving size is 1 cup.
- 1 point per cup.

330. Tamale Filling Green Chili Recipe

Serving: 20 | Prep: | Cook: 90mins | Ready in:

Ingredients

- Tamale filling green chili
- * 1 cup green chiles, roasted, peeled, seeded and chopped
- * 3 cups shredded Jack cheese
- * 1/2 cup green chile sauce
- * season to taste with salt, pepper, garlic powder, cumin powder.
- * You may want to double or triple recipe..

Direction

- I place this filling in my prepared tamale dough (using corn husks), in that order.
- Takes about 2 min. per tamale. About 90 min to steam a big pot full.

331. Tex Mex Chili Authentic San Antonio Recipe

Serving: 6 | Prep: | Cook: 40mins | Ready in:

Ingredients

- 3 tablespoon melted lard
- 3 lbs coarse-ground beef chili meat
- 1-1/2 teaspoons salt
- 1 teaspoon black pepper
- 3 tablespoons grated or finely minced onion
- 2 minced garlic cloves
- 3/4 teaspoon dried Mexican oregano leaves
- 1 teaspoon fine ground cumin
- 4-6 tablespoons Gebhardt's chili powder
- 6 cups beef broth
- 4 tablespoons all-purpose flour

Direction

- Heat the fat in a heavy bottom cooking pot. Brown the chili meat in the hot oil until the water has boiled away and the beef is sizzling. Browning the beef in this manner greatly improves the flavor of the chili.

- Add the salt, pepper, onions, Mexican oregano and cumin. Cook stirring until the onion has softened. Add the Gebhardt's Chili Powder and mix well.
- Mix the flour into the broth without any lumps. Add the beef stock and flour mixture into the chili with liquid to cover the meat.
- Bring the chili to a boil and reduce heat to barely simmering. While stirring to prevent scorching gently simmer for about 30 minutes or until the beef is tender.
- Adjust seasoning to desired taste and serve with crackers and beans on the side or use as a sauce for tamales, enchiladas, etc.

332. Thai Shrimp And Chicken Soup Recipe

Serving: 4 | Prep: | Cook: 20mins | Ready in:

Ingredients

- 3 cups fat-free, less-sodium chicken broth
- 1 cup bottled clam juice
- 1 tablespoon fish sauce
- 2 teaspoons bottled minced garlic
- 1 1/2 teaspoons bottled minced fresh ginger
- 3/4 teaspoon red curry paste
- 1 (8-ounce) package presliced mushrooms
- 1/2 pound peeled and deveined large shrimp
- 1/2 pound skinless, boneless chicken breast, cut into 1-inch pieces
- 1 (3-ounce) package trimmed snow peas
- 1/4 cup fresh lime juice
- 2 tablespoons sugar
- 2 tablespoons (1/2-inch) sliced green onion tops
- 2 tablespoons chopped fresh cilantro
- 1 (13.5-ounce) can light coconut milk

Direction

- Combine the first 6 ingredients in a large Dutch oven, stirring with a whisk.
- Add mushrooms; bring to a boil. Reduce heat, and simmer 4 minutes.
- Add the shrimp, chicken, and snow peas; bring to a boil. Cover, reduce heat, and simmer 3 minutes.
- Stir in lime juice and remaining ingredients. Cook 2 minutes or until thoroughly heated.

333. The "cure For All Ails" Tomato Soup Recipe

Serving: 1 | Prep: | Cook: 5mins | Ready in:

Ingredients

- 1 can Campbell's condensed tomato soup
- whole milk
- 1 Tbspn butter
- A pinch of sugar
- a small shake of cayenne pepper
- Optional: I usually don't make this with anything in it, but that day I had extra cherry tomatoes I didn't want to go to waste.

Direction

- Before putting on the flame, pour out contents of soup can into a small pot, then fill the can back up with milk. Mix for a few moments to blend.
- Turn on flame to medium-high.
- Chop up the butter into small pieces so they melt better/faster in the soup.
- Put in the sugar and cayenne, mix well.
- Allow the soup to heat through but DO NOT let it come to a full boil.
- Serve immediately with toast or crackers and feel better.
- Just an FYI, you should probably soak the pot in soapy water as soon as possible, or you'll have a hell of a time trying to scrub it out later. I'm just saying.

334. The BEST Crockpot Potato Soup Recipe

Serving: 8 | Prep: | Cook: 480mins | Ready in:

Ingredients

- 5lbs. potatoes; peeled and coursely chopped
- 1 sm. onion; chopped
- 8oz. cream cheese; softened
- 3-14.5oz. cans reduced sodium chicken broth
- 1can cream of chicken soup
- 1/4t. pepper
- GARNISHES:
- crisp bacon; crumbled
- shredded cheddar cheese
- sour cream
- sliced scallions

Direction

- Put potatoes & onion in crock-pot.
- Combine the cream cheese, chicken broth, cream of chicken soup & the pepper. Add this mix to the crock-pot.
- Cover & cook on LOW for 8-10 hours or on HIGH for 4-5 hours.
- After cooking time, mash the potatoes if you want the soup to be thicker.
- Ladle into bowls and garnish with a dollop of sour cream and the cheese & bacon. Sprinkle with sliced scallions.

335. The Gypsy Stew Recipe

Serving: 8 | Prep: | Cook: 60mins | Ready in:

Ingredients

- 3/4 cup pearl barley, rinsed and drained
- 5-1/2 cups water
- 1-1/2 teaspoons salt
- 1/4 cup olive oil
- 1 medium onion, finely chopped
- 3 garlic cloves, minced
- 1/4 cup flour
- 1/2 cup red wine
- 2 tablespoons soy sauce
- 2 teaspoons paprika
- 1 teaspoon dried thyme
- 1/2 teaspoon ground cumin
- 1/2 teaspoon cayenne pepper
- 2 potatoes, peeled and cut into bite-sized pieces
- 3 large carrots, peeled and chopped
- 1-1/2 cups green beans, trimmed and cut into 1-inch lengths
- 2 cups broccoli florets (about 1 small head)
- 2 cups coarsely sliced cabbage (about 1/4 head)
- 3 cups spinach, washed and dried

Direction

- Place the barley, 1-1/2 cups of the water and 1/2 teaspoon of the salt in a medium-sized saucepan.
- Bring to a boil and then reduce the heat to low.
- Cook for about 40 minutes until all or most of the water is absorbed and the barley is cooked. Set aside.
- Heat the olive oil over medium heat in a large, preferably non-stick pot.
- Add the onion and garlic and cook, stirring occasionally, until the onion just begins to wilt (about 3 minutes.)
- Sprinkle the flour over the onions and stir to mix it in thoroughly.
- Cook, stirring frequently, for 5 to 7 minutes until the flour is a tan color (approximately the color of peanut butter), taking care not to let the flour burn.
- Add the remaining 4 cups of water, remaining teaspoon of salt, wine, soy sauce, paprika, thyme, cumin, and cayenne.
- Bring to a boil; then reduce the heat to a simmer.
- Add the potatoes and carrots and return to a simmer. Simmer, partially covered, stirring occasionally, for about 10 minutes.
- Add the broccoli and green beans and cook for another 7 minutes.

- Add the cabbage and cook for 5 minutes more. If the sauce thickens up too much at any point, simply add more water and adjust the seasonings accordingly.
- Finally, add the spinach and barley and cook until the spinach wilts and the barley heats through.
- Serve warm.

336. Three Sisters Stew Recipe

Serving: 6 | Prep: | Cook: 240mins | Ready in:

Ingredients

- 1 small sugar pumpkin or 1 large butternut or carnival squash (about 2 pounds)
- 1 tablespoon olive oil
- 1 medium onion, chopped
- 2 cloves garlic, minced
- 1/2 medium green or red bell pepper, cut into short, narrow strips
- 14- to 16-ounce can diced tomatoes, with liquid
- 2 cups cooked or canned pinto beans
- 2 cups corn kernels (from 2 large or 3 medium ears)
- 1 cup homemade or canned vegetable stock, or water
- 1 or 2 small fresh hot chiles, seeded and minced
- 1 teaspoon each: ground cumin, dried oregano
- salt and freshly ground black pepper
- 3 to 4 tablespoons minced fresh cilantro

Direction

- Preheat the oven to 400 degrees.
- Cut the pumpkin or squash in half lengthwise and remove the seeds and fibers. Cover with aluminum foil and place the halves, cut side up, in a foil-lined shallow baking pan. Bake for 40 to 50 minutes, or until easily pierced with a knife but still firm (if using squash, prepare the same way). When cool enough to handle, scoop out the pulp, and cut into large dice. Set aside until needed.
- Heat the oil in a soup pot. Add the onion and sauté over medium-low heat until translucent. Add the garlic and continue to sauté until the onion is golden.
- Add the pumpkin and all the remaining ingredients except the last 2 and bring to a simmer. Simmer gently, covered, until all the vegetables are tender, about 20 to 25 minutes. Season to taste with salt and pepper.
- If time allows, let the stew stand for 1 to 2 hours before serving, then heat through as needed. Just before serving, stir in the cilantro. The stew should be thick and very moist but not soupy; add additional stock or water if needed. Serve in shallow bowls.

337. Tinks Chili Cheese Balls Recipe

Serving: 15 | Prep: | Cook: | Ready in:

Ingredients

- 1/2 clove garlic
- 4 -ounces cheddar cheese
- 4 - ounces pepper jack cheese
- 4- ounces cream cheese
- 1/4 cup chili powder
- 1- tablespoon chopped green chiles drained well

Direction

- Mince garlic in food processor
- Cut cheeses into chunks add to food processor
- Pulse until cheeses are grated
- Then process constantly until creamy, add green chiles and mix well
- Shape into marble sized balls and roll in chili powder
- Chill until serving time
- Yields approx. 15 balls

338. Tom Ka Gai Thai Coconut Chicken Soup Recipe

Serving: 3 | Prep: | Cook: 20mins | Ready in:

Ingredients

- 6 cups good-quality or homemade chicken stock, low sodium is best
- 2 boneless, skinless organic chicken breasts
- 3 lemongrass stalks
- 6 kaffir limes leaves (fresh or frozen)
- 2 cups oyster mushrooms, roughly chopped
- 2 thumb-size pieces galangal, thinly sliced
- 2 tsp. Spiracha paste
- 1 can coconut milk
- juice of 1 or more limes
- 2+ Tbsp. fish sauce
- 2 tsp. brown sugar, plus more to taste
- pinch of fresh cilantro (we don't really like it, but if you do, add more)
- a few fresh thai basil leaves (optional)
- 2 spring (green) onions, sliced

Direction

- In a heavy bottomed pot or Dutch oven, sauté whole chicken breasts over medium heat until nicely browned and just cooked. Remove from pot and set aside.
- Add a little chicken stock and scrape up the fond in the pot, then add the rest of the stock, turn up the heat and bring to a boil.
- Meanwhile, slice and mince the lower portion of the lemongrass stalk. Retain the upper stalk for the soup pot.
- Add mushrooms, prepared lemongrass (including upper stalk pieces), kaffir lime leaves & galangal. Boil 5 minutes.
- Turn heat down to medium. Add coconut milk, fish sauce, and Sriracha. Slice reserved chicken and return to pot with any juices. Stir well. Simmer gently 1-2 minutes.
- Turn heat down to minimum. Add sugar, lime juice and stir.
- Do a taste test. Look for a balance between spicy, sour, salty, and sweet flavors. Start with salty, adding more fish sauce if not salty enough (1 Tbsp. at a time). If too sour, add a little more sugar if you need it. If too spicy (hot), add a little more coconut milk. If not spicy enough, add more Sriracha. If not sour enough, or to brighten the flavours the next day, add more lime juice.
- Ladle soup into serving bowls. Sprinkle a little fresh cilantro, basil, and spring onion over each bowl.
- **Note: if serving this to guests- especially those not familiar with Thai food, be sure to explain about what to eat and not to eat in the soup. While it is all technically edible, most people don't eat the lime leaves, galangal or lemongrass tops. You could explain that only the broth, chicken, and mushrooms are eaten, or, you could cook the soup with the galangal, leaves & stalks in a cheesecloth bouquet. I also usually leave the lemongrass stalks quite long (3 inches or so) so they don't make their way into the bowls. Otherwise, my husband & I just pick around the rest, and my dear Dad eats the whole shebang. Enjoy!
- **Another note: no, no, NO you really can't substitute ginger for galangal, or lemon zest for lemongrass, or lime juice/zest for kaffir lime leaves. The flavours are not really all that similar. Believe me, you really can find these ingredients near you, even if you don't live in a large Metropolis or somewhere with a large Asian population. Take a real good look through your ethnic aisle or market, and expect to see some variations is spelling and preparation. Do a google search before you go, and familiarize yourself with what they might look like and brands you might recognize. The lime leaves are often sold frozen or dried- frozen is best as the essential oils containing all that lovely aroma are vastly diminished in the dry variety. Even so, dry is OK, just double the amount and simmer a little longer. Same goes for galangal, I've seen it dried and powdered as well as fresh, and they will do in a pinch. Fish sauce is crazy easy to find, but try to get a

brand made in Thailand as Japanese & Chinese varieties have a different flavour. And before you ask, yes, the fish sauce really should smell that bad- what do you expect, it's fermented fish juice! Believe me, you won't notice the badness of it, just the goodness, I promise!

- If you insist on using fresh chilies, use 1 for mild, 2 for medium, and 3 for spicy.

339. Tom Ka Soup Recipe

Serving: 6 | Prep: | Cook: 20mins | Ready in:

Ingredients

- 1 or 2 cans coconut milk (12 oz), depending on how coconutty you want your soup.
- 2 cups chicken stock
- 1/2 pound boneless skinless chicken, cut into bite size pieces OR
- 1/2 pound shrimp, shelled, deveined OR omit meat altogether!
- 3 tablespoons vegetable oil
- 2 tablespoons minced fresh ginger root
- 4 tablespoons fish sauce
- juice of 1-2 limes
- 4 garlic cloves, minced
- 1 tsp - 1 Tbs red chili paste (I'm really loving Korean chili paste lately)
- 1/2 teaspoon ground turmeric
- 2 tablespoons thinly sliced green onion
- 1/2 cup mushroom, any type, sliced thin
- 1/2 cup carrot, in delicate slivers
- 1 package tofu, cut into chunks
- 1 tablespoon chopped fresh cilantro

Direction

- Heat the oil in a large pot
- Cook the chicken or shrimp until it's done
- Toss in the mushrooms and carrots, cook for a few minutes
- Add everything else, bring to a boil, then reduce heat and simmer for about 10 minutes.

- Serve and enjoy!

340. Tom Kai Gai Recipe

Serving: 5 | Prep: | Cook: 90mins | Ready in:

Ingredients

- 1 tablespoons soybean or vegetable oil
- 1 medium onion, minced
- 1 clove garlic clove, minced
- 1 stalk lemongrass, 1/4 " slices
- 2 tsp. Thai red curry paste
- six 1/8" slices galangal or ginger
- 3 kaffir lime leaves
- 4 cups chicken stock
- 3/4 pound chicken breast, sliced into thin strips
- 2 cups of oriental mushrooms (straw, shitake)
- 1 2/3 cups of unsweetened coconut milk
- red spicy peppers, sideways sliced (optional, to taste)
- 3 scallions, thinly sliced
- juice from 2 limes
- 2 tablespoons Thai fish sauce
- 1/4 cup minced cilantro
- 1/4 cup minced cilantro

Direction

- In a medium heavy saucepan sauté the oil, garlic and onion until becoming transparent.
- Stir in the lemongrass, curry paste, galangal (ginger) and lime leaves and continue stirring for 3-4 minutes.
- Add the chicken stock and bring to a boil then reduce the heat to medium and cook for 15 minutes.
- Add the mushrooms, then turn it off for 30 minutes to an hour to let the flavors meld a bit and allow the mushrooms to soak in the flavor.
- Heat the soup back up, add the coconut milk, chicken, mushrooms, peppers, and scallions. Cook for about 5 minutes or just until the

- chicken is cooked. Add the fish sauce and lime juice.
- You can either take out the flavor items that you won't eat (galangal, ginger, lime leaves, lemongrass), or leave it in to be take out by those enjoying the soup.
- Sprinkle in some cilantro and serve! Enjoy.

341. Tomato Soup Exotica Recipe

Serving: 4 | Prep: | Cook: 60mins | Ready in:

Ingredients

- 1 white onion, sliced thinly
- 1 jalapeno chili, seeded and minced
- 4 cloves garlic, slivered
- 3 lb plum tomatoes, cut in half
- 1 tsp kosher salt
- black pepper
- 1 cup water
- 1/8 tsp saffron threads, crumbled
- ½ cup quinoa, thoroughly rinsed
- ½ cup vegetable stock, hot
- ½ tbsp curry powder
- 1 tsp brown sugar

Direction

- Preheat oven to 375F.
- Lightly coat a cookie sheet with baking spray.
- Spread onion and chili pepper pieces on sheet.
- Slip garlic pieces in tomato halves, place tomatoes cut side up on sheet.
- Sprinkle with salt and plenty of pepper, mist lightly with baking spray.
- Bake 1 hour.
- Meanwhile, bring remaining 1 cup water to a boil. Add saffron and quinoa, stir and reduce heat to low.
- Cover and simmer 15 minutes.
- Scrape all cookie sheet contents into a blender or food processor, add stock, curry powder and brown sugar. Puree until smooth.

- Ladle tomato mixture into 4 serving bowls, evenly divide saffron quinoa mixture between them and serve immediately.

342. Tomato Soup Recipe

Serving: 6 | Prep: | Cook: 30mins | Ready in:

Ingredients

- Butter – – – – – – – – 1 cup
- Onion – – – – – – – – 1 finely chopped
- Tomatoes – – – – – – – 1 kg
- Tomato puree – – – – – 1 tsp
- Stock – – – – – – – – 30 oz or 1 1/2 pint
- cloves of garlic – – – – – – 3
- Bay leaf – – – – – – – – 2 leaves
- Potato – – – – – – – – – 1 large
- Carrot – – – – – – – – – 1 sliced
- salt and pepper to taste
- Sugar – – – – – – – – – 1 tsp
- corn flour for thickening – – – 1 1/2 tsp
- milk with extra cream – – – 2 oz

Direction

- 1. Melt the butter in pressure cooker.
- 2. Add onions, sliced tomatoes, carrots, spices, potato and cook for 10 minutes.
- 3. Add liquid and seasonings and stir well.
- 4. Cover the cooker, bring to pressure cook on high pressure 10 minutes and then allow to reduce to room temperature.
- 5. Sieve the soup and blend the residual, and add to the soup.
- 6. Add the corn flour, blended milk with corn flour.
- 7. Add sugar to taste.
- 8. Serve with cream poured in after the soup has been dished out and garnish with croutons.

343. Tomato And Cream Cheese Soup Recipe

Serving: 10 | Prep: | Cook: 60mins | Ready in:

Ingredients

- 2 (29 oz.) cans of diced tomatoes
- 2 stalks of chopped celery
- 2 cloves of minced garlic
- 1/2 lb. of chopped mushrooms
- 1 finely diced onion
- 1 chopped red bell pepper
- tbsp. of margarine
- 2 tbsp. of all-purpose flour
- 1 tsp. of white sugar
- 8 c. of beef stock
- 1/2 tsp. of dried basil
- 1/2 tsp. of dried rosemary
- 1/2 tsp. of dried thyme
- 1 (3 oz.) package of cream cheese
- salt and pepper to taste
- 3 tablespoons chopped fresh parsley

Direction

- First you want to put the tomatoes with the juice in buttered baking dish.
- Now you can add in the celery, garlic, and the red pepper.
- Now put a lid on this and cook for about 25 min.
- Then you want to melt some butter over medium flame.
- Next you can add in the mushrooms and onions cooking for approx. 8 min.
- Now add in the flour, sugar beef stock, basil, rosemary, and the thyme.
- Stir this constantly until it boils, then add in the baked potato and let boil.
- Put a lid on this and let this cook over low flame for approx. 30 min.
- Blend your cream cheese in the blender.
- Once this is creamy, add into the soup.
- Salt and pepper needed before serving.

344. Tortellini Soup Recipe

Serving: 6 | Prep: | Cook: 25mins | Ready in:

Ingredients

- 1 pound ground beef
- 3 1/2 cups water
- 1 can (28 OUNCES) diced tomatoes, do not drain
- 1 can of French onion soup, undiluted (can also substitue cream of mushroom soup if desired)
- 1 package of frozen green beans (9 ounces)
- 1 package of frozen cheese tortellini thawed (9 ounces)
- 1 medium zucchini, chopped
- 1 teaspoon dried basil
- salt and pepper to taste

Direction

- In a large sauce pan, cook beef over medium heat, until no longer pink, drain, add the remaining ingredients; bring to a boil cook 5 min uncovered until tortellini are tender,
- Serve with bread sticks or crescent rolls sprinkled with parmesan cheese before baking.

345. Turkey Carcass Soup Recipe

Serving: 0 | Prep: | Cook: 2hours1mins | Ready in:

Ingredients

- turkey carcass
- 4 Whole carrots, cut into pieces
- 1/2 large onion, diced
- 2 Stalk celery, diced fine
- 2 clove garlic, minced
- 2 boxes chicken broth, (64 oz)

- 1 Can fat free chicken gravy (10 oz)
- 1/2 Bag egg noodles
- 1/2 Teaspoon pepper
- 2 Tablespoon fresh parsley, chopped

Direction

- Put turkey carcass in large stock pot, cover with chicken broth. If not enough to cover carcass, add some water. Sauté onion, celery, and garlic in skillet with 2 T. butter until soft and transparent. Add to chicken broth. Add about one carrot to broth and carcass. Bring to a rolling boil on medium high heat. Lower temperature to medium low and cook for about 1 hour or until carcass is white looking.
- Remove bones from pot and discard. Mash carrot pieces. Stir in chicken gravy and pepper. Add remaining carrots and continue to cook until tender, about 15-20 minutes.
- About 1/2 hour before you're ready to serve, bring broth back to a boil, on high heat. Add egg noodles and parsley. Boil for 10 minutes. Scoop into bowls and let stand for 5 minutes.
- Serve with rolls or crackers.

346. Turkey Chili With Four Beans Recipe

Serving: 6 | Prep: | Cook: 40mins | Ready in:

Ingredients

- 1 lb. ground turkey
- olive oil
- 1/2 bottle of beer
- 1 chopped onion
- 1 chopped green bell pepper
- 1 can kidney beans (drained and rinsed)
- 1 can pinto beans (drained and rinsed)
- 1 'small' can garbanzo beans (drained and rinsed)
- 1 can black beans (drained and rinsed)
- 2 cans of diced tomatoes
- 1 can water or broth
- 1 1/2 t. cumin
- 1 cup of frozen or canned corn (frozen is better)
- salt to taste
- freshly ground black pepper to taste
- 2 T. chili powder

Direction

- In a large pot or Dutch oven, sauté the peppers and onions in olive oil until slightly limp.
- Add turkey and cook it until almost done.
- Now add in the beer (!), bring to a boil then let simmer for a few minutes until turkey is entirely cooked.
- Go ahead and add in all the beans, tomatoes and water as well as seasonings.
- Taste and adjust seasonings as necessary.
- Simmer for at least 30 minutes (or even longer if you have the extra time...will taste much better).
- If necessary, the chili can be thickened with tomato paste or thinned with water.
- Add corn about 15 minutes before serving.
- This chili tastes wonderful as a leftover.

347. Under Pressure Split Pea Soup Recipe

Serving: 10 | Prep: | Cook: 30mins | Ready in:

Ingredients

- 2 1/4 cups green split peas (about 1 pound)
- 2 cups chopped onion
- 1 cup diced peeled carrot
- 1/2 cup diced celery
- 1 bay leaf
- 2 - 3 meaty ham hocks, (depending on their meatiness)
- Cold water (everyone should have this ingredient in their home)
- salt and pepper, to taste (I add this at the end, to taste, as ham hocks have different salt and smokiness levels all the time)

Direction

- If you are in a hurry, put the split peas in the pot with the about 8 cups of cold water and start the fire. You can chop and add the vegetables as they get done.
- Add the vegetables, bay leaf, ham hocks and enough water to cover by 2 inches.
- When it comes to a simmer, close the lid on the pressure cooker; allow it to come to pressure.
- When pressure is reached, lower the heat to low, and allow to cook for 30 minutes.
- Turn off the heat; allow the cooker to cool naturally, about 5 - 10 minutes.
- Release the existing steam, uncover and check for doneness. Remove the ham hocks and set aside to cool. Allow the split peas and vegetables to just simmer on top of the stove for a few minutes until the peas are mere mush. (It's o.k. if the carrots still look like carrots, as a matter of fact, it's preferred). Add water if the soup seems too thick.
- Allow the ham hocks to cool until they don't burn your hands anymore, then, carefully cut, pull or otherwise extract the meat from the bones. Chop the meat into little fine pieces and add back to the soup. Stir well. Taste and adjust the seasonings. Serve with some good Rye bread or make some Rye Bread Croutons. YUM!
- Be sure to check your pressure cookers manufacturer's directions.
- Did you know that whoever gets the bay leaf is the boss that night? Yep, old family tradition.

348. Vegan Lentil Stew Recipe

Serving: 4 | Prep: | Cook: 30mins | Ready in:

Ingredients

- 4 to 5 cups water (start with 4 and add as you it cooks if necessary)
- 1 cup raw lentils
- 2 large carrots, thinly sliced
- 2 stalks celery, chopped
- 1 large onion, chopped
- 3 to 5 cloves garlic, crushed
- 1 tsb olive oil
- 1 14oz can Italian tomatoes
- 1/4 tsp cumin powder
- 1 tsp coriander seeds
- 1/2 tsp sea salt
- 1/4 tsp black pepper
- 3 tbs balsamic vinegar

Direction

- In a saucepan over medium heat, combine all ingredients and cook for 30 minutes, until all the ingredients are soft.

349. Vegetarian Chili With Honey Cornbread Recipe

Serving: 6 | Prep: | Cook: 60mins | Ready in:

Ingredients

- For Chili:
- 2 tablespoons olive oil
- 1 sweet onion, chopped
- half a small butternut squash, peeled and diced
- 1/2 red bell pepper, seeded, chopped
- 1/2 green bell pepper, seeded, chopped
- mild fire roasted green chilies, minced (about 4 1/2 tablespoons)
- 1 chipotle chile pepper in adobo, minced
- 1 28-ounce can diced fire roasted tomatoes with added puree (Organic Muir Glen is the brand I use)
- 2 15-ounce cans organic black beans, undrained
- 2 15-ounce cans organic pinto beans, undrained
- 2 tablespoons red wine vinegar
- 3 garlic cloves, minced

- 2 tablespoons chili powder (Trader Joe's brand is super good)
- 2 turkish bay leaves
- 2 tablespoons dried Mexican oregano
- 1 1/2 teaspoons ground cumin
- 1 1/2 teaspoons ground coriander
- 1/2 teaspoon ground cinnamon
- garnish: grated monterey jack cheese, sour cream and green onions
- ~~~~~~~~~~~~~~~~~~~~~~~~~~~~~~~~~~~~~
- For honey Cornbread:
- 1 cup all-purpose flour, sifted
- 1 cup yellow cornmeal
- 1 Tbsp baking powder
- 1/2 tsp kosher salt
- 2 free range eggs, beaten
- 1 cup half and half
- ¼ cup melted unsalted butter
- ¼ cup honey
- ¼ cup granulated sugar
- 1/2 teaspoon vanilla (optional, but I like it!)

Direction

- For Cornbread:
- Preheat oven to 400° F. Thoroughly grease and flour a 9" × 9" baking pan (or use a nonstick baking pan or a flexible silicone pan).
- Sift together the flour, cornmeal, baking powder and salt.
- Combine the half and half, eggs, butter, honey and sugar.
- Add the liquid ingredients to the dry ones and mix just until the flour is moistened, no more than ten seconds. The batter should be visibly lumpy — leave it that way! It's extremely important not to overmix the batter.
- Once the liquid and dry ingredients have been combined, pan and bake the cornbread immediately.
- TIP: The dry and wet ingredients, respectively, can be mixed in advance, but as soon as the wet and dry ingredients have been combined with each other, the liquid will activate the baking powder and the batter must be baked right away.
- Bake 25-30 minutes or until a toothpick inserted into the center of the cornbread comes out clean and the edge of the bread starts to separate from the pan.
- ~~~~~~~~~~~~~~~~~~~~~~~~~~~~~~~~~~~~~
- For Chili:
- Heat olive oil in heavy large pot over medium-high heat. Add onion, butternut squash, bell peppers, and chili peppers and sauté until onion and butternut squash are almost tender, about 8 minutes. Add all the spices and garlic and sauté until fragrant. Add tomatoes, beans, and vinegar. Taste for seasoning and adjust if needed. Bring to boil. Reduce heat to medium-high and cook, uncovered, until mixture thickens, stirring often, about 45 minutes. Note: you may need to add water if it's too thick, it depends.
- Ladle chili into bowls, top with cheese, sour cream and green onions and serve with cornbread.

350. Vegetarian Tagine Recipe

Serving: 8 | Prep: | Cook: 120mins | Ready in:

Ingredients

- 1 head garlic, chopped
- 2 onions, chopped
- 2 large carrots, peeled and cut into 1/2 inch thick pieces, or about 1 1/2 cups cut baby carrots
- 1 celery rib with leaves, chopped
- 1 tablespoon olive oil
- 1 lemon, juiced
- 1 teaspoon cinnamon
- 1 teaspoon cumin
- 1 teaspoon paprika
- 1/2 teaspoon turmeric
- 1/4 cup chopped parsley
- 1/2 cup chopped cilantro
- 1 14 ounce can diced tomatoes

- 3 cups vegetable stock (I used Trader Joe's individual vegetable stock concentrate and added water)
- 1 14 ounce can chickpeas, drained and rinsed well
- 1 red pepper, chopped
- 1 pound butternut squash, cut into roughly 1 inch cubes
- 1 medium eggplant, chopped into roughly 1 inch cubes
- 1 cup sultanas (golden raisins)
- 1/2 teaspoon crushed red pepper flakes
- 1 box prepared couscous

Direction

- Heat up olive oil in large stew pot over medium-high heat. Add celery, carrots, onions and garlic. Stir for 1 minute, then turn heat down to medium. Let cook about 7 minutes. Add dry spices and let cook 1 minute until fragrant. Add lemon juice.
- Add parsley and 1/4 cup cilantro. Add tomatoes and bring to boil. Add in vegetable stock, chickpeas and butternut squash. Cook, simmering, 1 hour.
- Salt eggplant pieces, let rest 2 minutes then rinse well with water and add, along with crushed red pepper flakes, and chopped red pepper to stew.
- Chop up sultanas and add to stew. Cook additional 1 1/2, or until vegetables are tender. Add additional seasoning to taste. Stir in remaining 1/4 cup cilantro.
- Serve over prepared couscous.

351. Warming Ginger Soup Recipe

Serving: 4 | Prep: | Cook: 15mins | Ready in:

Ingredients

- Warming ginger Soup
- 1 cloves garlic, minced
- 1.5 tbsp fresh ginger, minced
- 4 cups good vegetable stock
- 1/2 c rice wine vinegar
- 1/4 c soy sauce (or tamari)
- 1/4 tbsp freshly cracked black pepper
- A few ounces of your favorite noodles
- A few mushrooms

Direction

- In sauce pan, add garlic and 1/2 cup of the vegetable stock. Simmer for 3 minutes. Add remaining ingredients, bring to a boil, and simmer for a minute or two. Add noodles, vegetables, or tofu as desired.

352. Weight Watchers Taco Soup Recipe

Serving: 12 | Prep: | Cook: 75mins | Ready in:

Ingredients

- 1 lb. ground turkey or lean beef
- 1 large onion, chopped
- 1 (1 oz.) package hidden valley ranch dressing mix
- 1 (1 oz) package taco seasoning Mix
- 1 (16 oz.) can pinto beans
- 1 (16 oz) can chili beans (either hot or regular)
- 1 (16 oz) can whole kernel corn
- 1 (8 oz) can Mexican-style tomatoes
- 1 (8 oz) can diced tomatoes (any flavor)

Direction

- Brown meat & onions and drain.
- Mix Ranch & Taco seasonings into meat.
- Add rest of ingredients, undrained to mixture.
- Simmer 1 hour.
- 2 Weight Watchers points per cup.

353. West African Style Chicken Stew Recipe

Serving: 6 | Prep: | Cook: 60mins | Ready in:

Ingredients

- 6-8 boneless, skinless chicken thighs
- 2 tbls olive oil
- 1 medium onion finely chopped
- 2 cloves garlic minced
- 2 medium zucchini sliced
- 2 cups chicken broth
- 1 6 oz can tomato paste
- salt to taste
- 1/2 tsp ground cumin
- 1 tsp curry powder
- 1 tsp smoked paprika
- 1/2 cup natural peanut butter, no salt added
- 3 large sweet potatoes, peeled and cut into chunks
- 2 tbs butter
- 1/2 cup finely chopped peanuts

Direction

- Boil sweet potatoes in salted water until tender, drain and mash with 2 tbsp. butter and keep warm
- In a 3 quart Dutch oven brown chicken in olive oil and set aside
- Sauté onion and garlic in remaining drippings until translucent
- Add chicken broth, tomato paste, curry powder, cumin and paprika mix and bring to a boil over medium high heat
- Add zucchini, and chicken thighs turn heat to low, cover and simmer for 45 minutes to 1 hour until chicken is tender.
- Take off heat and stir in peanut butter until melted and combined, put back on low heat until heated through
- Serve on a bed of mashed sweet potatoes and garnish with chopped peanuts

354. White Bean Turkey Chili Recipe

Serving: 8 | Prep: | Cook: 20mins | Ready in:

Ingredients

- 2 T. olive oil
- 1 large onion, finely chopped
- 2 (4-oz.) cans mild green chilies, chopped and drained
- 6 cloves garlic, finely chopped
- 3 cans great northern beans, drained
- 3 cans white kidney beans, drained
- 3 cans low-sodium chicken broth
- 1-1/2 tsp. ground cumin
- 1 tsp. dried oregano or italian seasoning
- 1/4 tsp. cayenne
- 1-2 cups cooked turkey or chicken (white meat) coursely chopped
- salt

Direction

- Heat oil in a large kettle and add onion and garlic.
- Cook for a few minutes until tender.
- Stir in beans, broth, cumin, oregano, and cayenne.
- Bring to a boil, reduce heat, cover and simmer 10 minutes.
- Add chicken.
- Cover and simmer for another 10 minutes.
- Salt to taste and add more cayenne, if needed.
- Garnish with sour cream, green chili sauce, chopped green onions, shredded Monterey jack cheese, crushed tortilla chips, or any combination of these. We like fat-free sour cream.
- Note: The cans of beans can be substituted with 1 lb. dried Great Northern Beans. Soak beans in 8 cups of cold water overnight in a covered pan in the refrigerator. Drain and rinse.
- Note: As chili simmers, you can mash the beans slightly to thicken the chili. I don't do this because I prefer it chunkier.

355. White Chicken Chili Recipe

Serving: 4 | Prep: | Cook: 20mins | Ready in:

Ingredients

- 1 tablespoon vegetable oil
- 1 onion, chopped
- 3 cloves garlic, crushed
- 1 (4 ounce) can diced jalapeno peppers
- 1 (4 ounce) can chopped green chile peppers
- 2 teaspoons ground cumin
- 1 teaspoon dried oregano
- 1 teaspoon ground cayenne pepper
- 2 (14.5 ounce) cans chicken broth
- 3 cups chopped cooked chicken breast
- 3 (15 ounce) cans white beans
- 1 cup shredded monterey jack cheese

Direction

- Heat the oil in a large saucepan over medium-low heat. Slowly cook and stir the onion until tender. Mix in the garlic, jalapeno, green chile peppers, cumin, oregano and cayenne. Continue to cook and stir the mixture until tender, about 3 minutes. Mix in the chicken broth, chicken and white beans. Simmer 15 minutes, stirring occasionally.
- Remove the mixture from heat. Slowly stir in the cheese until melted. Serve warm.

356. Winter Minestrone Recipe

Serving: 6 | Prep: | Cook: 40mins | Ready in:

Ingredients

- 2 T olive oil
- 1 onion, chopped
- 2 carrots, peeled, chopped
- 2 celery stalks, chopped
- 3 ounces thinly sliced pancetta, coarsely chopped
- 2 garlic cloves, minced
- 1 pound swiss chard, stems trimmed. leaves coarsely chopped
- 1 russet potato, peeled, cubed
- 1 (14.5 oz) can diced tomatoes (or roast your own)
- 1 fresh rosemary sprig
- 1 (15 oz) can cannellini beans, drained, rinsed
- 2 (14 oz) cans low sodium beef broth
- 1 oz piece parmesan cheese rind
- 2 T chopped fresh Italian parsley leaves
- salt and pepper

Direction

- Heat the oil in a heavy large pot over medium heat. Add the onion, carrots, celery, pancetta, and garlic. Sauté until the onion is translucent, about 10 minutes. Add the Swiss chard and potato; sauté for 2 minutes. Add the tomatoes and rosemary sprig. Simmer until the chard is wilted and the tomatoes break down, about 10 minutes.
- Meanwhile, blend 3/4 cup of the beans w/ 1/4 cup of the broth in a processor until almost smooth. Add the pureed bean mixture, remaining broth, and Parmesan cheese rind to the veggie mix. Simmer until the potato pieces are tender, stirring occasionally, about 15 minutes. Stir in the whole beans and parsley. Simmer until the beans are heated through and the soup is thick, about 2 minutes. Season w/ salt and pepper to taste. Discard Parmesan rind and rosemary sprig (the leaves will have fallen off the stem).
- Ladle into bowls and serve!

357. World Championship Chili Cook Off Winning Chili Recipe

Serving: 8 | Prep: | Cook: 190mins | Ready in:

Ingredients

- 2 1/2 lb lean ground chuck
- 1 lb Lean ground pork (I've made it with all beef)
- 1 cup onion, finely chopped
- 4 garlic cloves, finely chopped
- 1 can beer (12 oz.)
- 8 oz. can tomato sauce
- 1 cup water
- 3 tbls. chili powder
- 2 tbls. cumin
- 2 tbls. beef bouillon granules or 6 cubes
- 2 tsp. oregano
- 2 tsp. paprika
- 2 tsp. sugar
- 1 tsp. cocoa, unsweetened
- 1/2 tsp. coriander
- 1/2 tsp. louisiana hot sauce, to taste
- 1 tsp. flour
- 1 tsp. cornmeal
- 1 tbls. Warm water
- I like beans in my chili so I add some

Direction

- In Dutch oven, brown half the meat and pour off fat
- Remove meat
- Brown remaining meat and pour off all fat, except 2 tbls.
- Add onion and garlic and cook and stir until tender
- Add meat and remaining ingredients except flour, cornmeal and warm water
- Mix well
- Bring to boil, then reduce heat and simmer covered 2 hours
- Stir together flour and cornmeal, then add warm water and mix well
- Stir into chili mixture
- Cook covered another 20 minutes

358. Yayla Yogurt Soup Recipe

Serving: 5 | Prep: | Cook: 15mins | Ready in:

Ingredients

- 1/4 cup rice
- 5 cups of water (if you wish you can use half chicken stock, half water)
- 2 cups of plain yogurt
- 1 egg yolk
- 1 tbsp flour
- 2 tbsp butter
- 2 tsp dried mint or fresh mint thinley sliced
- 1 tsp salt
- 1 tbs red pepper

Direction

- -Boil rice in 5 cups of water with salt until (very) soft.
- -In a bowl, beat the egg yolk and flour well, and then add yogurt and mix. With 1-2 tbsp. water lighten up this mixture.
- -Add to yogurt mix in a boiled water and rice and start cooking on medium heat and stir with wood spoon until soup is boil. It's important that, otherwise yogurt would curdle. Cook soup after boiled like 3 minutes.
- -Heat butter in a pan. Once it sizzles, add mint flakes and red pepper stir for 20-30 seconds (don't let it burn). Then, pour it into soup.

359. Yummy Homemade Hotdog Chili Or Sauce Recipe

Serving: 8 | Prep: | Cook: 10mins | Ready in:

Ingredients

- 1 tablespoon butter or margarine
- 1 1/2 pounds lean ground beef
- 2 medium onions, chopped
- 1 clove garlic, crushed
- 1 tablespoon prepared regular mustard
- 1-- 6-ounce can tomato sauce
- 6 ounces water
- 1 tablespoons chili powder
- salt and pepper to taste

Direction

- Combine everything and simmer until thick. Do not brown ground beef first.
- Cook 5 minutes longer, stirring often.
- Put over cooked hot dogs in a warm bun.

360. Yummy Moroccan Lentil Soup Recipe

Serving: 8 | Prep: | Cook: 70mins | Ready in:

Ingredients

- * 2 tablespoons butter
- * 2 tablespoons olive oil
- * 1 large onion, finely chopped
- * 1 small green pepper, finely chopped
- * 2 medium carrots, shredded
- * 1 1/2 cups peeled and finely chopped eggplant
- * 4 cloves garlic, minced
- * 2 full teaspoons cumin
- * 1 teaspoon curry powder
- * 1 teaspoon allspice
- * 1 1/2 teaspoons cinnamon
- * 1 teaspoon red pepper flakes
- * 300 ml water
- * 1 tablespoon vinegar
- * 1 liter chicken broth
- * 1 can diced tomatoes, drained
- * 1 16-ounce bag dried lentils, any variety
- * 1/2 teaspoon salt
- * plain yogurt or sour cream, for garnish
- * Chopped fresh cilantro, for garnish

Direction

- In a large stockpot over medium heat, combine the butter and oil and stir until the butter has melted. Add the onions, green pepper, carrots, eggplant and garlic. Stir well. Add the cumin, curry powder, allspice, cinnamon and red pepper flakes. Sauté, stirring, until the vegetables have softened, about 10 minutes.
- Add water, chicken broth, vinegar, tomatoes and lentils, and bring to a boil. Reduce heat to low, and simmer, uncovered, 1 hour, or until the lentils have softened. Season with salt. To serve, garnish each bowl with a dollop of yogurt or sour cream and a sprinkling of chopped cilantro.
- Enjoy!

361. Zuppa Maritata Wedding Soup Recipe

Serving: 6 | Prep: | Cook: 30mins | Ready in:

Ingredients

- For the meatballs:
- 1/2 lb ground beef
- 1/2 lb ground veal, pork or turkey
- 1/4 cup commercial bread crumbs (or grate your own from stale Italian bread)
- 1 egg
- 1 tbs parsley, finely chopped
- 1/2 clove garlic, minced (optional)
- 1/2 tsp paprika (optional)
- 1/2 tsp salt and pepper to taste
- For the soup:
- 4 cups chicken broth
- 2 cups spinach, chopped
- 1/4 cup grated pecorino romano cheese
- Orzo - small grains of pasta shaped like barley (optional)

Direction

- Combine the ground meat, bread crumbs, egg, parsley, minced garlic, salt and pepper in mixing bowl.
- Mix well with a fork and form into tiny meat balls (about the size of marbles) with your hands.
- *(Place meatballs on a greased baking sheet and bake for about 25 minutes at 350? F, until brown.) ALTERNATE METHOD FOR MEATBALLS)
- About ten minutes before serving, bring the chicken broth to a boil, add the spinach and cook until tender.
- Add the meatballs and return soup to a simmer.
- Stir in the Pecorino cheese and serve.
- *Note: you can sauté the meatballs in virgin olive oil until brown, or bring your chicken stock to a low boil, add the uncooked meatballs, simmer for about 25 minutes, add the spinach, cook until tender, stir in the cheese and serve.

362. Zuppa Toscana Soup Olive Garden Recipe

Serving: 4 | Prep: | Cook: 35mins | Ready in:

Ingredients

- 5 1/2 cups chicken stock or broth
- 1/2 cup light cream
- 2 medium russet potatoes
- 4 cups chopped kale
- 1 lb hot Italian sausages
- 1/2 teaspoon salt
- 1/2 teaspoon crushed red pepper flakes

Direction

- Combine the stock and cream in a saucepan over medium heat.
- Slice the unpeeled potato into 1/4-inch slices, then quarter the slices and add them to the soup.
- Add the kale.
- Grill or sauté the sausage. When cooked and cooled, cut the sausage in an angle about 1/2-inch thick. Add the sausage to the soup.
- Add the spices and let the soup simmer for about 2 hours. Stir occasionally.

363. Butter Chicken Recipe

Serving: 6 | Prep: | Cook: 35mins | Ready in:

Ingredients

- 1 kilogram chicken breasts
- 1/2 cup plain yoghurt
- 2 tsps ginger and garlic paste
- 1 tsp ground black pepper
- 1/4 cup butter
- 20ml oil
- 1and 1/4 cups fresh cream
- 30ml lemon juice
- 1tsp white pepper(ground)
- 1 and 1/4 cups tomato puree
- 1 tsp salt
- 1and1/2 - 2 tsps red chillie powder (to taste)
- (

Direction

- Wash cube chicken in big bite sized pieces drain
- Mix yoghurt, oil, ginger & garlic paste, 1/2 of lemon juice and spices
- Smear chicken pieces and leave overnight
- Cook in pot on medium heat until almost dry
- Sauce:
- Add rest of lemon juice, tomato puree and any leftover marinade to melted butter
- Cook sauce until thickened
- Just before serving add cream to sauce
- Place chicken on platter pour sauce over
- Decorate with cut fresh cilantro leaves

- Serve piping hot with naan and a green salad
- Enjoy!!

364. Chinese Hot And Sour Soup Recipe

Serving: 2 | Prep: | Cook: 20mins | Ready in:

Ingredients

- 1 tofu, julienned
- 1 cup of pork, julienned
- 1/2 cup of bamboo shoots, julienned
- 1/2 cup of Wood Ear mushroom, julienned
- 1 chilli pepper
- 7 cups of water or broth
- 1 tsp salt, or to taste
- 1 tsp granulated sugar
- 2 Tbs soy sauce
- 2 Tbs chinese rice vinegar
- 1 tsp sesame oil
- 1 Tbs cornstarch dissolved in 1/4 cup water
- 1 egg, beaten
- 1 spring onion, finely sliced
- 1 tsp of white pepper to taste

Direction

- Bring the water to the boil, add the pork, bamboo shoots, mushrooms, and tofu.
- Stir in the salt, sugar, soy sauce and vinegar and sesame oil.
- Cook for around 15 minutes, taste,
- Mix the cornstarch and water. Slowly pour the cornstarch mixture into the soup, stir well, add in the beaten egg, and stir again
- Garnish with spring onion. Serve hot.

365. Chinese Wonton Soup Recipe

Serving: 2 | Prep: | Cook: 30mins | Ready in:

Ingredients

- ready made wonton skin
- wonton filling;
- 300 grams of finely minced pork
- 100 grams of minced spring onion
- 20 grams of finely chopped celery
- 20 grams of fried shallots
- pinch of salt
- generous pinch of white pepper powder
- 1 egg white
- 2 tbs of soy sauce
- 1 tbs of sesame oil
- soup base;
- 4 cups of stock
- salt & pepper to taste
- pinch of hon dashi (to replace msg)
- 1 teaspoon of fried garlic
- roughly chopped celery

Direction

- To make the wonton filling, mix all ingredients in one direction with a big wooden spoon
- Knead with the wooden spoon for at least 10 minutes
- Wrap 1 teaspoon of filling on each wonton skin
- Bring stock to the boil, add all the seasoning, add wontons cook for around 5 minutes, add celery, and serve

Index

A
Apple 3,7,14,44,159
Artichoke 4,58,77
Avocado 3,45

B
Bacon 4,67,132
Baking 145
Barley 3,21,24,33
Bay leaf 32,110,182
Beans 3,6,7,26,46,152,184,188
Beef 3,4,5,6,7,21,22,23,24,29,62,70,72,76,84,88,94,96,112,116,117,131,161,172
Beer 6,152
Beetroot 6,132
Black pepper 143
Bread 4,52,61,107,185
Broccoli 3,4,5,28,52,55,87,111
Broth 4,7,71,106,156
Butter 3,6,8,30,88,129,150,182,192

C
Cabbage 3,4,5,6,7,31,79,92,149,167
Cake 3,4,43,54
Cardamom 81
Carrot 3,4,6,9,17,32,33,78,151,182
Cauliflower 4,5,58,64,104
Celery 99
Champ 7,190
Chard 3,4,5,21,70,106,107,132

Cheddar 3,18,28,42,43,50,98,104
Cheese 3,4,5,6,7,25,28,32,33,34,42,52,55,58,93,99,111,130,132,142,179,183
Chicken 3,4,5,6,7,8,12,14,18,30,34,35,36,37,38,39,40,41,42,43,45,56,60,62,69,78,80,84,90,91,95,104,105,109,110,117,132,140,143,160,161,162,165,166,168,177,180,188,189,192
Chickpea 6,118,120,121,124
Chilli 4,46,81
Chipotle 3,4,27,43,48,66,166,176
Chorizo 10,73,113,167
Cinnamon 7,159
Cloves 81
Cocktail 5,113
Coconut 3,7,34,171,180
Coriander 4,46,75,107
Couscous 6,117
Crab 3,4,7,43,54,99,107,170
Crackers 96
Cream 3,4,5,7,10,18,32,33,54,55,56,57,58,59,60,69,104,111,132,142,183
Crumble 48,136
Cumin 46,69,107,153

D
Dijon mustard 87
Dumplings 3,7,23,24,32,33,40,161

E
Egg 4,51,69,70

F
Fat 140
Fish 4,6,7,33,55,74,75,115,116,125,137,154,159,180
French bread 20,61,73,76,77,94,99,109,141
Fruit 6,117

G

Garlic 6,7,99,107,130,132,150,159

Gin 5,6,7,105,151,187

H

Ham 5,85

Heart 5,81,87,88,89,90

Honey 5,7,92,185

J

Jam 3,5,6,7,20,98,110,140,163,168

Jus 18,87,97,111,130,137,149,164,170,177,179,192

K

Kale 6,124

L

Lamb 3,4,5,6,16,70,81,101,102,103,121,130

Leek 4,5,6,10,57,66,78,104,127

Lemon 4,5,6,75,83,104,105,106,107,151

Lentils 3,21,106,107

Lime 3,5,43,102

Ling 73

Lobster 3,5,15,108

M

Madeira 109

Marjoram 30

Marrow 5,112

Meat 3,5,6,31,43,97,103,114,120,158

Milk 88,132

Mince 18,37,38,169,179

Mint 5,102

Mozzarella 131

Mushroom 4,5,6,9,54,56,57,77,83,129

N

Noodles 5,92,106,147

Nut 89,157

O

Oil 99,106

Okra 7,158

Olive 8,18,106,116,192

Onion 3,4,5,13,20,61,73,76,88,99,107,132,182

Oxtail 76

Oyster 3,6,33,99,127,154

P

Paprika 5,94,167

Parmesan 3,6,19,30,39,40,43,61,97,130,131,189

Parsley 99,132,146

Parsnip 4,78

Pasta 5,6,107,114,125,128

Peach 3,4,6,46,78,129

Peas 3,27

Pecorino 192

Peel 19,41,69,76,101,129,132,140,145,148,153,154,157

Pepper 4,5,6,67,69,71,98,99,102,107,116,132,147

Pie 6,42,55,141

Pizza 6,130

Pork 4,6,47,48,61,135

Port 6,132,136,137

Potato 3,4,5,6,7,9,10,34,42,43,57,58,59,62,66,100,108,122,124,127,128,132,135,138,147,157,178,182

Pulse 121,132,159,179

Pumpkin 3,4,5,6,7,24,58,63,64,87,112,113,141,171

R

Rabbit 5,86

Ratatouille 6,143,144,145,148

Rhubarb 107

Rice 4,5,6,48,56,70,75,80,114,116,130,143

Rye bread 185

S

Salsa 3,5,44,102

Salt 6,35,43,51,80,82,98,99,107,116,119,138,143,144,153,154,159,183,187,188

Sausage 3,5,6,7,38,96,99,109,127,133,134,140,155

Scallop 7,156

Seafood 5,6,7,113,122,156,157,158,164

Seasoning 107,110,153,170

Seeds 46

Sesame oil 143

Sherry 132,133,156

Shiitake mushroom 37

Shin 160

Sorrel 14

Soup 3,4,5,6,7,8,9,10,11,12,13,14,15,20,21,24,25,26,27,28,30,31,32,33,34,35,36,37,39,40,45,46,47,49,52,53,54,55,56,57,58,59,60,61,62,63,64,65,66,67,68,69,70,71,72,73,76,77,78,79,80,82,83,85,86,87,89,90,91,92,93,96,97,99,100,102,104,105,106,107,108,111,112,113,114,115,116,117,118,119,120,121,122,124,127,128,129,130,132,133,135,137,138,141,146,147,148,149,150,151,154,155,161,165,166,167,169,170,171,172,173,175,176,177,178,180,181,182,183,184,187,190,191,192,193

Spaghetti 5,115

Spinach 4,7,59,107,171

Squash 3,6,30,150

Steak 6,130

Stew 1,3,4,5,6,7,9,12,16,21,22,23,24,29,33,42,48,62,70,74,81,84,86,88,89,94,95,101,103,104,115,117,118,120,122,125,127,130,131,133,134,136,142,151,154,159,160,161,164,172,178,179,185,188

Stock 5,6,7,76,91,99,108,132,150,162,182

Sugar 182

Swiss chard 21,107,189

T

Tabasco 17,27,31,36,46,66,110,113,122,147,160,170,174

Taco 4,7,68,176,187

Tea 32,115,184

Thyme 99

Tomato 4,7,46,78,177,182,183

Tortellini 7,183

Truffle 132

Turkey 4,7,60,66,183,184,188

V

Vegan 3,7,13,31,185

Vegetables 5,24,32,85,102,145

Vegetarian 7,185,186

W

Water chestnut 143

White pepper 143

Wine 3,20

Worcestershire sauce 20,29,33,38,61,68,128,130,143,154,168

Conclusion

Thank you again for downloading this book!

I hope you enjoyed reading about my book!

If you enjoyed this book, please take the time to share your thoughts and post a review on Amazon. It'd be greatly appreciated!

Write me an honest review about the book – I truly value your opinion and thoughts and I will incorporate them into my next book, which is already underway.

Thank you!

If you have any questions, **feel free to contact at:** *author@limerecipes.com*

Mona Scott

limerecipes.com

Printed in Great Britain
by Amazon